the Ghosts of Italy

The Ghosts of Italy

A MEMOIR

❦

Angela Paolantonio

The Ghosts of Italy

Copyright © 2016 by Angela Paolantonio
www.angelapaolantonio.com
All rights reserved. No part of this book may be reproduced in any form without written permission from the publisher.

First Edition: September 2016
Photography by Angela Paolantonio
Book design & website design by Doug daSilva / www.dougdasilva.com
Chapter titles set in Bickham Script. Text set in Granjon.

The Library of Congress has catalogued the paperback edition of this book as follows:

Paolantonio, Angela, 1959
The Ghosts of Italy / Angela Paolantonio

Library of Congress Control Number: 2016914737
CreateSpace Independent Publishing Platform, North Charleston, SC

ISBN-13: 978-1537410913
ISBN-10: 1537410911

For my father

What counts is what we are and the way we deepen our relationship with the world and with others, a relationship that can be one both of love for all that exists and of desire for its transformation.

– ITALO CALVINO

Prologue	*1*
Cerca Trova (Seek and Ye Shall Find)	*5*
Spigolare (To Glean)	*23*
Via Sant'Antuono, 49	*37*
Santo Spirito (Holy Spirit)	*53*
La Portressa (The Doorkeeper)	*69*
Winter in the Old Village	*83*
Woodstoves in Winter	*99*
Five Letters, the Road to Macchiursi	*113*
Camera Matrimoniale (Marriage Bedroom)	*123*
Sacred and Profane	*133*
Fireworks and Lucciole (Fireflies)	*149*
Tramandare (To Hand Down)	*163*
San Nicola, Falling Far from Home	*173*
Head of an Italian Girl	*191*
Cera Una Volta (Once Upon a Time)	*205*
Sense and Sensibility in the Old Village	*217*
Questa la Vita (That's Life)	*227*
Fatta Bene (Well Done)	*237*
Sex, Food, Laundry	*253*
A Stone, a Leaf, a Door	*261*
Four Seasonal Alta Irpinia Recipes from Calitri	*271*
Author's Note	*283*
Acknowledgements	*285*

Prologue

A warm summer breeze lifts pale blue sheets and a host of marshmallow clouds float over my balcony. It's early June in Calitri and each afternoon the bells of Saint Anthony are rung by hand from the small yellow church at the base of the hill.

I am sitting here after a post-*pranzo riposo* contemplating nothing, or maybe something. Wouldn't it be nice? I dared dream years ago, conjuring an image of one day living in a stone house on a hillside in Italy, a flock of sheep grazing in a field beyond a balcony.

Well, now I have them in view.

Yet it is not just any view, nor any stone house on a hillside in Italy. It is the house where my grandmother was born, the balcony view of her youth. And if you asked me then, whether this wistful dream might come true, I would have nodded and smiled and stayed dreamy. *Domani o dopodomani*, tomorrow or the day after tomorrow, we all know in Italy nothing is in our control. So when the plates and silverware stop clinking and *la Tredicina di Sant'Antonio* begins, I'll dream of other dreams to come on this hillside in Italy.

I always felt someday I would find my spirit in Italy. It was tangible. Italian fairy dust seemed to be floating around the corners of my life at an early age. Maybe it was the spirit of my grandmother, a generational pull toward her spiritual roots from across the pond.

When I was born, I was the first child to be named for a grandparent. I entered the world just two months after my grandfather Nicola died. Until that point he had forbidden any of his other grandchildren to be named so.

Pop, as my father used to call him, loved America, New York, and baseball. He wanted his children and grandchildren to assimilate to the American ways and values that he believed in. Leave the village behind, he said. Some of his own children were named after their grandparents, probably to assuage his wife and the traditions of family back in the old country. But that was as far as it went, until he passed, and my mother was given the green light to name me for my paternal grandmother, Angela Maria.

As a child, I always felt the presence of invisible spirits. Or maybe they were just dead people. They hovered in our basement boiler room on Long Island or in a friend's home when I visited, especially when I was around some of my Italian relatives. I didn't want to admit that I could feel ghosts or that they were ghosts, just otherworldly presences, say over my shoulder, but unmistakable, even a bit creepy. Yet they always seemed benevolent.

After a while, I would suss out a place for its ghost potential. I found myself wondering, sometimes apprehensively, of whether I would have a ghost experience in some new apartment or city I had moved to. I also discovered that I was sensitive to a whole host of other empyreal information. People would find me and tell me things about myself or my past self, or my romantic relationships, present or past. At first the stories seemed fanciful, farfetched. They were never elicited by me. But they kept happening. I wasn't yet willing to believe any of it as a reading into my Italian spirit. But one story specifically, the one about the princess and the warrior, that one followed me around for oh, say thirty years. Beginning in my junior year of college, then resurfacing every eight years or so, never coaxed by me, until my first trip to Calitri.

My first foray into my grandparents' village was over a decade ago. Since then their hilltop *paese* has become my home. I spend most days photographing my way into the lives of the villagers, documenting a lively yet serene world in deep contrast to my American life. Each season I drop into the daily world of their Italian liturgical and agricultural calendar, rituals that have changed little since my grandparents' time. Saints and feast days mingle with the waxing or waning of the moon, the weather, and whether today is the day you will plant the onions or pick the walnuts.

Always invited to feast with families as they enjoy the fruits of life that they work very hard for all year long, I am L'Americana in training. Yet no matter how many questions I ask or photographs I take, I might never truly understand all that is involved—unless of course I were to marry one of their own and become a true *Calitrana*.

If the quote says you can't go home again, then I believe I may have found a middle place. Between the world left behind by my paternal ancestors and the life I have created from out of their past.

Cerca Trova
(Seek and Ye Shall Find)

I t seems I may have come to this small hilltop village in Campania in reverse.

I arrived for the first time one day in late November just after celebrating Thanksgiving alone on a rooftop in Rome—where I savored the best tuna fish sandwich I had ever eaten in my life.

Thanksgiving was on a Thursday as usual. But in Rome it was just another day and my order just another *panino* to the young confident guy behind the counter. Fresh arugula, large Capri capers, and olive oil smothered the pink tuna on thick-crusted bread. Bought with a bottle of white wine at a crowded corner deli near Campo dei Fiori, the sandwich was big enough for me to split into two meals. But rather than find it sodden a few hours later, and really enjoying my prosaic solitude on this day of American family feasting, I devoured both halves while sitting on a folding chair with the sounds of the neighborhood wafting up to the roof.

It was the last day of the closing week of the Millennial Jubilee in 2000, marking two thousand years of the Roman Catholic Church. All week the Eternal City had been quiet and withdrawn, her museums and churches nearly empty. The couple in the window below my perch were just boiling the water for their pasta. I poured myself another glass of wine and thought of my parents and my first daring adventure away from home alone on the holidays.

In a week I would find myself almost two hundred miles south of Rome in Calitri. And the simple days of rooftop wine and panini would be over. Not to mention freedom from familial responsibilities. I was meandering along on a personal journey that would lead me to discover another world, and fairly change the course of my life. But that wouldn't occur to me until much, much later.

My family had been split up on two coasts for more than ten years—my two brothers and their families lived on the east coast and my parents and I lived on the left. My younger sister, after a brief stint in New York City, not unlike myself before her, would eventually join us. Each year my parents or I would fly to the east coast to spend either Christmas or Thanksgiving with my siblings. This year I wanted something different. I wanted a break from the family and, truth be told, since I had recently rounded forty, a break from the established embarrassment of being the still unmarried Auntie at their table. I had the time and a plan to meet up with friends in Verona, just as I had a year ago when I celebrated my fortieth birthday in Venice. (What was the problem?)

For years I had conjured images of the place, but in reality I really had no idea what the village might look or feel like. Nor did I expect to find anyone who knew me, or my family.

The last person to make this journey was my grandfather Nicola, sometime in the early 1950's. Bearing boxes of clothes and shoes, any goods his family might need, he returned to his home village in those early years after World War II, when all of Southern Italy was struggling with abject poverty, recovering from the war's devastation. No one in the intervening years had returned. No letters were exchanged and, of course, no phone calls. There had not been any further contact between my Paolantonio family on American soil and those that remained in this landlocked region of Italy in more than fifty years.

I really didn't know when I landed in Rome how I would get there. I had no advance plan on how to reach the town nor knowledge of a bus route or train schedule. I just knew the name of the town and that it was on a hillside somewhere east of Naples. I planned this quick detour as a short day trip. Once in Sorrento, I thought I would simply make my way inland before I headed north again.

I had tried to research our family in Italy before using only our last name with scattered results. A few months before I left, I'd had a brief phone conversation with my father. I called him from my desk. I knew he was at his.

"Hey, Dad, what's the name of that town in Southern Italy where your parents are from?"

"Avellino," came his deadpan response. "That's the regional capital." A medium-sized city in the coastal province of Campania, Avellino is about forty miles inland from Naples.

"No, the other town, where they were born. What was it called again?"

"Calitri," he said. "It's a small hill town. Probably a lot harder to find." And it was true. I was never able to find it back then on any Michelin map.

I started to type.

"Calitri," my father repeated. "Pop always joked that everyone there had one leg shorter than the other from walking up and down that hill." I heard him chuckle. Then, "Why? Where're you going?"

Raffaele Freda, a distant cousin of an old Long Island friend of my mother's, and whom I had contacted by postcard from Los Angeles, accompanied me around Rome. He quietly arranged for his brother's family to put me up for a night in Avellino.

One evening after dinner, upon learning of my intent to locate the town of my grandparents' birth, Raffaele produced an Avellino phone directory from his foyer credenza. Together we looked up my family surnames. When we found Paolantonio and Cicoira—my grandmother Angela Maria's maiden name—still listed in the tissue-thin pages he simply ripped them from the book and handed them to me.

"*Cerca trova*," he said. Seek and ye shall find.

My trip began early the next morning in Sorrento, and wound me around the Southern Italian coastal peninsula with connections in the towns of Amalfi and Salerno. Capri and the Amalfi coast—gorgeously visible from my seat on the bus—were less than two hours south by car from the mountain countryside where I was headed, though traveling in Southern Italy, as I found out, was an adventure that took the whole day. In Salerno I was unwittingly separated from my luggage, and had to enlist the help of no less than the whole contingent of unionized bus drivers in Amalfi's beachfront parking lot—on their Feast Day no less—as the entire town looked on in full Renaissance regalia. From there the road took me back inland for another hour or two to the main depot in Avellino.

Raffaele's brother Carlo Freda and his wife Carla were impossibly warm and kind. They spoke no English and I spoke very little Italian. We passed the evening nearly silent with a simple dinner followed by a traditional *passeggiata* window-shopping, then a *caffè* and a gelato under the glow of street lamps.

It was a pleasant and relaxed evening spent with strangers after the dazzling bus ride.

The next morning Carlo accompanied me to the bus stop on a quiet side street of suburban Avellino. I carried only my camera—my OM1—and a shoulder bag. Inside the bag were the two torn pages from the phone directory with the highlighted surnames of my paternal grandparents, and a scribbled bus schedule from Carlo securing my return by 6pm that same evening. I was fully intending to be back in Avellino in time to have dinner with the Fredas. Carlo simply informed the driver where I was headed, paid for my ticket, and was gone.

Barely awake, nursing a nagging trepidation, I boarded the big blue bus. The driver peered down from his perch like a stern but benevolent uncle, took the ticket from my hand and I was firmly in his charge. I was his lone passenger. Gazing blankly out the window, I settled in for the two-hour ride.

Apart from my underlying nervousness, my chief worry was how I would find a good meal at noon, knowing that in Italy in most towns and small cities, it grows deadly quiet between the hours of one and four p.m. Every family pauses at *mezzogiorno* for their four-hour lunch. An errant tourist without a plan is often left wandering around the streets alone with meager options; a dark bar with a few thin *tramezzini* and hopefully a cold beer. After I considered those few options, wishing I had packed at least some fruit, I closed my eyes to the still-early hour and tried to sleep for a while.

Climbing through Apennine passes covered in forests of chestnut and acacia, the bus made slow progress as the driver paused to pick up school children and commuting workers just beginning their day. One by one they glanced at me, *la straniera*, (the stranger). Seemed I was a dead giveaway.

Along the route I recalled stories from friends years ago, on vacations or honeymoons in Italy, cantering through small towns and villages looking for proof of their provenance. Some got as far as locating a name on a doorbell, then went no further.

"Didn't you ring the bell?" I would ask.

"No…" would come the answer.

Sometimes the end of a journey remains forever hidden, the search for a connection infinitely subtle. To be so close and not follow through seemed incredible to me. Although I had to admit, I had been to Italy twice already without making any effort to find the place of my family origins and I wondered now if I would do the same.

As deep green and brown forest hues gave way to distant white outcrops dotted with stone hamlets and villages, I felt the pull of my grandparents' past.

Those two brave kids. Leaving a deep landlocked village on a hillside precipice warm with Italian life. The handsome Nicola pulling behind him what can only be surmised as his pliant, supplicant new wife, Angela Maria, who perhaps had waited years for the moment of his decision, his assurance that he could pull it off in the new country. Or was it her they waited for? Her *corredo*, her dowry? At age twenty-five when they married she had had ample time to be sure. So no, they were not waiting for her home and hearth goods to be secured. And what could they bring aboard ship but a satchel or perhaps a small trunk? No, it had to be Nicola. Age thirty, sure of his ability to provide. Maybe he had asked his mother to find him a suitable girl once he was ready for marriage.

Nicola's first journey to America was before age seventeen to join his three elder brothers. Sailing alone from Naples on the three-masted schooner the Prinzess Irene, he landed in New York Harbor on July 4, 1907. He then traveled back and forth, brought or sent back money for the remaining family. With that money they bought land and built their village homestead. They remained in the village for a while. Their rock-solid father—in the one photo, my great-grandfather's countenance was much like my grandfather's, that of a field marshal in full command of his brood. All boys. My great-grandmother was a renowned beauty. With a full head of lustrous black curls and dark eyes, dressed traditionally beside the hearth in an impeccably embroidered black wool skirt, vest, and white blouse. I am certain she maintained full disclosure for her family.

What they imagined would come could not have been foretold. How we have now all grown up could not have been dreamed. But they did embark, the four boys together leaving their beloved parents and their countryside behind.

I put my hand to my heart. Was it fear or love? This powerful pull there in my breast. It was almost as if someone knew I was coming, and they were drawing me in.

Morning sun shone through mountain mist as the driver pulled up to the center of town. *Pensionati* in dark suit jackets and 1940s fedoras stood tethered in twos and threes under a wide stone portico. A fruit-and-vegetable store owner, a *fruttivendolo*, in his cap and apron, swept the clean sidewalk out front. He glanced at the Pullman arriving in the *piazza*, then went back to his work. It was 8 a.m.

The driver glanced in his rear-view mirror. Most everyone else had left the bus.

"*Signora*..."

Louder.

"*SIGNORA*..., this is your stop."

Startled at the sound of his command, I leapt up and all but ran down the aisle of the bus, then felt my knees give way as I stepped down to the curb. My heart lightly pounded, alternating between its rightful place in my chest and as a lump in my throat. I hesitated there for a moment, wondering about the day before me, when a voice called out in my head,

"Well, you made it. You're in this town called Calitri. The birthplace of your paternal grandparents." Pause. "Now what?"

My family and the one photo of my grandparents felt very far away. Until this moment—traveling around the tourist mecca of Rome and then the azure beauty of the Amalfi Coast—I hadn't allowed myself thoughts of longing for them. Now I wished for them to be near. The bus driver slammed the door behind me and roared off. And with that I felt really on my own. Scanning the street filled with elderly men, I quickly adopted an air of urbane purpose and, with all those male eyes on me, casually made off down the street.

On my right was the fruit and vegetable store. On my left and up the street a bar-pasticceria not quite open for business. *Caffè e dolce* was just what I needed to allow me time to collect myself. Here I had the whole day in front of me with absolutely no plan. This would be perfect, if only I were in Florence or Siena or back in Rome. But I was high on some mountain ridge in deep-country Campania. There wasn't a *palazzo* or *museo* around for a hundred miles. At that moment, I knew I was struggling with the combined fear of the unknown discoveries before me and the possibility of wandering aimlessly in a town where everyone could see I didn't belong.

I wandered into the center of the street, glancing back at the square I had arrived in. I was torn whether to follow that road up towards what looked like the barren old city or down another toward some shops and general village activity. It didn't matter which direction I headed, really, as I was suddenly at a complete loss where to begin this journey into my past.

"Excuse me," I heard myself say in halting Italian to the fruttivendolo. "My name is Paolantonio." Those simple words of self-identity caught in my throat. I felt myself beginning to wobble.

With the folded page from the phone directory in my hand, I continued, "Can you help me find my family?"

The fruttivendolo finally noticed the bewildered young woman before him and sprang into action. He motioned for me to wait, pulled on the strings of his apron, and backed to his store, and in a moment he had returned. Through the group of gathered men we walked, up onto a sidewalk and into an apartment hallway adjacent to another bar with more gathered men, just across the street from where the bus pulled in. There we stood in the dark as he rang the apartment bell. It could have been any dark hallway from my early childhood in Brooklyn. In fact, for a moment I felt I was there. After he conferred with the petite elderly woman who answered the door, we were back across the street as she had instructed. He stopped at a small appliance shop. *Elettrodomestici*, the big white sign said. It too had not yet opened for the day.

The fruttivendolo assured me the owner of the shop would be able to help me, then gently suggested I wait for him, motioning toward the bar across the street. I walked to it, entered, and sat alone at a table to wait.

Still in a mild state of shock, an unusual timidness had gripped me—I found myself unable to order a simple coffee from the woman behind the counter. Townsmen drifted in and ordered their espressos or beer with confidence as they glanced at la straniera with nothing at her table. I sat stock still, not wanting to miss a thing. Quiet murmurings came behind me. So here I was, in the no-longer mythical town of my grandparents, my father's parents, nervously awaiting what would happen next.

A small white pickup bounded up the street and stopped squarely in front of the store as I watched from inside the bar. The fruttivendolo walked over to meet the driver and said a few words as he pointed across the street. Without a moment's hesitation, the man made his way over to the bar. At the sight of him and the fruttivendolo coming towards me, I started for the door. The three of us met halfway in the middle of the street.

"*Buongiorno. E che bella mattina, eh?* I am Vito. And you? How can I help you?" the man said rapidly, mixing Italian and English.

My brain stumbled for just a second. "Did you just say Vito? That's my father's name!"

"*Piano, piano!*" he commanded. This startled me, though I had no idea what it meant.

"I am Vito Cestone, not Paolantonio, *io.*" He pounded his hand to his chest. "My mother, she is Paolantonio. *E il tuo nonno?* Grandfather?"

"My grandfather was Nicola Paolantonio," I said.

The fruttivendolo nodded, then quietly slipped away, his mission complete.

Vito ushered me back to the table. He instructed the woman behind the large glass cases filled with row upon row of fresh pastry to deliver whatever I wanted. The espresso machine immediately began to whir as she pulled my caffè.

Now assured of my place, the other villagers, all men, slowly began to leave.

"*Allora,*" Vito said. "What is your name?"

"Angela," I said. "Angela Paolantonio."

"*Ah, sì.*" His next question was direct, probing. "*Dimmi, quanti anni hai?*"

Wait. Did he just ask how old I was?

He smiled, but seeing I was mildly put off, he worded it another way, though no less forceful. "*Che anno di nascita?*"

Defeated, I told him the year I was born. "1959."

"*COMPLIMENTI!*"

He quickly offered his own statistics, that he was just a few years younger than myself, married with two young boys. I sat perplexed across the small hard cafe table from this stranger who seemed only interested in personal facts. Yet within a few minutes, he would ceremoniously usher me around the village in search of distant relatives, some of whom were contemporaries of my paternal grandparents.

"Wait one moment, please." Vito raced back to his store across from the bar. When he returned, we climbed into his small pickup and took off down the street.

The first house we stopped in was that of a grandmotherly woman, small and round with what I thought were easy Neapolitan features of dark, curly hair and large soulful eyes. Vito fired off something to her in their local language and in another flash he was gone, assuring me from over his shoulder he would return.

Here I was left alone in the small spare kitchen of a woman I didn't know and could not communicate with and who immediately began making me coffee in the tiniest mocha pot I had ever seen. Since I had just had a strong cappuccino in the bar, I gently declined her offer with a shake of my head and a smile. But with a scoff and a wave of her hand she canceled my plea. So I sat dutifully drinking the strong, sugared coffee and ate from a plate of her soft, homemade cookies that I realized were flavored with a hint of anisette just like my favorite Stella D'Oros. My smile widened. Better than Stella D'Oros. I was feeling a little closer to home already. Stella D'Oros, as anyone knows, are a luxury in any Italian-American kitchen. My mother served them for company. It wasn't often they were put out for us kids.

"*Sono buoni?*" the woman asked.

"Delicious!" I said.

I made attempts at conversation in petrified Italian, though she understood none of what I said. It seemed I was simply in her charge. And she politely attended her duty.

Turned out her last name was Paolantonio. Treasured photos were soon pulled from living room drawers and credenzas. Boxes of family memories were cheerfully shared. Men proudly stood in uniforms and children posed in faded dresses. Groups of people, young and old, at parties with family members visiting from America, where they had emigrated years and years before. As each photo drifted before me I strained to find some connection to the grandparents I never knew. Unfortunately, none of the people in the photos seemed familiar. *La signora* Paolantonio was not a relative. How could that be? Even she looked disappointed.

I wondered if the rest of my day would be like this.

Vito returned as promised, declined a coffee but grabbed a cookie, and off we went again, zipping through the town in his tight pickup. He carried on a conversation with me in a jumble of Italian and forced English. He couldn't help but remind me of my younger brother: open, gregarious, willing. I appreciated his eagerness to help me as my personal ambassador, delivering me around the town, but I hardly paid attention to his banter. I barely understood what he was trying to convey anyway. With my head in the clouds, daydreaming of my family back home and then my long-forgotten grandparents, I turned toward the window and watched as the streets of the town zoomed by.

The first section of road we drove along was a tumble-down ruin. The hillside and the stone houses built into it were oddly all in an advanced stage of decline. In fact they seemed to continue to crumble as we drove by. Certainly a marked difference from Sorrento or Amalfi or even where the bus dropped me off in the center of Calitri earlier. Stone stairways and iron railings were exposed, suspended high above the street, leading nowhere. A bright red Campari sign caught my eye from a block of abandoned upper balconies. Whole rooms of ceramic tiled kitchens were exposed to daylight in a kind of surreal Lewis Hine photo void of people.

"What happened here?" I thought, but I didn't ask. The present was much more distracting.

We drove on through the town down a long, main street lined with stores then turned up into a cul-de-sac neighborhood lined with modern brick apartment buildings. An older woman waved from her third floor balcony as we drove up. Smiling, she looked as if she had always known this day would come, although she would rather have had it happen years ago. Her declarations and questions were rapid fire as soon as I stepped foot in her apartment.

"*Nipote di Nicola!*" she said all in Italian, which Vito translated.

"Where have you come from? And why has it taken you so long to come here to visit us? You are alone? And your parents? Why didn't they come with you?"

I barely had the courage to answer before she began the ubiquitous process of making us caffè.

At once demanding and compliant, Giuseppina Paolantonio was a study in old-world characterizations. She spoke no English and barely any Italian. Yet as we sat down to her kitchen table I found I was unusually at ease with her, and as my father's first cousin she immediately took possession of my well-being.

As I nursed my third *espresso* in less than two hours, she began with her version of the family legend of the four Paolantonio brothers who immigrated to America, and how the oldest brother, Francesco, Sr., her father, was called back home. Then she began to tell me stories of my grandfather.

With a toss of her head and a glint in her eye, she mimicked how she remembered her own *zio* Nicola. "*Un bello uomo*," she said, all but giggling. "*Alto e forte*."

Easy on the eyes and a hit with the ladies, the young twenty-something man she remembered, not yet married, had a determined gait and flirtatious smile. As I sat in her kitchen and listened to her tales of long ago, I was amazed at how much she knew and remembered. On this journey so far, she was the first person I had met with tangible memories of my grandfather Nicola and the life and parents he left behind. And her eagerness to share all that she felt and recalled was both a joy and heartbreak for me.

Then all at once she wanted to know about his life in America. Perhaps she assumed I knew something about him that she did not. But I was at a loss. Somewhat more gently, yet still frank, she wondered how he got on after my grandmother Angela Maria had died. But my heart was blank. She then asked,

"Didn't he have any girlfriends?"

My eyes went wide. But Giuseppina didn't flinch.

I gently shrugged and offered, "I don't know."

Nicola was still a powerful man in his early fifties when he lost his wife. So I suppose to Giuseppina he was capable of having relationships with other women. It was an innocent question, her voice filled with easy hopefulness. A man needs a woman, after all, she seemed to intimate. I put my hand to my heart. It suddenly felt as if someone else knew I was here and they were drawing me out. Then, I remembered a companion of my grandfather's who visited our family on Long Island when I was still a very young child. I could see her in my mind's eye. She was present at birthday parties, baby showers, and other family gatherings. Also in a few old black-and-white photos in my parent's big black photo album, womanly plump and rosy-cheeked, with and without my grandfather. Her name was Mary. My Aunt Mary Number 2, I used to call her.

Although I never saw her and Nicola together, she was the closest I had come to having the feeling of a grandparent in my life. Unconditional love. From her it flowed, was flowing now.

A sudden warmth from this childhood memory rose through me like a light-wave, though I didn't share—couldn't have shared—my thoughts with Giuseppina. I could never have expressed all of its poignant feelings to her in her language, nor the full bloom of my longing that caught me by surprise that moment in her kitchen. She just smiled. Across from her kitchen table a wall of wood and glass doors opened onto a balcony that looked out over the town and fields beyond. I didn't know it then but I would enjoy many summer evenings out there after dinner with her and her husband, zio Giovanni. There we would sit in the quiet dark night or watch late afternoon thunderstorms crackle and roll through the hills and valleys in the distance.

Vito returned. He tossed back his coffee while he motioned to me and began again for the door. I got up to follow him just as he and Giuseppina exchanged a brief conversation in their insiders language.

Then he said from the door, "*Allora*, see you tonight, *zia!*"

She called and waved as we descended the marble stairwell, "*Ciao, ciao. Ci vediamo stasera. Ciao...*"

She then continued watching from the kitchen balcony until we were gone.

Vito swung his pickup around to the main street of the town. I had no idea who we were scheduled to meet next. The morning had stretched to well past eleven and I felt I had already had a full day. I was famished and confused by all the espresso I had consumed. I didn't think I could accept another coffee, no matter what the protocol. Surely a bite to eat would revive me for an hour or so longer before we moved on.

But instead we parked along the main street halfway into town, and entered a double wood door at street level with a small nameplate on the wall. *Buongiornos* were exchanged between Vito and the young women seated behind the high front reception desk. They were typing at computers, answering phones, and navigating our unannounced—and I supposed by their faces—highly curious visit. Vito breezed past them with authority once he secured permission to enter the inner chamber of the office.

"*Permesso?*" he said confidently.

With a wave of his arm he held open the door for me to walk through. Squinting through a thick cloud of cigarette smoke I spied a well-dressed man standing behind an imposing black desk. I was quite anxious at the thought of another new introduction and now dumbstruck at the site of this tall, handsome, and proudly erect man before me. And again I felt this powerful pull. Was it fear or love? He turned slowly in my direction as I haltingly stepped into the room.

He did not speak first, so I offered a meek, "*Buongiorno*" with my hand outstretched.

Then, instead of fumbled Italian I told him my name in English.

Pause.

"*Buongiorno, signorina,*" he replied. *Signorina* was not something I'd been addressed as so far on this trip.

Long pause. I stood silent.

Then he took an equally long pull on his cigarette. Drama seemed his forte.

Francesco Paolantonio slowly rounded his desk and gently took my hand in greeting while he spoke in slow, deliberate English, "Your grandfather Nicola was a very great man."

Another long-suppressed wave rose from my chest to my throat. Still holding my hand, Francesco seemed to steady me. His eyes then smiled a warm welcome and I finally melted from exhaustion.

He offered me a seat in one of the black leather chairs opposite his desk. From behind it, he reached into a tall glass case filled with volumes of books and framed dedications and pulled out a vintage red, silk-lined case. Inside was a shiny black fountain pen.

"This was a gift from your grandfather," he said. "Forty years ago."

Tears welled in my eyes. I steadied myself through the cloud of emotion in the room. Weak and without breakfast, or anything to nibble on since early this morning, I could barely concentrate on this moment.

Francesco pulled another long drag from his cigarette filling the room with new ribbons of thick white smoke.

"Would you like a coffee?" he asked.

Cerca Trova (Seek and Ye Shall Find)

Spigolare
(To Glean)

"*Buon Pranzo e ci vediamo più tardi!*" Vito said. His final obligation complete, he left us with his salutations and hurried off.

I had been delivered successfully to Francesco Paolantonio, who asked me to call him Franco.

Franco had dispatched an old friend of his to the office with some photos of the two of them taken years ago. As the friend entered the inner chamber, he stopped short in front of Franco's big black desk, absolutely flummoxed to find me seated behind it, busily firing off emails to my family.

I looked up from my typing just as he wordlessly handed me a few small black-and-white photos. "*Molto bello ragazzi!*" I couldn't help but blurt out, incorrectly.

The friend, still perplexed, only relaxed when Franco reappeared with a tray of coffee, smiling in approval of my compliments of their handsome good looks as young men.

"This is Francesco, my cousin," Franco said.

I rose from my seat with a, "*Piacere*."

Francesco was much shorter than Franco but no less impeccably dressed. The two were no more than twenty years old in the photos, perhaps younger. It must have been the mid-1950s. They were walking in a seaside town wearing custom-made suits, looking as handsome as can be.

"Here we are in Salerno," Franco said.

"*Bello*," I repeated.

Then, another photo showed my grandfather Nicola and Franco's father, Vito Sr., with Franco's older sister between them. All three were seated on the edge of a beautiful marble fountain. I was a little taken aback when I saw my grandfather there between the two. The photo must have been taken on one of his last trips back to his hometown, in the years after World War II. I didn't think then, that the photos of Francesco and Franco, the handsome first cousins, could have been taken by my grandfather. That it might have been his own camera, or my father's, brought with him from America all those years ago, that had taken these images. Or that Franco, having seen that I had made my solo journey with just a shoulder bag and a 35mm camera in hand—my OM1, given to me by my father for my eighteenth birthday—made the connection, linking that long-ago day to me and my grandfather on his own.

Franco and I were now laughing together as he made copies of the photos for me to take to my family back home. He was clearly enjoying this unexpected sojourn into his youth on what might have been an otherwise normal day in his office. And by now everyone else in the office had left for lunch, so he put out the last of his many cigarettes before we headed out the door to his car on the street. Still with my nervous politeness, and lack of complete comprehension of most of the morning, I did not fully understand we were on our way to his home for the midday meal. I was just in everyone's charge. And though Franco spoke in English, he explained in the car that this was the first time in many years he had to recall the language.

Slowly we drove down the main street. Inside his car the center console ashtray overflowed with spent cigarettes and ash dusted the leather seats. I noticed too that by now most of the residents had headed home. Shops were closed or closing. There were no restaurants visible in town for tourists because there were no tourists in town. We drove past the piazza where I had arrived by bus early that morning. There was the fruttivendolo closing the gate of his corner fruit market. The men gathered earlier on the street outside the bar and under the portico were all gone. Schoolchildren with enormous backpacks walked in twos and threes. Elderly women disappeared behind closing curtains.

Slowly, we drove.

Winding down the same switchback road I traveled up to the town, we arrived at very near the bottom of the hill and pulled in front of a stand-alone, four-story apartment building. To the left was a professional-sized soccer field. Across the street was what looked like a high school. Behind the school rose the town, what the Romans once called *Aletrium*, stacked with row upon row of crumbling stone houses, built to follow the ascent of the hill, ending at the top in the ruins of a centuries-old castle. The castle was originally built by the Langobards who ruled Italy from the sixth to eighth centuries. It was one of a few strategic Southern Italian strongholds from their southern expansion in the late sixth century and had had some three hundred rooms, before being completely destroyed in an earthquake in 1694.

Slowly we climbed the marble stairs up three flights to an apartment door. Franco's wife Raffaela was waiting just inside.

A quiet and kind woman with soft, lineless features, she politely ushered us in. She led me first into the dark living room on the right and asked if I needed to freshen up before we sat down for lunch. I was grateful to be moments away from the first meal I'd had since the evening before. Though, after the long inland journey and a morning filled with first-time meetings, all that coffee and heightened emotional confusion, my appetite had plunged.

I retired to their bathroom. After splashing fresh water on my face, I ran my fingers through my tousled hair in the mirror. All at once I was exhausted and embarrassed. What was I doing here? Raffaela and her home were refined and dignified. Franco in his office had been the same. I looked at myself, dressed in jeans and a brown leather jacket and what seemed now to be a little over-the-top red, white, and blue Hush Puppies boots, warm and waterproof. I seemed an ersatz hipster, an errant Wonder Woman allowed into the inner sanctum of a well-tended Italian home. I struggled to hold it together.

Raffaela prepared and served lunch in their warm sunny kitchen. Three simple courses with a strong local red wine. At the table, Franco began to ask about my family and my life in America. I recounted a few facts about my mother and father and my three siblings; where we lived, how old we were, and how many grandchildren there were. Franco and Raffaela were polite and patient, yet curious that I had traveled all this way alone to discover my roots. What was I looking for and what did I expect to find?

They told me of their children, who were grown, married, and starting families of their own. Franco seemed fascinated and more than a little concerned that I was a single, independent woman, a kind of artist traveling alone in Italy. Southern Italy. Eventually the question came up about why I was not married. I could see the wheels turning in their heads as they tried to come up with some reasonable answer to my singleness.

Then, almost in unison, they asked, "Don't you want to be married?"

I winced at having been put on the spot. "Yes, of course. I was close twice. That is, I've been asked twice. But I decided against it. In the end, they weren't the right choices." As soon as I said this I wondered why I, a single American woman in the prime of her life, had come all this way alone.

Unfazed, Franco simply nodded. "Well, since you are a princess, you must wait up there for your prince." He gestured in the direction of the French doors at the opposite end of the kitchen. I turned, perplexed, to look out their balcony at an unobstructed view of the strong and gracefully arching hillside of Calitri. "Perhaps you should wander around up there until he appears."

Interesting. Who doesn't want to be a princess?

After our meal Raffaela busied herself with putting her kitchen back in order. She gently refused my offer to help, so I followed Franco to the living room where we continued our conversation. In his slow English and my halting Italian, we labored through our language handicaps to get to know one another. As in his office, the room held an impressive collection of encyclopedias, volumes of collected literature, and a component stereo in glass cases.

We sat down on adjacent sofas and after a moment he opened the conversation.

"What type of music do you like?" he asked as he lit a cigarette.

"My favorites are jazz and the blues. Both original American music. From New Orleans."

I smiled. "I like jazz, too. And most other popular music. But I love the Beatles. My father bought me all their early records. I learned big band jazz from my parents' record collection." Franco nodded. "My parents still listen to Frank Sinatra, Count Basie, Gene Krupa." I added. "My father loves Ella Fitzgerald too."

In the brief time we sat together, we discussed art, entertainment, and American politics. Particularly, his disdain for the death penalty, which he insisted was a barbaric and unjust form of American jurisprudence.

Then Franco leaned in with an unexpected question. "Do you think the Mafia assassinated Kennedy?"

It caught me by surprise, yet I recognized his concern. Of being lumped in with the doings of nefarious members of his—our—Southern Italian heritage. I was only four at the time but I remember everything that black day. The sorrow of others. Watching the funeral. The sober glow of my Aunt Rose's black-and-white television set in her darkened living room in East New York. My father had already moved us to Stewart Manor, a suburb on Long Island. I don't remember who else was there in her apartment that Monday. Maybe they had all gone to Mass. Venerated, romanticized, the Mafia. Someone always wanted to know if you were in. I never understood why. My family, my childhood, was far from this kind of occlusion. We were a product of President Kennedy's Camelot. My Italian-American aunts and uncles had served in two wars, were blue collar earners with American hopes and dreams. The Mafia? We children never thought of it, or were shielded from it. And then, a scant three months after the assassination, the Beatles arrived, and with the release of "Please Please Me" everything changed. But Franco was waiting.

I pulled out of my private reverie and shook my head no. "I don't think they" (we Italians) "had anything to do with it."

He turned to light another cigarette and that concluded our discussion.

Raffaela appeared in the living room not to join us but to offer me a place to lie down for a while. With appreciation, I accepted her offer and followed her to the adjacent bedroom. There she lowered the shutters to block the room from afternoon light, turned down the single bed, and left me to myself. I lay down, emotionally and physically exhausted, yet my mind continued to race. I suppose it didn't help that I had had enough espresso to fuel a small locomotive. Still, I must have drifted off, because upon awakening I felt a deep heaviness in my bones. When I realized again my whereabouts, and my tentative relationship to everyone here, tears welled in my eyes as I faced the darkened room alone. But I wasn't alone.

A soft knock came at the door. It was Raffaela. She offered to have me freshen up with whatever I needed from her dressing room. Once composed, I rounded the hallway to the kitchen where she was making coffee. In a few moments Franco appeared in the kitchen doorway with his equally tall older sister Teodolinda from her family's apartment below. She was trailed by her son Vito, my emissary of the morning. The kitchen was now filled again with the sounds of the Calitrian dialect as Vito went over our morning adventure in his pickup truck for the first time with his mother and Raffaela.

Teodolinda Paolantonio had a large frame and jovial face. Her manner was both cheerful and imposing. She smiled broadly at me while following the events as described by her son, occasionally interrupting him to ask questions: "How did she get here?" "She's alone?" "Who has she met?"

Out of the corner of my eye another person had entered the now crowded kitchen. It was *nonna* Migliorina, Francesco and Teodolinda's mother. She lived upstairs in the top loft apartment. The Paolantonio family owned the entire apartment building as well as the family businesses on the ground floor. Behind the 1980s era building was the one-hundred-year-old *casa di campagna*, or country house, and their fields, where most of these immediate Paolantonio relatives, including my grandfather, had been raised.

The level of conversation and emotion in the room rose around me. Where Raffaela and Francesco were quiet, dignified, and reserved, Teodolinda and Vito were vociferous and excitable. Tiny nonna sat quietly at the table and listened.

Then the doorbell rang and Raffaela excused herself to answer it. After a moment or two, nonna Migliorina slowly rose from the table and rounded the doorway to see who had arrived. Eventually I was drawn out of the room. I rounded the door to the hallway as if willed by a benign force.

Raffaela appeared to be begging forgiveness from the women at her front door, as was the courtesy, as she deemed it not a particularly convenient time for visitors. Italians, I have come to learn, are fiercely private in their own homes. Visitors outside the immediate family rarely, if ever, make unannounced calls. Even a neighbor across an immaculate hallway might never knock on an adjacent door unless an unusual circumstance exists. But it seemed this was no ordinary circumstance. Concetta Borea and her daughter Maria Cicoira had come from across town to meet me.

Concetta, tall and regal, her long silver hair pulled back in a round braided bun, dressed entirely in widow's black, projected a deep reserve of energy. Maria was at least twenty-five years or so her junior, shorter, with slightly graying hair. They smiled hopefully at the chance to enter and introduce themselves, and as I approached from behind, Raffaela finally acquiesced and invited them in.

Concetta Borea's sighs of delight were soft and resigned as she entered the apartment. She grasped my hand tightly and brought her softly wrinkled face to mine in a long singsong of whispered murmurs. Who she was and how she came to know of my arrival today in Calitri was a mystery to me, yet she stayed fixed by my side.

We all made our way back into the kitchen as Concetta quietly began speaking in dialect. As she spoke, she pulled two photobooth-style photos from her large black vinyl handbag. She handed the first one to me and I nearly fainted from another sudden wave of energy. It was as though something or someone had passed through my body and said,

"Look at me."

Was it recognition? Or was recognition wanted from me?

In my hand was a photo of a man who immediately reminded me of my father. He had hard, masculine features with large dark eyes, and a crop of platinum hair that framed his stern face. But he was tougher than my father, hard-bitten, clearly of another time. Concetta's long-dead husband Pasquale Cicoira had looked directly into the lens with an old-world seriousness.

Concetta explained, he was Angela Maria's younger brother, Pasquale Cicoira.

Until that moment, I hadn't really thought about my grandmother's side of the family. I had introduced myself as a Paolantonio, thought of myself as a Paolantonio, and from my first moments in town, Paolantonio relatives had usurped all my time. With Concetta's arrival, I was thrust headlong into the lost world of my grandmother for the first time since my childhood—nearly forty years. And I felt myself beginning to unravel.

I was ushered into the cool dark living room for a seat on the sofa. Concetta sat right beside me, taking my hand. Quietly she began recounting a story to the others who had gathered in front of us, encircling us, hovering just over our heads. It took place in Calitri. Somewhere in 1935 or 1936.

A dark energy filled the room. I surmised the tale was about my grandmother, as all the eyes in the room drifted gravely back and forth from Concetta to me as she spun her tale. With her cool soft hand in mine, I understood almost nothing but felt every heart-rending wave as she continued with her memories of her sister-in-law, Angela Maria Cicoira. Spellbound, I felt something pulling me in.

My grandmother, Angela Maria, was the biggest mystery of my life. The only memento I have of her is one photograph. Actually, it is a composite photo of two separate images of her and my grandfather Nicola created to look like a couples' portrait. Retouched by hand and signed by a studio artist, it looks like it was made in the late 1940s.

For years my parents had it tucked away in a long narrow credenza drawer in the dining room. No frame. No context. No reverence. I would stumble upon it every now and again while looking in that drawer for something that might help me complete a homework assignment or grade school art project. It was sort of a family junk drawer. There were odd pencils and rolls of tape, used greeting cards and old gift package ribbons up top; scattered coins, clips, and rubber bands resting beneath. Occasionally forgotten family snapshots made their way in there too. And then, tossed in carelessly with all the rest of the unclaimed items, was the 8"x10" black-and-white portrait of my father's parents.

In it, my grandmother's perfectly proportioned oval face holds a soft smile. Her eyes are warm and alert. She seems to have engaged the photographer as if she were his friend. An air of benevolent calm fills her side of the frame, bearing no trace of the few facts that were known about her. My grandfather is dressed in an elegant black wool suit and what looks like a handmade silk tie. He holds himself proudly, erectly; his gaze rests off in the near distance, somewhere out of the frame. Brought together by a trick of the darkroom, they look as if they were sitting in separate rooms of life. My grandfather's right shoulder is tucked just behind my grandmother's left. It is the only visual evidence in the photograph of their union. Whenever I came upon this photo, never having had any stories or memories to accompany the people in it, I often just put it away in the drawer and forgot about it.

Or so I thought.

As a young girl I was reduced to fantasy about her. Along with the mystery of the one photo, I was named after her, my hair and features resembled hers, and so as a young impressionable child, I just assumed my destiny would follow hers. For years, I feared I too would end up lost and forgotten. Bereft and left to be sifted over in a family junk drawer by a curious grandchild.

It was my mother who would recall her favorite story as a

teenager about the crazy woman leaning out the window yelling down to the kids on the street below. As always, the young man she would marry, my father, who also played on that street, remained silent. Back in the 1940s, in East New York, didn't all immigrant mothers from little Italian villages lean out their windows on hot summer nights to call their children in for dinner, or to keep an eye on the goings on in the street? I'd seen this on television, in some movie or TV commercial. Yet somehow the story grew in legend in a young child's mind about her grandmother being in an unstable—even unruly—state of emotional balance.

Was it out of fear or love? That standard folk tale of the forbidden thing. I know now my parents were just trying to protect me from some sad stories about Angela Maria that I didn't need to know. But that was long ago. What about the good things? Her warmth? Wasn't she kind? What did she cook? Did she bake breads, cakes? It felt like the lack of love to be denied access to her. My Italian grandmother!

The only other paternal relative, living nearby in Queens, was my father's older sister Mary—my Aunt Mary, my godmother. Even she never spoke of her mother. No questions were answered and nothing, nothing was offered.

The only daughter born to Nicola and Angela Maria, my Aunt Mary was a formidable person on the outside, though over the years she too proved unresolved and withered on the inside. She too would be stricken by the mysterious family ailment—unrevealed to me; was it depression?—struggling for years in and out of hospitals and sadly dying, over medicated, in her own bed in relatively young middle age. She was just one year older than her mother had been when her mother had died. I remember Aunt Mary's funeral well. It was 1974. I was not quite out of junior high and stricken with a blow that confirmed my worst fears. Silence around the cause of her illness persisted and prevailed. No one offered an explanation. The chasms of repressed tensions between brother and sister passed down from my father were oceanic. As a teen, all I wanted to know was how far would I follow in their footsteps? Would I develop this mysterious ailment too?

There is an underlying and unfortunate provenance of the women of the Cicoira lineage. My grandmother Angela Maria, her younger sister Maura, her only daughter Mary, and even her first granddaughter Diana were all struck down in the prime of their lives with an unnamed ailment that isolated and hospitalized them and, with the exception of Diana, felled them in their early fifties. These ghosts of my grandmother's lineage and the secrets behind them haunted me for years. I've traveled far to forget them. The farthest, and most alien trip was turning out to be the most challenging to my hard-won sense of acceptance and calm. Italy. Calitri.

While I was remembering these things, Concetta was continuing her story of Angela Maria. "*Voi siete la luce*," she said at the end, having wound us all down this sad memory lane.

"What does that mean?" I asked.

" 'You are the light.' " Franco translated. Not an oblique comment. I had never felt the light before.

Concetta said something else. " 'You have come all this way to shed the light on our Angela Maria.' "

For she was long lost to Concetta too, having left Calitri for the last time more than sixty years ago, never heard from, or returning again.

So the journey was ordered up for me then. It was up to me to stumble upon Angela Maria, the unbeloved, at the age of forty, while I still had the chance to break the spell. I really hadn't known what I was looking for until I got here.

Italian fairy dust was pulling me in.

Spigolare (To Glean)

Via Sant' Antuono, 49

☙

Content with the success of her mission, Concetta Borea began her salutations of departure as she slowly rose from the sofa. Before she could make her way to the door, I jumped up to get my camera. I needed something of this ephemeral meeting to take back home with me. She and her daughter Maria Cicoira made themselves available as I directed them out onto a long balcony with the Southern Apennines behind them in the distance. Concetta assured me in my haste that we would have more time together, as they had arranged for me to come by Maria's tomorrow afternoon for caffè to meet more of my relatives on my grandmother's side of the family.

The following day? But I was scheduled to leave on a bus this afternoon. How was I going to honor this appointment and meet the other side of my family? Once Concetta and Maria left I could barely contain a new wave of confusion, and a new flood of tears.

Franco and Raffaela hoped I would pass the night with them. But they told me that with her invitation for dinner, zia Giuseppina had also laid claim to the honor of having me as her overnight guest. Since she was the elder relative, and more apt to be offended if I didn't accept, I acquiesced to sleep the night in her apartment. Then I made sure to ask Francesco to contact the Freda's back in Avellino.

Francesco drove me over to her apartment on *via* Cicoira. I arrived with the few items I had with me that day. I hadn't yet met zio Giovanni, her husband. A strong and intensely resolute man with few words and many skills, he looked pleased to meet me. Giuseppina had spent the whole afternoon cooking and preparing for dinner. As soon as I arrived, she asked me to set the table in the dining room and it made me feel right at home.

Shortly after, her son Berardino and his wife Rosetta arrived. New greetings were expressed all around. Berardino spoke halting yet correct English. Rosetta, though cordial and curious, barely uttered a few words. Their teenage daughter Giusy, who became the official translator, would soon follow. Vito Cestone, my morning emissary, his wife Lucia, and their two young sons were also on their way over.

With their arrivals, dinner was soon underway.

Ten distant relatives—newly met strangers—tightly arranged around the dining table, all clamoring for my attention. Questions in dialect were bantered about. Giusy Giovane, as I came to affectionately call her, named after her grandmother Giuseppina, dutifully translated as much as she could. Their curiosity about their newly acquired American cousin from Los Angeles was boundless.

Noticing that I carried a camera, they began to ask me about my personal life.

"Are you a photographer?" someone asked.

"Why are you single?"

"What's it like living in Hollywood?"

"Do you take nude pictures?" That last question came from Berardino.

The table collectively scoffed, as did I, and he seemed to momentarily slink into embarrassment.

Truth was—how did Berardino know?—that I owned a number of nudes, hung on the walls in my bedroom; even one taken of me. Nude. They were artful images, gifts from friends and photographers I worked with or managed. Nudes. But I scoffed with the others to project a simple, personal chasteness. As an emissary, *a parente lontano*, a distant relative come all this way, I wouldn't have wanted to give them the wrong impression of my life in America.

At a peak moment after dinner and several glasses of zio Giovanni's peerless homemade wine and then a strong digestivo, a homemade *limoncello*, I got the nerve to make the transatlantic call to my parents in California, and rouse them out of bed to say hello to their relatives for the first time.

Zia Giuseppina handed me the phone. The din at the table was at its loudest. All eyes were fixed on me. The moment I motioned that I had a connection to the U.S., they fell immediately, dutifully silent.

It was 7 a.m. in Los Angeles. I surmised my father could detect the long distance connection just as he picked up the receiver.

"*Buonasera*," I said, a slight lilt in my voice.

"You mean *buongiorno*," was his casual but present reply. My father never lost his Brooklyn accent after more than forty years on Long Island and at least a dozen in California. "How are you doing over there?" he asked.

I could hear my mother in the background rousing out of sleep, "Is that Angela? Is everything alright?"

He passed the phone to my mother.

"Of course, everything's fine. I'm sitting around a dining table in Calitri with about ten of Daddy's relatives, and they all want to say hello!"

As I handed the phone to zia Giuseppina, everyone clamored to be part of the conversation. I watched and listened closely as she and my mother—on the other end of the transatlantic and cultural line—were locked in simultaneous misunderstandings. It was beautiful.

"This is Marie, Angela's mom. It's morning here. We're not quite awake yet," I heard my mother through the other end of the receiver. "How many are you all? Hello?"

"*Salve. Sì, sì...sono Giuseppina.*" Zia Giuseppina could barely keep up. "*Sì, sì.* Good, good."

"Take care of our daughter for us!" Then Giuseppina handed the phone back to me.

"Dad?"

"Hello, I mean ciao," he said.

"Dad, everyone in Calitri says hello," I said. "And they all remember your father."

"That's good," he said. "Take care of yourself there now."

"Of course. Don't you want to talk to anyone?"

The conversation lasted only moments but it was enough to elicit a new round of questions and inquiries from the group about everyone back home. My parents, lost to the translations, merely continued to enlist my safety on the trip, asked for a postcard, and then were gone.

When at last I climbed into the impeccably fresh single bed, I hardly thought rest was possible after this seemingly endless day of new and old emotions. My heart and mind reeled. Zia Giuseppina first made sure I was comfortable then left me to my privacy in the spare bedroom with its panoramic view that overlooked the darkened hills of Campania.

I thought about my conversation with my parents and how my father didn't want to talk to anyone. My relatives were surprised and saddened when they learned I wasn't raised in the company of my Italian-born grandparents. Most of them hadn't had to forge ahead in life without the loving and often practical guidance of their family elders. I supposed they imagined it an unfortunate by-product of the immigrant story.

With determination and spunk, my parents raised their four children without their own parents. Their first apartment was on Himrod Street in the Bushwick section of East New York, Brooklyn, then an area largely populated with Italian immigrants and their extended families. They married six months earlier than planned in the winter of 1955 to qualify for a vacancy in a building on their street. Early photos of my brother and me being bathed in the kitchen sink or happily playing on the linoleum floor are a black-and-white substitute for any memories I have of those early years.

Then, when I was two years old, my father moved us to a 1920s duplex on a wide shaded street in Stewart Manor on Long Island. My mother was the first of her multi-sibling family to live in a house in the suburbs. In 1961, the small incorporated village of Stewart Manor was a charming tree-lined enclave of mostly Irish Catholics. We would remain one of the few Italian-American families in this neighborhood, thirty minutes from Manhattan by the LIRR, for thirty years.

Being Italian-American in Stewart Manor had little impact on my early development, or so I thought at the time. Large family gatherings at our house on Sundays or holidays were the norm. While my mother's older sisters commanded the kitchen, my uncles retired to our backyard in summer, the sofa in winter. Freshly made meat sauce over #8 Ronzoni spaghetti or frozen Star ravioli were Sunday staples. While these details were instrumental to my upbringing, I missed out without any real grandmothers in the kitchen.

The following morning I awoke to the sounds of zia Giuseppina quietly rustling around the kitchen as she prepared coffee for breakfast. Zio Giovanni was already dressed for his morning rounds of first tending to his olive grove and vineyard in the fields of the casa di campagna, then to gathering with his fellow pensioners around the porticos and small piazzas in town.

For now it was just the three of us in their sunny kitchen, the long-lost American *nipote* and two elder *parenti* who spoke not a trace of English. Still we had an easy time with each other. After a double espresso and several homemade soft and dunkable biscotti, I followed zio Giovanni out on to the balcony. The morning sky of this late November day was bright, crisp, and clear as we sat in the silence of our culture gap, taking in the countryside. As far as the eye could see, rolling wheat fields graced the horizon with the ancient hilltown of Calitri in the near distance. And not a sound could be heard.

To my surprise, an elder relative, Angelo, Giuseppina's cousin, arrived at the apartment to offer his services as a driver. Seemed zia had planned an outing for us. We left the apartment, climbed into his immaculate late model Fiat, and took off down the street. I had little idea what the plan was so I just sat back and watched again as the town slid by the car window. I was beginning to recognize my surroundings a bit more as we once again passed the piazza and its large stone portico filled with men where I first arrived. This time though, we continued straight up the main street heading straight toward the *Centro Storico*.

Winding around and around town in the car, I was soon lost in the visual maze of narrow cobblestone streets, vertical layers of ancient houses, and elderly women dressed in widow's black standing on corners or in doorways. It was only a few minutes drive into the center of the old village, yet visually it was of a completely other time.

"There's zia Concetta!" I called out from the back seat.

As we whizzed past her tall frame too quickly, I craned my neck out the back window and waved. I think she saw me, and I was happy to recognize her. Angelo parked the car up a narrow street that barely fit his Fiat. We then took a route by foot. I was completely distracted by the other-worldliness of the old village, as if we had stepped back in time at least one hundred years.

We walked up a narrow stone-paved via, on a slight curve, the other half rounding its way down from the further upper reaches of the hill town. On the right, an arched stone carriage entrance to a patrician mansion from at least the sixteenth century, its enormous, weathered wooden doors were closed to the street. Above the entrance was a medieval-style loggia, long and curved to follow the street, with white columns that supported wide open arches. Across from the mansion was a lovely ochre-painted outer wall of a smaller home, obviously recently restored. The lintel of this house was of carved stone, too. A simple, eight-petaled, antique flower motif repeated at the four corners of the doorway. Two terracotta pots of bright red geraniums graced the entrance.

Then, just ahead on the right stood two much smaller, dilapidated houses. They appeared to have been uninhabited since the beginning of time.

We three stopped at this point in the via. Pointing upward toward one of the doorways, Giuseppina wasted no time in announcing that this house in front of us was the past residence of "*il tuo nonno Nicola.*" At first I was a little confused. Perhaps it was the language barrier. I reflected a few seconds to understand what was being said. And then, taking in the scene, it hit me.

Did the sign on the front door say "*Vendesi*"—For Sale—? I gasped and immediately ran to climb the dozen or more heavy stone steps to the landing. Sure enough, there was a long, faded, handwritten sign nailed to the door. I quickly turned to call down to Giuseppina and Angelo, "This house is for sale!"

"*Attenzione!*" They expressed more than a little concern that I was about to plunge to the street from excitement.

But I could not contain my glee. First I took a photo of the two of them standing on the pavement below from the top of the steps. For posterity? Then I shouted down my immediate decision. "I'm going to buy this house!"

From the very first time I had traveled in Tuscany several years before, I had the natural and overwhelming desire to return again and again. Strolling the streets of the medieval towns, I was captivated by the sights smells and sounds of those living, cooking, and eating just out of reach. I felt a fully qualified sense of belonging to their secret society, cut off from the wayward tourists below. I daydreamed of living on a Tuscan hillside with sheep grazing in a field below my windows. But how to reveal myself to the locals then of my feelings?

Suddenly, standing before the house for sale, it occurred to me how much easier it might be to set up house in a town where relatives were easily available, for counsel, for comfort, in the event there was some need. With this third trip to Italy and my innocent journey to Calitri, it seemed I had hit some mark, or maybe I had unknowingly struck a deal with the universe.

But zia Giuseppina and Angelo were not as convinced. In fact, they dismissed my declaration easily and quickly, as if the mere idea were preposterous.

Angelo shrugged with a "*Beh*." Giuseppina laughed nervously. Then, pausing as if for a moment they were actually considering the thought, they both said, "Don't be crazy."

At the time, I assumed it was nothing more than another communication barrier. Could this be how you were absolved of a past lives sins? How you stumbled upon absolution? Could I now qualify as a real Italian, fully vested in all its dividends?

Angelo and Giuseppina called me down from the landing and made to leave. I glanced up to appeal to the heavens. Whoever was up there was unimportant. Certainly they realized how this immediately qualified as an imperative. Not even they could dismiss this opportunity to lay some claim to the origin of my ancestry, my Italian roots. But I was in their charge.

Without any further comments from Giuseppina and Angelo we headed back to the Fiat, passing a small chapel tucked into a corner on a tight curve in the via. To change the mood I asked, "Zia, what's the name of this little church?"

"*Chiesetta di Sant'Antuono,*" she said.

I admired its simple facade, one large round window set above heavy wooden doors. Creeping jasmine in terracotta pots wound up the walls on either side of the single stone step. I thought it was probably once the private chapel of the family whose medieval palazzo was behind us, back up and around the bend. I imagined my grandfather as a boy, thinking he might have grown up nearby, playing on the stone step, or even marrying my grandmother at the altar inside.

Black-and-white funeral posters lined the adjacent walls as we continued down the lane. I kept looking back, visually retracing our whereabouts so as not to forget the spot. The Centro Storico with its labyrinth of *vie, vicoli,* and *scali* proved impossible to navigate without a guide. It would take me at least two more separate visits to the village years apart before I found that corner again on my own.

With Angelo behind the wheel we headed off again but in another direction out of the old village. No sooner had we arrived in Franco's office than the scoop was out. I was now officially the daffy American with crazy plans. In his office, Franco quietly ushered me into his private chamber as if he had heard nothing. Once inside he offered me his computer to email my family. He pulled on his cigarette and wandered aimlessly around his office while I commandeered the use of his captain's desk and black leather chair.

"You are writing a novel," he joked, seeing how much I was writing to my family back home. He offered me a coffee and then a cigarette. I accepted both and began to entreat him to my plan.

"I'm serious about the house." I said. "It was once *nonno* Nicola's! I'll need photos, and to contact the owner."

He listened gravely, silently, from the opposite side of his desk, the client side, pulling on his cigarette once, twice. He was nothing if not a dramatist.

Then he gently changed the subject.

Back in her kitchen on via Cicoira, zia Giuseppina was busily preparing for my last afternoon meal with her family before I headed back to Avellino and my waiting hosts, the Freda's. Only a day and a half had passed since my arrival here, but my heart and soul had traversed generations. Francesco once again delivered me by car from his office to Giuseppina's apartment. He made the three flights of stairs to the apartment with me then stood by as I rounded the door of the kitchen. There on the table in front of a happily smiling Giuseppina and her daughter-in-law Rosetta, was a tremendous mound of homemade *tagliatelle*. The two women seemed dwarfed by its abundance.

Pale golden ribbons of fresh pasta were heaped onto a large round wooden board. The room and my senses were filled with the aroma of fresh semolina and eggs. It all seemed to glow from within. On the stove simmered a bright red *sugo di pomodoro* and in the oven was a freshly roasted chicken that Giuseppina told me she had killed just yesterday. (I had spied her curious activity in the gardens below the living room window at Franco and Raffaela's.) My eyes went wide. The sight of the pasta, the intoxicating aromas, this realization, all came to an audible gasp. Visibly pleased with my astonishment, Giuseppina turned to the stove to put the water to boil.

This final lunch with zia Giuseppina, zio Giovanni, and their family was enormous; the tagliatelle alone could last me a lifetime. After lunch, Vito Cestone came by for a last caffè, followed by Francesco.

The two men held court over Giuseppina's small kitchen, now crowded with my new relatives offering their last salutations. Angelo Cirminiello from that morning came by with his wife Lucia and there was Berardino and his wife Rosetta too. Most everyone made time to come and say goodbye before Francesco escorted me back to Avellino.

Everyone stalled for time.

In the last conversations around the kitchen, I promised to send them all some of my very own Italian almond biscotti, a baking tradition I keep at Christmas. It would be but a small repayment of gratitude and thanks for all they had done for me in these brief thirty-six hours. Finally, Franco hedged to leave, explaining he wanted to reach Avellino before dark. Slowly we all went into the hallway, hugging and murmuring final goodbyes as I fought back tears.

Zia Giuseppina broke away for a moment and rushed to her pantry to bring me two home-cured *sopressata*.

"One for you," she said, smiling, with tears in her eyes. "And one for your parents."

Down the staircase and onto the street they continued their goodbyes, then called and waved from the balcony. Once we were in Franco's car and he rounded the curve in the cul-de-sac, we spotted zia Teodolinda with her daughter-in-law, racing around the opposite corner just in time to say goodbye.

I jumped out of the car and I gave them both hugs of thanks, took photos of their warm smiles, and again we were off. We made one more stop at Franco's apartment building at the bottom of the hill for a last goodbye to his wife Raffaela and his mother, nonna Migliorina. Up the stairs I climbed one last time. Raffaela, still quiet and reserved, with a trace of sadness in her eyes, gave me a gentle hug and a double kiss on both cheeks. I could tell there was still a lot there to discover, and all at once I did not want to leave.

Up further still to nonna's loft apartment, where she was waiting with a small sepia-toned portrait of her husband, Vito Paolantonio, my father's first cousin. His young leonine profile, strong, proud, and handsome. He shared the name of my great-grandfather Vito Paolantonio, Sr., with my father—the elder patriarch of our families, both Italian and American. The father of the four emigrating brothers who made it possible for our lineage to exist and for my contemporary discovery to unfold on this incredible journey inland to this small mountain village in far eastern Campania.

I had the photo of Vito Paolantonio framed when I arrived in Verona the following day and placed it on my desk at home in Los Angeles to remind me of these moments until I could return to Calitri.

Franco was waiting downstairs at the wheel of his car to escort me back to Avellino. With a last glance I spied an illustrated *stemma*, or coat of arms, on the wall of nonna Migliorina's apartment. The Paolantonio family name was clearly written, with a declaration from the mid-1700s revealing an earlier incarnation of our surname that combined two first names; Paolo and Antonio. No surprise there. Perhaps two brothers? The white ground of the shield was divided in three by two wide black bands. The top band held two six-pointed stars. The middle ground held three round charges that looked to be Renaissance-style caps and in the bottom ground two crescent moons. Crowning the top of the shield was a knight's helmet topped with the opulent feathered plumes of a prince.

I wondered if my father knew about this?

Later, I learned the combination of the names Paolo and Antonio occurred in the late Renaissance, in the city-state of Gubbio. Gubbio was an important stronghold of the Romans.

Independent and landlocked in central Italy. An original Roman settlement, it belonged to the eastern provinces just inland from the important trade ports along the Adriatic Sea. The nearby towns of Perugia, Assisi, Spoleto, and Todi were rich in religious, artistic, and political intrigue of pre-Roman and medieval history. I could practically feel the ghostly mists of reincarnation.

But Franco was waiting. Raffaela and *nonna* Migliorina shooed me down the stairs. I was learning in Southern Italy, a woman doesn't keep a man waiting.

Once I was in the car, I pulled out a small journal from my bag and a pencil from the glove box and quickly recovered the illustration from memory. Franco was curious. I asked him, "Is the shield authentic?" While thinking to myself it was far sexier to have ancestral lineage in a beautiful city in Umbria during the Renaissance than contemporary roots in rural Campania.

Franco dismissed the document. "It's a fabrication," he scoffed. "A strictly opportunistic and commercial fake. Greedy, dubious historians will trace your family history for a price." I had obviously struck a nerve. We drove out of town and discussed it no further.

A few minutes later Franco's energy seemed to change when he turned on the car stereo and a Whitney Houston CD began to play. It was the soundtrack to *The Bodyguard*. Franco and I listened in silence, as I followed his somber lead. I was finally heading out of town, thoroughly changed by all these new feelings, new meetings. Then without preamble he revealed that he and Raffaela had lost their youngest child and only daughter just three years ago, when she was twenty-three. He didn't mention her name. And he didn't say how. I was struck by his sad admission.

"I am so sorry," was all I knew to say.

We drove on down the two-lane Ofantina toward Avellino. He leaned in to turn up the volume on the song "*I Will Always Love You.*" I kept the pull in my heart to myself as we both let the song carry us through. When we reached the Freda's apartment,

Franco saw me up to where Carla Freda waited with freshly made caffè. Franco personally thanked Carlo and Carla for hosting me, and I felt the emotional crumbling begin. The final goodbye would come soon. And I wasn't ready.

Finally Franco rose to leave. "It's nearing dark," he said. "I must return to my family."

We all rose for the door, my heart sinking fast. Franco looked me in the eyes as I lowered my head. "Don't cry," he said. All I could muster was a nod. "Remember. Don't cry."

The front door shut and I collapsed into tears.

Via Sant'Antuono, 49　51

Santo Spirito
(Holy Spirit)

I returned to Italy in June of 2001 for three months when I rented the house of an American friend in Verona. Carol was a freelancer, a color press supervisor at Mondadori, married to a Veronese man named Lucio. When I stopped in Verona on my way back from Calitri last fall, I had had dinner with them, and so recounted my recent adventure in the small Southern town, everyone I had met and all that had happened.

"Something strange happened to me on the flight from Naples to Verona," I told her. "I was sitting next to a very attractive guy."

"That's not unusual in Italy," Carol said.

"He was gorgeous..."

Earlier that morning, I boarded a plane in Naples along with mostly business travelers and husbands and wives of a certain class, few solo passengers like myself. Walking down to my seat, I hoped the flight wouldn't be full. Settling in, I had pulled out a small compact to check my reflection, when I glanced up to see a gorgeous guy towering above me, wearing a suit that strained across his athletically tight build. Smiling down, he motioned with his head at the numbered seats. Oh, *dio*, I thought. Like some archangel sent from heaven, this guy would sit right next to me.

The seat could hardly contain his left thigh, which had no where else to go but firmly against my right leg. Sigh. I smiled as casually as I could. Like all good Italian men, though, he knew just what his leg was doing to the blood in my veins. I was transfixed.

He glanced innocently at our touching thighs blending together as if on some transcendental plane and opened a conversation.

He was extremely polite with a hint of smoldering allure; no wedding band on his finger. It would be my first time in Verona. He lived and worked in Brescia, a city just west of Verona.

Then he politely urged me to visit his beautiful city; a place rich in history of the Langobards. Langobards? Seemed I had heard of them before.

Only a moment or two had passed when he leaned over from his magazine to show me an article inside, about an exhibit of the Langobards in his hometown of Brescia, the *Barbari D'Oro*. He then offered me the magazine so that I could read more about it. It was written in Italian in the main body with a column on the right side of each page in English. What a coincidence, I thought. In the first paragraph were names and places now familiar to me, considering the recent life-changing events in Calitri.

First there was mention of an ancient monastery of San Salvatore in Brescia. Then I read about Queen Teodolinda, who along with her King Authari—they were married in a field outside Verona—ruled the Kingdom of the Po Valley in the late sixth century, attributing to the grand flourish of civic and cultural arts of that period, and strengthening the role of Christianity throughout the then still-pagan Italian peninsula. Later their rule expanded to the Southern regions as far as Salerno and Benevento just east of Naples.

A tingling in my veins came in waves as I read. Recent real-events-cum-prophecies rolled about in my head: passing through Salerno; seeing the Langobard castle at the top of the hill in Calitri; meeting my zia Teodolinda; and even my empirically-minded, European-History-Master older brother, whom I had emailed back in Franco's office. The princess was traveling. Who was this handsome Angel from Brescia?

The plane hummed along; the sky outside my window seat had not a glimmer of blue. I relaxed into the comfort and heat of my companion's thigh and read the article completely, scanning the images and illustrations and their descriptions again and again. Apparently the Barbarian horde had been deeply misunderstood. More than their plundering and pillaging, their reign had produced artists and intellectuals that later influenced the Carolingian court at Aix la Chapelle.

There was even mention of the Benedictine monk and historian, Paolo Diacono, or Paul the Deacon, who chronicled the years of Langobard rule, achieving his masterwork *The History of the Langobards* at the end of his life. I had found this very book by chance in a Los Angeles library while browsing for travel information just before I flew to Venice, over a year ago. As I read the book that night in bed, the tingling began. A pious and intellectual man, Paolo Diacono—chronicler to the kings and queens of Bavaria—retired to the Abbey di Montecassino near Benevento to live out his days in peace after the dissolve of the empire.

Ancient Aletrium and the Langobards. Queen Teodolinda and her holy scribe. What was going on here?

Carol began to sense some deeply held, newly surfaced information around me, about the places I had been to and the people I had just met. In light of the last two days, my feelings were clearly easy to detect. But as she began to ask me questions, something began to tug in my chest. She tossed out Renaissance marriages, a scheming duke, an uncle planned as my betrothed. And the room started to close in around me.

Leaning in, she finally said, "I'm a psychic, you know."

"Really?" I drank a bit of wine. What would I want with a psychic?

Nonplussed, she continued to probe. "Do you believe in past lives?"

After dinner Carol told me she had been offered a job in New York City. Was I interested in subletting?

My life in Los Angeles was occupied with the lives and creativity of the photographers I represented, managed, and produced from my home office, but I wanted something more. I lived what seemed half of a Hollywood Hills life in one of five Robert Byrd-designed 1940s ranch houses on Mulholland Drive, on six acres of land tucked down a quiet cul-de-sac from a long private driveway. Wild, early Southern California land, cleared and built by first-generation Italian-Americans, the Luciani family; their parents came from the town of Campobasso in Southern Italy.

Up on their ranch, the Hollywood sign was to the left, the Capitol building to the right—one up and across, the other down and below the Cahuenga Pass hill. Tony landmarks to be sure, but very much home. Home of the Beatles and Frank Sinatra's legendary recordings. Ed Ruscha's LA scapes, his Standard Stations. Fante's "Bandini Quartet." Wallace Stegner and Mary Austin's lost untrammeled Wild West. And beyond the hill, the lights of the City of Angels there for dreaming. If you dreamed of Hollywood.

The ranch had a wide grass *campo* with a long wood pile to one side, an overgrown kitchen-garden in *mezzo*, which when I first moved there, towered with raised beds of tomatoes, zucchini and haricot verts, protected from critters both on the ground and in the air by an elaborate wood trellis canopied with bird netting. Then after years of neglect, it was transformed into a thick and tangled cactus garden dedicated, no doubt, to Rodella Luciani, the original den mother of the four sibling families who were raised on the property. Rod died very unexpectedly in her rocking chair of a brain hemorrhage. Her husband Dan, had been sitting next to her. I was working from home when it happened. Watched from my living room window as the emergency fire truck pulled into the driveway. It was four o'clock on a sunny Los Angeles afternoon, not long after I had returned from an earlier trip to Italy.

Here I lived my version of the California wildlife. Coyote, brown deer, and bobcat ruled the open, unpopulated hillsides. They walked up my driveway, came to my door, stalked my two cats, everyone's cats. I gardened. I planted tomatoes and roses and dahlias. I cleared dead trees and brush on weekends with the rest of the Luciani clan and created a shaded gravel patio for client entertaining and barbecues. There were fruit and nut trees; orange, avocado, and nespole; grapefruit, walnut, and persimmon. What we could harvest was ours for the taking unless the foraging deer got to them first. But wild was relative until I got to Calitri.

I reveled in these peaceful yet accessible urban surroundings. In summer it was all sun and heat and garden work. In winter the brick fireplace in the kitchen warmed my hearth. It was straight out of *Sunset* magazine. I promised myself then, that I would not leave this L.A., Walden-esque ranch until something else, someplace else, was created for me to land. I loved it up on the hill. I was not about to move myself again without some karmic ally, some divined place for me to go.

Then, once I set foot in Italy, I knew I would never go anywhere else. It was always an organic process of discovery and returning and intention. Italy was where I felt I needed to be. My soul indeed already floated in the air and land and frescos there. It was certainly in the aroma of the food that drifted down from high Gothic windows to the street below where I wandered, beckoning me with a truth I could not deny—I belonged inside those medieval homes. I was not a tourist. I was a child of their ancestry. The heart and head of an Italian girl. My heart waited. Your time will come, it said. I felt it in my bones. But I did not know how or when, until my trip to Calitri.

In the summer of 2001, from Verona I traveled down to Calitri twice, by train and bus, stopping for a night in a much cooler Naples to visit an Italian friend and stroll down old via Chiaia.

Zia Giuseppina and zio Giovanni were kind enough to host me again in their 1970s apartment just off the main Corso that leads out of town and east toward the plains of Puglia. In June the high rolling fields were already golden; the honeyed aroma of sun-ripening wheat carried to their third-floor balcony as if on a sea breeze. All around the town at nearly every street corner and *vicolo*, just beyond the edges of apartment buildings in the modern quarter, or sliced between ancient stone houses of the Centro Storico, the expansive landscape of Alta Irpinia was revealed. I was continually caught by surprise when first experiencing this constant reference of place and improbable beauty. Was it magic? The surrounding hills seemed to have two simultaneous points of perspective. Enveloped in a protective blanket of soft tawny light from the wheat fields, reflected toward the endless sky above, and then the solid mass of rounded earth below that stretched on forever. The colors and atmosphere changed hourly, the effect continuously gratifying. It was a region rarely visited by tourists and blessedly so. The world was at ease there. There was an immense silence, a vast ocean of wheat-field stillness shimmering in the sunlight.

At this early juncture, zio Giovanni and zia Giuseppina still felt like pinch-hitting grandparents to me. They offered a living link from my dad's memories of his baseball-loving father Nicola, to him as a young man and to his young life in Calitri. Zia Giuseppina too had been instrumental as my first guide last fall, when she took me deep into the Centro Storico and unwittingly sparked the quest for the house on via Sant'Antuono.

Our ability to communicate was still limited given our language barrier yet her house was a quiet respite for me to unwind, enjoy occasional lunches, and from there explore the town. Retired for at least twenty years, zio Giovanni was very old world and still active. He made very good red and white wines in his garage *cantina* with grapes cultivated from the land near the casa di campagna—the one hundred year old Paolantonio homestead. Back and forth from their apartment he drove every day, except Sundays, in his apple-green, Vespa-made, three-wheeled *Ape* to work the fields by hand and sickle.

Once in awhile I would hitch a ride, always at Giuseppina's command, for he would never have offered himself. Tucked inside the small cab built for one, he reluctantly transported me to the center of town or carried me back up the steep hill from the homestead.

"Ever ridden in the cab of a Ape?" he asked.

"No," I said. Zio Giovanni was my first.

"It's a bit tight. You need to be comfortable with the old guy driving or it could get embarrassing." Wizened zio Giovanni smiled at me. "Generally only the wives were given the honored and very narrow spot." There was only one rickety bench seat, "and sometimes not even then."

The joke went that some wives were made to ride in back, but I didn't believe him. Zio Giovanni turned the key, eased in on the clutch, and we buzzed down the street. Zia Giuseppina waved from the balcony.

I had returned this summer not only to visit all my newly discovered relatives, but to investigate the house for sale, at via

Sant'Antuono 49, purported to be where Nicola and Angela Maria lived with their young family some seventy years ago. I had nothing more to go on than this. Why, for how long, and to what end was not yet understood, and not revealed at the time. Did they sail back for a wedding? A funeral?

I had spent the better part of the last seven months obsessed with the few details I had, corresponding with Franco by letter about my determined plans. Over those months Franco had indulged me by taking and then sending the much-asked-for photos of the house behind the little church on via Sant'Antuono.

So when I arrived, armed with the photos and an American's can-do spunk, I had naively assumed everyone was expecting me to secure plans about the house. Who was the owner? How did I begin the process? Of course, I was thrilled when what had previously sounded like an improbable and daft plan to most of my new relatives—"Buy that house?"—finally seemed a dream that was very close indeed.

One week day morning I set out after breakfast to take a walk into the old town. It was a cloudless June morning, the sky a *Della Robbia* blue, with just a hint of the heat that the afternoon might bring. I collected my camera and surreptitiously made for the door.

"*Dove vai?*" Zia Giuseppina caught me.

"For a walk in the town, to take pictures." I hoped I wasn't too obvious.

"*Eh, mo, da sola no,*" she quickly replied.

As was the ancient protocol in a Southern Italian town, I was learning, Giuseppina insisted that I be accompanied by her two teenage granddaughters on what I tried to explain would be a simple walk along the main Corso into the center of town. What with her old-world persistence, and my still ingénue status, I acquiesced. She may have been on to me after all.

Giusy and her cousin Antonella, both visiting their grandmother from the northern city of Torino where they lived, joined me.

I soon had the pair following me into the Centro Storico. From the bustling main thoroughfare into the nearly deserted streets of the old town we meandered, winding deeper and deeper into its center. By then I was happy to have them along, as it became clear I would never have found this narrow sloping lane again all on my own. And as they followed me they began to openly speculate about my desired destination.

"How far are we going?" asked Antonella. She looked at her watch. "It's getting near lunch."

When finally we rounded the narrow corner in the bend of the via and arrived in front of the old house, I was relieved, if only for a fleeting moment—for as soon as I looked up at the door, I found the For Sale sign gone.

I stared intently up at the doorway, rooted in my tracks. Happy just a moment ago, my heart now pounded in confusion. I remembered how excited I was last November when the brave idea struck me to buy this house, then I had waited, planned, all winter to return. That day Franco and Giuseppina had discouraged my willful glee to buy it. I didn't understand why. After all, I was the first in our family to return to our roots, the first to retrace the steps of our grandparents. It seemed providence, perfect luck, meant to be. Franco had simply put his arm around my shoulder, squeezed me tightly and gently changed the subject. Now here I was, come to close the deal, but something was wrong.

I turned to Giusy.

"What is it?" she asked.

Antonella eased closer in.

"I need to find out who owns this house," I said.

"What house?" Antonella asked, looking around.

"This one here," I said, pointing up toward the door. "Number 49."

"Oh?" Giusy said. "Why?"

Soon after I had returned to Los Angeles last fall, I found two ceramic house numbers in a boutique in Studio City—the numbers 4 and 9. Blue numbers on an antique white background. I smiled to myself, took them home and leaned them against the splashback tiles in my vintage ranch kitchen in the Hollywood Hills, which had been ironically, completed in 1949. I looked at them each morning as I made coffee and every evening as I made dinner. A very early site map, I thought, for the dream of buying the house on via Sant'Antuono, a reminder of the provenance of the place, and my pluck in having shown up in time. It was my first conscious sitemap—to me, everything up to then had been a sort of beginner's luck.

I daydreamed about the meaning of the number 49, looking for clues. The Buddhist belief in the number of days before your spirit or soul is reborn when you die. That I didn't want to have to wait until I was 49 to live in Italy. Then I thought of the death of my grandmother, Angela Maria. I don't know why, as I hadn't thought about it in a very long time. Come to think of it, I had never been encouraged to think about it at all. How old was she and what year did she die?

Odd, but I still did not know. I didn't even have one of those Italian *ricordini* for her, those Italian funeral remembrance cards with the birth and death dates and Catholic condolence prayers, for the dearly departed. There were plenty of those in my mother's dresser drawer. But none for my father's mother.

"Ask your father," my mother always said, whenever I had a question about my grandmother.

But I didn't want to pester him with this daydream of mine. So I calculated as best I could. Then it came to me. She must have been about 49 years old, or that she died in 1949. A sign? It was early for signs. I wasn't really following signs or totally aware of all the signs yet.

On our way down the lane, Giusy, Antonella and I passed an old stone bench fastened against the wall. It was empty just a moment ago, but I glanced back now to see two women sitting outside their door shelling peas. They seemed to appear out of nowhere. Just then another woman came out her door in front of us. She headed directly across the lane to the cantina below the steps of number 49, and she had a key.

I suddenly felt a bit nervous, not sure how to do this. As the three women called greetings in dialect to one another across the lane, I made my way over to the woman with the key to talk to her about the house. Giusy and Antonella were right behind me. They were still unaware of why I needed to inquire further about the dilapidated place before us, and involve these three grandmothers in the process.

As she opened the cantina door, the woman turned to greet the three of us, first nodding to me like the stranger I was, with a smile and a bit of skepticism.

She addressed Giusy, "What is going on here, *figliola*? What do you want?"

With Giusy translating and the woman's curious glances, I asked,

"Do you know how to contact the person who owns this house? I am here to buy it." It was a bold move, I knew, to directly address this elderly woman, as a stranger. It was just too forward, too impolite.

The woman looked askance at me, and in the next instant I knew. She announced with certainty, "The *padrone* was indeed here just this morning, though much earlier, to sell this house."

"Today? But to whom? Did he know in advance I was arriving?" The three watched my face as a mixture of surprise and fear clouded my expression. And then a look of bemused pity entered the old woman's eyes. With that look my heart sank, and for just a determined second more the thought raced in my head that the house could be mine.

"Was I just hours too late?" I had waited all winter for this chance—my entire life—and suddenly it was over. I had returned this summer eager to carry out my desire to secure the house for sale and thus take hold of a piece of family history, retrieve a legend. Now it seemed I was only a contestant in the games the ghosts of my past seemed to be playing with me. Thoughts teetered back and forth with only furtive holds on the clues, clues of my Paolantonio and Cicoira legacy, and where these ghosts were leading me.

All the women, young and old, gathered around me now in the narrow lane. They were all talking, consoling, as I fought back tears. I could hardly focus on what they were saying. I was alone in my head, alone in my disappointment. This narrow lane, the stone bench, what was here for me now? A faint voice, then a sudden gust of warm wind whirled over my head, overwhelming my instinct to cry. I glanced up toward the narrow slice of blue and the numinous sound, and spied a bird fluttering between the stone houses. I felt my wounded heart literally being carried away from the scene. And in that moment, somehow I knew—my dreams in Calitri were yet to be fulfilled.

The elders began their inquiry about me and my origins, and with the news that I was a niece of zia Concetta Borea on via Fontana, their conversation brightened. Giusy filled in my paternal relations, and with all antecedents mentioned and accounted for, recognition was complete and offers of a communal caffè soon followed. But by now it was mezzogiorno. The two cousins gently declined, offered explanations that we were expected home for the family meal, and the elders smiled knowingly. We said goodbye, securing invitations for coffee another day.

So we continued farther down the lane away from via Sant'Antuono 49. Camera in hand, I accepted emotional support from the two cousins but said little. I did not return to the lane again until later that summer to find the three-story stone house gutted, the cantina filled with tools and stacks of *mattone*, and a hand-crank cement mixer just outside the door. The new owner, it seemed, was wasting no time getting to work on the restoration of the house.

We quickly rounded the corner where Chiesetta Sant'Antuono stood. I was pleased to see this small elegant chapel again. I remembered it from my first visit when, zia Giuseppina, her cousin Angelo, and I hurried past it to his parked car.

At this bend in the road, via Sant'Antuono either sloped down wide stone steps to the left, or continued straight through to another narrow corridor, wound up to the right, and led to who knows where. On the landing of the stone steps stood an old iron fountain, the first I had seen, with a slight pool of water rippling at its base.

Giusy and Antonella led us straight through the corridor. We took the steep and narrow steps that led up to the right, continued through a dark narrow vicolo, and arrived farther up two more levels onto a street called via Giuseppe Tozzoli. Here we continued up toward Piazza della Repubblica from where we had entered the old village, until suddenly we came upon a huge wooden portal open onto the lane.

There in its cool shadow sat an elder woman in her summer apron, shelling peas. The ancient and cavernous entrance of this once patrician palazzo was open wide to the street. And as we walked up to it, the woman, dwarfed by its size, greeted us with a beaming smile and an open, friendly manner as if to welcome us into the courtyard of her lord's manor. We stopped briefly to say hello. With her invitation we stepped through the huge carriage doors into the cool courtyard and out of the bright sun.

Unlike the damp dark courtyards of centuries-old buildings I'd just visited in the heart of Naples—echoing with women's voices from the crowded apartments above—inside here was silent. The walls were sun-bleached dry and crumbled. Weeds grew out of the stone walls and ironwork several stories above. No voices lived here now, nor did it seem had they for many years.

Eager for a distraction and curious about the provenance of the place I stepped in behind *la portressa* to examine the abandoned courtyard then asked if I could go up the stairs to get a better look. She obliged and up I went, straddling the tumbledown stone steps with care, camera poised to record.

Giusy and Antonella did not follow me in.

"We have to get home for lunch," Giusy said. "My grandmother is waiting."

"It looks dangerous." From Antonella.

I peered around a stone wall to see three more mighty wooden doors. I had been away from Giusy and Antonella long enough though. I would return later to this abandoned palazzo to get a better sense of its bygone grandeur. It was another side to Calitri that I had not yet explored.

La Portressa

(The Doorkeeper)

I did go back the next day alone, as I knew I would. La portressa was there in her usual spot when I walked down the quiet vicolo from the opposite direction of the day before. Glad to have found my way, I called out as I approached her.

"*Buongiorno.*"

"*Buongiorno, anche a te!*"

La portressa lived just across the narrow lane in a small dark house opposite the palazzo. Again she was beaming and very pleased to see someone. This morning, however, I found her with some sewing across her knees. A small rush chair, darning basket, and a broom were nestled on the stone floor beside her.

"Can I take your photo?" I asked in Italian while I had the chance.

"*Certo!*" she said very enthusiastically. "*Così?*"

I stood with my back to the wall across the too-narrow space. She stood in the grand portico, held her arms open wide, and smiled wonderfully like an indulging aunt greeting a long-lost niece. She certainly was the most gregarious person I had met so far walking around Calitri. I couldn't help but wonder who she might be and if she had a special message for me from my past.

She did not press me for information, though, about who I was or what brought me here to the Centro Storico. She just welcomed me into the small world between her home and the abandoned patrician palazzo, which she commandeered as her own. I took one or two frames. Then, without a word, la portressa offered me the key to one of the doors up the stairs. She nodded, and I smiled and accepted. She knew I had come to explore the abandoned sixteenth century palazzo. She only called after me to be careful, then left me to myself.

Up the crumbling stone steps I went. Inside the apartments were large, rambling rooms that showed years of decay. Some were wallpapered with designs I could date from at least the turn of the century. Wide deep doors between large ample rooms, wood-paneled wainscotting and double window frames fixed with thickly carved, interior wood shutters. Delicate Victorian glass gas lamps hung from the high, vaulted ceilings. Glass sconces, too, hung about the walls of what may have been the women's sitting rooms. There was a large kitchen room with a fireplace and a long, white, tiled wood stove, a *fornacella*, which I would find common to the town. It was built low into a stone arch cut high into one wall. And then a tiny closet sized room tucked in a corner with a single commode inside.

This interior was certainly a far cry from the poor, two-room, lightless dwellings far below in the town. Neglected as it was, it nevertheless firmly declared itself of the patrician class. While I wandered in the rooms taking photos, I wondered what it had been like for the different classes to live in this remote hill town centuries ago. I couldn't help but think of the contrast between two Italian novels that reveal views of life in Southern Italy, though at very different points in history. *Christ Stopped at Eboli* was written by Carlo Levi, a journalist, political activist, and painter forced to live in exile in a remote hill town of the then lifeless Lucanian South. *Il Gattopardo* published in 1958 and made into a film by Luchino Visconti, was written by Giuseppe Tomasi Lampedusa, a member of the patrician class, who described the slow decline of his beloved Sicilian culture. The two novelists portray the immeasurably different lives of two vastly different worlds in equally isolated regions of Italy.

It seemed that these lives, these different classes, collided right here in Calitri. They had flourished together for a few a centuries within the walls of the village, from Langobard rule starting in the sixth century to the royal Bourbon line of the Gesualdo's and Mirelli's of sixteenth century Napoli. Calitri hugs a rocky hillside in the far eastern region of Campania, yet is within walking distance to what is described as the strange, sometimes feared, and always forgotten desolate region of old Lucania, new Basilicata, depicted by the painter Carlo Levi and writer Ignazio Silone.

Oddly, now the *contadini* seem to be the victor. Still proudly, stubbornly, inhabiting their family homes and land while these grand *palazzi* lay abandoned. Their owners long gone. And in their leaving released the town from their fiscal grasp. The cultural class wars and its damaging legacy are still evident in the locally underdeveloped economy and startling lack of respect for their own legacy.

I climbed back down to the carriage entrance to find la portressa waiting for me.

"*Vuoi un caffè?*" she asked.

"*Con piacere,*" I said. I had learned a few new phrases while living the summer in Verona. I was also learning that in the South an offered coffee was always accepted.

For the few more days I was in town, I explored the streets with my camera. Calitri's Centro Storico was still fresh for me. And it helped alleviate my disappointment about losing the house on via Sant'Antuono.

Later in August, very near the end of my three months in Italy, I traveled down from hazy, hot, and unbearably humid Verona to Calitri a second time for just a few days. Calitri's weather by contrast was sunny, bright, breezy, and dry. I was hosted this time by Raffaela and Franco, waking each morning to a view of the Paolantonio casa di campagna from their spare bedroom window. I would walk out there after breakfast with Dorina as she puttered and tended her chickens. Zio Giovanni had already arrived hours ago with zia Giuseppina in their three-wheeled Ape. They worked together in their field garden gathering greens, feeding the feral cats, and picking fresh figs. It was a party some mornings. All of us there on the grounds, with a panoramic view of the Apennines that surrounded the interior valley on one side and the graceful arch of the hill town rising nearer on the other.

These were the stone houses where zia Giuseppina and her older siblings and cousins grew up. She recalled with great flourish one morning who of her cousins lived in which houses as their mothers and fathers worked the land. She opened the door to the one in the middle.

"I spent most of my childhood in this house here." A small cracked mirror hung from a thin nail on the door. We stepped inside onto well-worn, unglazed terracotta paving. Farm implements stood against the stone walls. It was cool and dark and, though very primitive, somewhat cozy too.

"Cousin Angelo and his family lived here." She pointed to the house next door that made an L in the low earthen structure.

They were a warren of slightly tumbledown, one-story, one-room houses with beamed lofts for sleeping and cubby holes for provisions. A single ground-level hearth was built into one corner. Its chimney had the conical shape of an indoor *trullo*, reaching up through the roof. There was a climbing rose-covered pergola in bloom. A Cecile Brunner! With a long, marble-top trestle table underneath for taking meals outside in summer. There were fruit trees of all shapes and sizes: black gelso, quince, and fig; pear, crabapple, and *biancospino* plum. And everywhere, fragrant bay laurel.

It was Franco who would give me the historic information of the place. He sat on a long split log under a wide shade tree one morning in well-cut trousers, solemnly smoking his cigarette down to its end, as he told us the tale of San Sebastian.

"This homestead, these three simple, stone structures," he said, "were built atop an eleventh century *convento* named for San Sebastian." Military martyr, soldier saint. Once a Roman soldier under Emperor Diocletian, San Sebastian turned defender of the Christian faith. He suffered the slings of their arrows but survived. Twice martyred, he is named patron saint of archers, athletes, and Roman soldiers—the legionnaires.

Franco continued, "The legionnaires marched south and east on a stretch of the via Appia just below the town." He pointed to the Ofantina that could be seen in the valley below.

"Did they stop in for a beer?" I wanted to ask. Franco stopped short of claiming that as a boy he could still hear their hobnail boots crunching on the road.

"Ancient ghosts and spirits in our midst!" I said. "What stories these monastery stones could tell."

Turns out San Sebastian's feast day on the Italian liturgical calendar is January 20. Nicola and Angela Maria's wedding anniversary. As a very young man, my grandfather Nicola served as a sergeant in the Italian cavalry under King Victor Emmanuel

III. After emigrating to America he became an ardent baseball fan, idolizing Joltin' Joe DiMaggio. He took my dad, over countless summers and autumns in 1940s New York, to games at Yankee Stadium in the Bronx. Soldiers and athletes, San Sebastian indeed.

Nicola, the youngest of the four brothers, helped build this homestead by pulling stones from the ancient monastery ruins themselves, and with money from his early years, working in New York as an unmarried man, that he diligently sent back home to Calitri. I wondered, did he choose to marry on San Sebastian's feast day for posterity? Or was it San Sebastian who sent down his martyred graces upon the couple?

⁕

With my Paolantonio relatives holding sway, I didn't make it up to the upper town that easily. Franco went off to his office in the early morning, and zia Dorina didn't drive. But late one day, strolling around the town, I ran into Benito, the father of my cousin Adolfo, in front of the post office. Benito's wife Angelina was a Cicoira, my father's cousin on my grandmother's side. He quickly called me aside.

"I didn't know you were back in town," he said. Then just as quickly he invited me to lunch at their house the next day.

The following morning, I went to see zia Concetta with unresolved feelings about the house on via Sant'Antuono. I persuaded her and zia Angelina to walk with me to the house one last time. There seemed to be something there I still needed to know, something still pulling me in.

Zia Concetta called for the key from one of the women on the lane, and we soon climbed the stone steps to the house. A tumbledown mess of a place—all exposed rock, no electricity or water, no bathroom or kitchen, just a one-room hovel with a meager fireplace hearth as a hole in the wall, a stall in the back for the mule; left exactly as it was when the last person living there had expired. A kind of grim mausoleum, it was more like an abandoned brigand's cave than a proper dwelling.

Once inside, Concetta reenacted the desperate pleas of my grandmother—pounding the stone wall with her fist—when she found her little Mussolini dead that early summer evening.

"Dead?" It was the first time I had heard of a fallen child. Then I thought to myself, "They called him Mussolini?"

Southern Italians are particularly enamored with Mussolini's civil contributions as Prime Minister: roads, bridges, and community centers like Calitri's *Casa del exEca*, a large communal hall where private weddings can be celebrated by any and all townspeople free of charge. When Mussolini invaded Abyssinia and Ethiopia in October of 1935, many Southern Italians were on the frontlines. On the main Corso Garibaldi, and all around the old village, remain small porcelain house numbers—*i facciati*—blue numbers on a white ground, with the then fascist symbol in the upper left corner. Some of the symbols have been burned or chipped away. Many remain. Mussolini left his fascistic mark too on the personalities of elders in the town: zia Giuseppina's *"Avanti!"* echoing the name of the Italian Fascist newspaper published throughout her childhood.

Then I realized Angela Maria's story must have been the one Concetta had enthralled us all with that first day I arrived in Calitri. It was 1935. My grandmother Angela Maria's last time in Calitri, with her husband Nicola and her four older children.

"Why did little Mussolini die?" I asked Concetta, knowing full well the mortality rate must have been very high. And just then felt wobbled by a surge of deathlike energy overtaking the dark, dank room.

"Era solo nu' picc'nin." She sighed with a shrug and her high feminine lilt. Meaning it was a long time ago, and that she didn't remember much more.

She moved toward the door.

"And he's buried in the cemetery here?" I countered.

"*Eh sì, ma nessun ricordava dove.*" Yes, but no one remembers where.

Sometime later I went to the Comune records office. *Paolantonio, Vincenzo Nicola. di Nicola e di Cicoira Angela Maria deceduto 28 giugno 1935 in via S. Antuono, numero 49. Alle ore 18:40. Nato circa 3 mesi prima.* He had been three months old.

As zia Concetta, Angelina and I started to leave 49 via Sant'Antuono, the owner of the house suddenly appeared. An overweight, greedy-looking guy, he seemed to be offering me the tumble-down house for 10,000 lira. "Furnished," which meant, "as is."

Zia Concetta waved him away.

Later, Adolfo came to pick me up at the bottom of the hill in a faded red Fiat. His mother Angelina, was waiting at the door when we pulled into their driveway. They lived in a two-story ramshackle house on a far northeastern precipice, the farthest spot in the Centro Storico, just above *la ripa*.

After a lunch of handmade raviolis and home grown salad greens—their wine, olive oil, tomatoes for the sauce; everything, they were proud to tell me, was home cultivated—Adolfo and Angelina decided to take me on a leisurely drive out to the countryside. It was a golden August afternoon. The air was rich with the hot smell of freshly cut hay and turned earth. Cicadas whirred lazily in the grasses. I rolled down my window and leaned out in awe as wave upon wave of rolling fields sped by the car window. We were headed toward *contrada Macchiursi*, "the place of wild bears."

We came to a dusty halt amid a cluster of stone buildings and a few yard dogs. An ancient volcanic crater loomed hazily in the distance. I got out of the car in my summer skirt and sandals and immediately scanned the area for photo opportunities.

We were soon greeted by a woman named Rosa, a friend of zia Angelina's. As was the custom, Rosa invited us into her farmhouse for a bit of hospitality. It was fresh and cool inside, the great room sparsely furnished. She brought out a strong chilled limoncello and a plate of cookies. We took our seats around the dining table, drinking and making small talk. Well, zia Angelina made friendly small talk with Rosa in the local dialect. I mostly listened, nodding occasionally when the conversation clearly centered on me and my travels, or my connection with the town of Calitri. Adolfo simply sat quietly among us women.

Then a couple of heavy steps were heard coming up fast on the porch. One of Rosa's sons, long-legged and hurried, just home from town, bounded into the house.

He stopped briefly and nodded his greetings, yet seemed slightly awkward around the women. The flow of conversation at the table was not broken. Rosa did not introduce him. Yet a small shock wave went through my body as he advanced through the room. Not much later he re-emerged in a change of clothes from a room in the corner of the house, stole a look at me, and headed out the door again.

We lingered a bit longer in the cool main room, enjoying a second plate of biscotti and another limoncello. Once or twice, the tall, handsome son stole another moment to enter the house. Though his duties pulled him toward the responsibilities of the farm and his work tending the animals.

Finally, we three women and Adolfo walked outside to the still warm, late afternoon sun to accompany Rosa to the barn. The farm had a dozen or so milking cows, one hundred sheep to graze, and a pen of *maiale* to provide pork for their table. It was a working *latteria*, hard won and not taken for granted. I wandered about the yard where we had pulled in earlier. I was slightly woozy from the strong aperitifs we had just taken and still struck by the huge form of the dormant volcano that dominated the horizon. And now too by this robust and handsome man standing in his field clothes surrounded by the elements of his family's livelihood, with the seemingly improbable powder-blue sky gently vibrating a halo behind his head.

Our eyes locked. My knees buckled. This must be heaven, I thought.

"Giuseppe," he said, indicating himself.

"*Piacera*." I smiled. "Angela." We stared calmly at each other for another moment. Then he went back to his work.

Curious as always, and certainly interested in this tall, handsome figure going about his chores, I gingerly poked around in the yard in an effort to help, albeit with camera in hand. I watched as he fed the cows their grain from a huge bin outside the barn doors, then as he assembled their milking apparatus and hooked it to their teats.

Eager to be a part of his work, or maybe keep his attention, I offered to carry a full pail of fresh, warm milk over to a young calf crying loudly, incessantly, in a smaller pen across the yard. The poor thing drank ferociously. Giuseppe looked on at me in bemusement. Back and forth I went, sandals and feet now dusted brown, as I offered what assistance I could.

Finished with the calf, I strolled away from the group to steal a look at the huge pigs in their pen across the yard. Then I called over to Adolfo, "Are there any lambs?"

I remembered my first trip in Italy some years earlier, with a friend and his wife and their young son, hiking far into a brilliantly green, endlessly rolling glen somewhere in the region of Lago di Bolsena. The air was soft and wet from a morning rain. We were following a well-worn path in the tall grasses when suddenly we were overtaken by a cloud of mother sheep ushering their young around a hillside and into our view. The sweet sound of dozens of tinkling bells, bleating lambs, and soft hooves filled the valley until you could hear nothing else—and wanted nothing else to interfere with the blessed sight and sound of their daily migration from far fields to home.

Giuseppe quickly joined us as Adolfo obediently translated my request. "She wants to know if there are any *pecore*."

Giuseppe rushed over to a large, covered corral, empty save for one tiny lamb. He ducked inside and chased her down, then carried her over, cupped in his arms for me to coo over.

It seemed an offering that bridged two worlds.

"How old is she?" I asked. The smooth, wiry lamb squealed and tightly nuzzled Giuseppe's chest then calmed down at the sound and vibration of his deep voice.

"*È nato stamattina*," he said. He held her out for me to stroke. Whose eyes were more pleading, I could not tell. Joseph and the Lamb of God, I thought. Cradling a newborn animal was an everyday occurrence for him, I supposed, but it was the closest I'd come, save a few litters of puppies born in our basement when I was a young girl. We three stood for a while cuddling the animal until it was time for Giuseppe to get back to his work.

The transparent afternoon light had warmed to a muted amber. The shadowed volcano grew even darker on the horizon. Rosa and Angelina had gone back into the house.

Adolfo and I strolled around the house to the front yard where we came upon a strikingly handsome man in his late fifties, lumbering up from the neighboring field on a huge tractor. With bright and lively eyes, he called down in a commanding voice, "*Buonasera*."

"*Sera, signore*," Adolfo replied.

It was Rosa's husband, Michele Zarrilli. I watched as he pulled the giant machine to a stop in front of us, then smiled and nodded an amiable greeting.

Michele sized me up, then casually asked Adolfo, "Is the girl holding the camera your new *ragazza*?"

"No, she's not my girlfriend, but a *cugina lontana* visiting from America."

Michele Zarrilli was clearly delighted. Without missing a beat, he asked, "Has she met my eldest son, Giuseppe?"

As it turned out, the girl with the camera took only two photos that day. One of the sun-golden fields racing by as I leaned out the car window on the way toward the farm. The other of Giuseppe bemused in the moments of our hasty departure. I cheerfully offered Giuseppe a newly turned phrase, "*Ci vediamo!*" He replied, "*Tutto apposto.*" Clearly he was expecting to see me again. Unfortunately, I left Calitri the very next day.

We wouldn't meet again for nearly two years.

※

By end of my stay, as I was again saying goodbye to relatives, zia Dorina began, "*Perché ti devi sempre andare cosi presto?*" As always her peerless gentility. "*Resta ancora un po con noi.*"

"But I have a plane ticket," I said.

She teased me about staying longer, long enough to find myself a man, "*Non hai trovato un bel ragazzo?*"

Zia Dorina loved to banter with me about all manner of customs and culture of her hometown. I think too she was genuinely concerned that I was always alone when I visited, or perhaps she was just projecting her own loneliness and longing. A widow for more than twenty years, by custom she seemed always shut away at home. Yet as we stood face-to-face cheerfully making salutations in zia Giuseppina's kitchen, hers was a heartfelt wish that next time I come I should spend more time, find a man, and in that way I wouldn't always have to be saying goodbye.

Zio Giovanni too had made very strong declarations this summer about my single status. Slamming his fist on his kitchen table one evening, during a friendly conversation about the events of my day, the day I went walking in the Centro to look for the house, he declared, "Stay and live in Calitri! You'll be married, *subito!*"

Whoa. I had to chuckle. He reminded me of my father, but his suggestion seemed a bit out of reach. My relative's concerns and opinions about my welfare were clear and heartfelt. They wanted me socially protected. And the only way to guarantee that was to settle down, become someone's wife.

"But zia Dorina, where? And who?" I went along with her. Perhaps she could help me by finding this man for me. "After all, you know the town well."

"*Eh, sì*...but what should I look for?"

"Ah," I said. "That's easy. *Alto, bello e gambe forte.*" Echoing zia Giuseppina's earlier description of my grandfather. And secretly thinking of the handsome guy I had just met, the Handsome Man from Macchiursi.

"And," I promised, "once you find him, all you have to do is call me and I'll return, presto!" We both had a good laugh. Finally trumped, she broke into a huge grin, gave me a kiss on both cheeks, and with that I was off.

Winter in the Old Village

※

Lascia o Raddoppia? Quit or double?

With the loss of the house on via Sant'Antuono, I could have just never gone back, never made another trip to Calitri. Or at the very least let it go for a long while. There was a hugely popular Italian game show on television in the late 1950s called "Lascia o Raddoppia?" "Quit or Double?" I knew in my heart that there was more to come for me in Calitri. So, rather than stay defeated, I doubled my odds and began returning as often as I could. Not so much to prove myself or defend myself in the loss of the house on via Sant'Antuono; painful as it was, I had to let that go. But the love and friendships with my new found relatives continued to build. And my curiosity for their small village culture widened. I grew more conscious, more curious, with each visit. These *parenti lontani*, my relatives were, by their very lives, illustrating the personalities and character of the grandparents I never knew.

They indulged me. And I was learning to receive. It kept me going, kept me returning—opening myself further, immersing myself deeper into their world. I was fascinated. And they in turn were learning about me, L'Americana. I was dubbed this nickname quite early on.

By the fall of 2002 I had spent another summer, all of June and July, bridging business relationships with Carol and other photography industry colleagues in Verona, with only one long weekend down to Calitri. It didn't seem enough. With a November business trip that same year for the opening of an American photo exhibit in Verona's Scavi Scaligeri Museum of Photography and no Calitri visit, I decided it was time to immerse myself in the village of my ancestors. There was something there for me that was calling me. There seemed something more there that I needed.

In February 2003 I arrived to spend the month alone in an old stone house in the Centro Storico. (Without heat!) It was during this stay that I felt, I knew, I was getting closer to the spirit of my grandmother. Yet, and yet, I was still naive to the fact that zia Concetta lived in the house where she was born. I stood out on the narrow balcony of the bedroom on cold, dark nights, looking out over the barren street below, with abandoned and weathered door after door, as one mystery bled into another.

I had hoped months earlier to stay alone in the Centro Storico and was pleased that it was possible for my February return. The house on via Fontana belonged to zia Concetta and she agreed last summer to allow me to stay there on my return trip. At that time the town was bright with seasonal light; warm colors were evident at every turn. The characteristic stone houses and narrow *vie* and *vicoli* blithely offered themselves to my camera as I wandered around in a light skirt and sandals. Though I had enjoyed those two previous trips to the town that summer, they were brief, no more than a few days at a time. I knew the severity of the winter season would yield a treasure trove of images and emotions of another sort. I hoped that darker and more contemplative, the Centro Storico and resulting black-and-white photographs would reveal the hidden inner spirit of a once populous place.

In the small enclosed bedroom on the second floor of the house, simple French doors of wood and glass opened onto a narrow iron balcony that looked out over via Fontana. From that balcony, I could lean out to the left and look up a short way to see the stone arch of zia Concetta's front door. Farther up at the top of the street as it intersected with via Concezione stood the one-hundred-year-old dry-goods store with its wide, double red doors framed in little *lampadine* still closed from the night before.

On the first morning I awoke to softly falling snow. The world up there in February was incredibly silent. Winter fog muted any errant sound. Seeing this house for the first time in the bright summer light and heat of last June did not at all prepare me for its transformation during a cold damp Irpinia winter. If I poked my head out the French doors upon early rising, I could spy on the comings and goings of a nearly empty and narrow street. A few people might venture out bundled against the cold, moving like dark ghosts on their way to or from via Concezione. Elderly women gamely swept the street in front of their doors or put out meager leftovers for the stray cats. Occasionally they would see me, L'Americana, surprised at first and then nodding in silent greeting. I guess they knew then that anyone at this window would be a protégé of zia Concetta and therefore immune from any concern.

From the balcony I studied the door just across the way at different hours of the early morning or late into the night, when the cold room prevented me from any restful sleep. Focusing on its simple lines became a sort of meditation for me. Its facade possessed a sad yet utilitarian simplicity, long void of any warmth of color or sense of ownership. The sky too, the sliver of what I could see from the balcony, was cold, colorless. A thick fog enveloped this small area of the Centro in the wee hours of every morning. And as I stood there on the narrow balcony in the soft lamplight, my mind would wander.

This via, empty and silent as it was now, was one my grandmother would have frequented when she was a child or young woman in the years before she married my grandfather and then emigrated with him, leaving its life and circadian rhythm forever. Back then it would be a bustling, narrow thoroughfare, alive with the voices and workday activities of the families, women, children, and their livestock, who all lived, played, and expired in the small stone houses running its length. "If my grandmother were looking down on me now, what would she tell me of life on this street at the turn of the century?" I wondered. "Would she know I was here?"

I slept a stone's throw from places she would have walked, shopped, and laughed with her mother, siblings, and friends along these intimate streets. What would she think of her granddaughter, her namesake, returning once again, with her camera, her questions, and curiosity? Would she think of me as the visiting neophyte, a stranger to the rhythms and rituals of life here in the once grand Centro Storico?

Upon arriving and laying out my bags in the cavernous chill of the main room of the house, I immediately felt lost and found. From this stationary meditation at the window I progressed to walking studies of the neighborhood alleys and doorways, my heart leading me instead of a map. I climbed ancient and worn stone steps and explored connecting archways. Some led to enclosed vicolos and grottos or opened out onto the outer ridges of the steep hillside. On my first morning venture I walked through a wide archway just across the house on via Fontana. There at eye level stood an old chimney pipe wafting fragrant wood smoke against a pale gray sky, utterly silent against the morning. The hillside in the near distance was a blanket of snow. Some doorways were shut tight, but a face would poke out a window from above, curious as to the stranger with her camera.

Some mornings I would cover a lot of ground and find myself in the farthest upper corners of the earthquake-rattled sections, long ago abandoned. There, near the top of the ancient hill of the town once called Aletrium, just under the ramparts of the Langobard castle, weeds and broken porcelain teacups could be found tangled together on bare stone window frames. Wind-scattered trash and dust devils blew dirt against crumbled walls and crooked doorways. Thin stray dogs skittered around the corners as I walked by. I was more than a stranger here yet eagerly willing to follow clues that led to who knew where.

Other days I wouldn't make it to the end of via Fontana, fascinated and pulled away by the beautiful view of the snow-covered valley through a tall arch, or confused by the intricate switches and turns of the lanes. As the early morning progressed, elders gave the right of way to small roving bands of students who cut through the narrow lanes on their way to the Art Academy at the base of the hill. Their voices and muffled footsteps could be heard long before you saw them walk by, burdened by huge knapsacks. As it neared 9 a.m. the streets gradually became more populated and I'd make my way back to the house to shake off the chill and fill in the rest of my day.

By this time the electric water heater had had time enough to heat water for a quick hot shower to warm my bones. The dark stone house was colder inside than the winter street outside. Waking early to dress simply made the most sense since there was no heat other than the blood in my veins under layers of thin California woolens and a feeble *caldo-bagno* blowing out its most powerful blast that barely warmed the bedroom.

Morning routines in the cavernous house posed their own challenge, I was quick to find out. I could not keep the caldo-bagno turned on while I showered or while boiling the moka pot for coffee and have a single light bulb on all at the same time. In fact, no more than two electrical draws were possible at once. That left me with few options as I scrambled each morning from comparatively warm bedroom to cold bathroom or to the sub-zero lower floor to make coffee in the cantina on a sort of camp like double electric burner. At night I read or wrote by a palm-sized orange flashlight that cousin Adolfo left me, thank god. He instructed me rather cavalierly that I might need it if the power suddenly went out. It never occurred to me that it would actually happen or that I would have to carry that dim Girl Scout lamp from room to room, even as the sun shone outdoors. The stone house, built into the hill, had no windows from front to back. It was black as pitch inside in winter even at noon.

That first morning when I aroused myself from bed, I had no cozy chenille robe to pull on. I was in layers of sweaters and a pair of woolen sweatpants that luckily I had thought to bring with me that I slept in. I casually left the caldo-bagno on high to keep the bedroom warm as I knew I would soon return to it in order to dress for the day. Turning on the light in the main room I shuffled into the bathroom to prepare a shower. The bathroom was a dark, windowless space. Divided into two small rooms, one with the sink, mirror, and single light overhead, and the other with commode, bidet, and naked corner shower square with no *tenda* to keep the steam or spraying water in.

I stalled for time by first going downstairs to prepare coffee while the electric water heater rumbled alive in the bathroom. Once the mocha pot was on the hot plate and turned on conservatively low, I returned upstairs to take my shower and hoped the stream of hot water would thaw the frigid feeling this stone house settled overnight in my bones.

In the middle of this simple morning routine, the place suddenly went utterly black. Naked and wet without a sliver of light anywhere, I groped around in shock for a towel. I retraced my steps back to the bedroom for the flashlight, and then downstairs to the very far end of the sub-zero room to trip the fuse in the box on the wall. I turned off the mocha pot and then headed back upstairs to begin my shower all over again.

"I must be crazy!" I thought. Or brave. Or entirely ignorant of the meager resources the town had to offer in winter.

Eventually, I gingerly complained to Adolfo, since he was a Cicoira, that the house was too cold, too dark and too lonely. "Would you consider helping me find other accommodations for my visit?" He nodded his head as feebly as the caldo-bagno was warming the room and then offered, with just a raise of his chin, nothing by way of a concession.

"What about zia Dorina?" I suggested.

"*Non lo so*," he finally said.

Across town, zia Dorina was more demonstrably concerned. "*Ma come fai in quella casa di sera per il riscaldamento?*" She wondered out loud how I was doing up there alone, without anyone to properly look after me.

"There isn't any heat," I said.

"*Un camino?*" she countered. I shook my head no to the fireplace too.

"*Fa freddo!*"

Though, when I stared at her, wide-eyed and said, "Yes, it is freezing there. Can you help me?" she avoided my plea. I was baffled.

After a few more days of suffering and getting nowhere with subtle hints and whimpers, I finally ordered my timid cousin Adolfo to call zia Dorina again and campaign on my behalf, that it was okay for her to intervene.

Finally she agreed to find me a more suitable place. But it all transpired without my attendance. Within twelve hours I was repacked and on my way to a modern apartment near her with piped in gas for hot water and heat galore. And at the end of my stay, I paid her son one hundred euros for the convenience.

The subtle implications of embarrassing or insulting zia Concetta, or Adolfo for that matter, were lost on me here. I was still very much the ingénue. Adolfo was mutely incredulous, but he drove me over to the new place just the same. I put fresh yellow freesias in a glass and cooked him a nice lunch. Had I only been in Calitri for ten days? This simple act of survival was a *brutta figura* for my Cicoira family and would stick with me a long time.

⁓

Once I met local Professor of Art Fulvio Moscaritolo in the Centro Storico, I thought, I could do this. I could see myself taking an old place like his and make a studio. I'd be perfectly happy, maybe even teach art at the local Art Academy, just down the street.

I ran into him puttering out in a garage in an old white painters coat as I walked down via Concezione from Sant'Antuono, on my way to lunch with zia Concetta.

His studio-garage was adjacent to a wide stone-staired plaza that led up to a remarkable, abandoned, Renaissance era, double-vaulted medieval loggia. Who once lived up there? I wondered.

After exchanging buongiornos, I said, "I see you are working on something." He had a palette knife in hand, and just inside the door was a large figure he was modeling in clay. He soon asked to invite me up to his atelier, an inspiring one room cluttered space with an adjoining room as his personal gallery.

Fulvio Moscaritolo was a painter, ceramist, and sculptor. He was the sculptor of the local life-size bronze monument to the long-sailed emigrants in the center of town. He also restored saints. Those hand-painted, sixteenth century, Neapolitan paper mâche saints that were displayed in alcoves in small churches and then carried on feast days through the town.

A true renaissance man of art, Fulvio was humble, warm and kind, and extraordinarily, variously talented. He reminded me of my own art teachers in high school and college, champions of young talent.

"*A chi apartieni?*" he asked.

"Yes, I'm here visiting relatives." I answered. I had my camera with me, it seemed clear I was la straniera. But could he sense I was also an artist?

Calitri's *l'Istituto Statale d'Arte*, built with state funds and inaugurated in 1959, was at one time the best Art Academy in the region. With *l'Istituto Tecnico Commerciale*—the business school, that preceded the Art Academy in 1953; and *il Liceo Scientifico*—the Science high school, completed in 1961, Calitri had become the region's epicenter of higher education. Teens are still bussed from other smaller villages in Alta Irpinia to Calitri to attend the schools.

We talked about fine art and art history and photography. Perhaps there was room for another art professor in the town?

Before I left, Fulvio gave me a catalog of his work and a beautifully designed black-and-white photo book of turn-of-the-century families of the Avellino region titled, *Siamo Antichi*. I held back tears for his generosity or were they tears of recognition? I stayed on a bit more, conversing and absorbing the contents of his studio, thanked him and then moved on down the street to zia's for lunch.

༄

One morning, zia Concetta came to collect me at my door with the mild complaint that she was expecting me to come sit with her as she prepared our midday meal. She had invited me the afternoon before. I heard a gentle rap on the door.

"*Che fai?*" A soft Italian lilt in her voice.

"*Ciao zia.*" Surprised but pleased she had come to me, I explained that I spent the early morning walking the Centro Storico with my camera documenting the empty streets and enjoying the silence of the snow-dusted town.

"*Vieni con me.*" Unimpressed with my adventure, she stood just inside my door covered in black winter woolens, waiting patiently as I collected my things so we could return to her house together.

I followed her lead out the door to the left to a small back stairway I hadn't noticed before. We climbed up the stone steps and behind the house where I slept and to my surprise arrived again out onto via Fontana. Here was a *scorciatoia*, a shortcut, right under my nose. It brought us up onto a little vicolo, then gently sloped down to her front door.

Inside her warm kitchen the unmistakable aroma of my childhood filled the room. Atop her woodstove *ragu* simmered in a small cast iron pot. A tall porcelain pot filled with water waited its turn on the white gas stove to the right. Set across the kitchen table was a large wooden board with a mound of soft dry farina in the center. To my surprise and delight zia Concetta was about to make fresh macaroni for us for *pranzo*.

The fresh and fragrant semolina flour was from her own field—once tended by her husband Pasquale, my grandmother's youngest brother—now harvested by her daughter Maria and her husband Vincenzo, then milled in the molino at the base of town. The tomatoes for the sauce were homegrown too, preserved that summer and put up for the year in, strangely, brown beer bottles. Dozens of these bottles lined a top shelf in the basement cantina of Maria and Vincenzo's home across town. The wine at lunch was made of grapes grown and pressed from Vincenzo's vines. Slow food. The gathering of manna. Nearly all of the food prepared and presented that day had been cultivated from my relatives' own land. Land that had sustained my grandparents and generations before them for a few hundred years.

And now I felt included in that circle. A women's circle. Zia Concetta's circle. Watching her make pasta, I realized this was the age-old way of women handing down their wisdom, handing down tradition. *Tramandare*. From the old to young. Italian homemaking patiently demonstrated to their daughters. Not that I didn't know some of these things already. But it seemed Concetta's duty as an elder of the circle to show me what she knew. How to make fresh macaroni was essential in these parts.

Growing up on Long Island I never witnessed fresh pasta made by hand. Certainly never on a Tuesday, or any other day in the middle of the week. And certainly never by a nonna or any other relative, dressed entirely in black. But I was familiar with the aroma of tomato sauce—only on a Sunday—while we waited for the large contingent of extended family, mainly my mother's sisters and their husbands, Aunt Rose in her long black Cadillac, to drive out from Brooklyn or Queens.

With camera in hand I watched zia Concetta with the curiosity of a child and the lens of a photojournalist as she approached the kitchen table with a teacup of water and began to mix the farina with her hands. Then she began to fold and mix the dough. Its soft yellow color emerged as she rolled it back and forth on the board with her strong, lithe hands. Methodically she continued until the dough reached the consistency she needed. She divided and subdivided until she created two or three small rounds, and then subdivided them again with a simple, straight-edged iron tool, a hand-forged *paletta*, that neatly cut them in two. She worked this way until she had several small rounds the size of her fist, then began to roll them out into long tapered strands. She cut the strands with the paletta into small even pieces, almost little squares; then she set them aside on the board until she had all the dough cut and had created a large mound of bite-sized pieces.

With a fluid wave of her hand she dusted the mound with flour. She then set the teacup of water aside and began to select pieces two by two, rolling them toward herself with the tips of her middle fingers, then flicked them aside, all in one smooth motion. She continued this way, effortlessly pulling the dough pieces toward her two by two, creating what looked like little softly ridged convex gnocchi, or *l'cingule*.

L'cingule, boil up soft and plump and miraculously collect just enough sugo to satisfy each forkful. Just about every city or village of Italy, whether large or small, has a macaroni shape that is indigenous, and l'cingule have been made by the women of Calitri for generations. No 'cingule, no party, they joke here. No 'cingule, no husband. Maybe that was the point. I was single.

I imagined my father was raised on l'cingule, though he never spoke of it. One day, when describing a black-and-white photo that I had taken in zia Concetta's stone-walled kitchen, I recounted the motion of her hands across the table and the little forms she made with her fingers.

"*L'cingule'!*" my father cried out. Then his voice softened, "My mother made them nearly every day." It was one of the rare times my father spoke of his mother, Angela Maria.

That afternoon in zia Concetta's kitchen I shot frame after frame with my camera as the gray February light entered through the double windows of the front door, one curtain pulled back and hooked on a nail. What natural light there was, was barely reflected against the white ceramic tile of the walls. My OM1 advanced while her hands made swift motions across the table. There was no conversation, just two artists working away at their craft. Zia Concetta indulged me with this quiet ritual of making us lunch and, too, of allowing me to take photo after photo of her without comment or objection. After I exhausted a roll of film, I put my camera aside.

"Can I help you?" I asked.

In dialect she gently declined my offer.

"*Meglio no.*"

"But why not, zia?"

"It tastes better with only one pair of hands," she said.

A moment or two passed as I sat silently at the edge of the table and watched. Then without a word she set aside a small pile and allowed me to give it a try. Eagerly I attempted to imitate the swift, smooth motion that she had perfected over a lifetime. I rolled the small pieces two by two as she did. Zia Concetta was much faster, however, and in no time she had a large quantity of perfectly uniform l'cingule. Mine were thin and floppy, but she shrugged that they would do. When all the macaroni were made, she gathered them to one side of the large board and set them aside. There seemed too much for just the two of us. Later she set a steaming, covered plate aside for Adolfo.

All the while the pot of water simmered on the stove, readying itself for the macaroni. She tossed in two generous handfuls of salt and a moment later gently lowered l'cingule into the rolling water. She raised the massive board off the kitchen table and let whatever small scraps of dough and flour that remained fall to the floor, then stored the board behind it. With the macaroni now immersed, zia Concetta took a moment to remove her apron. She pulled a simple cotton tablecloth from the drawer along with two plates, two small wine glasses, and utensils. She placed a large bottle of chilled spring water and an even larger bottle of fresh, homemade red wine on the cloth. There was a half round of fresh bread too, green olives in herbs, and a bit of fruit.

Lastly came the grating of the cheese. A large round tin about seven inches across with grating spikes up top doubled as a storage container for the *pecorino*. Concetta grated in strong, smooth circles, paused once or twice to check beneath the cover to assess the volume she had produced, then emptied the grated cheese into a small bowl. The meat for the sauce—the *braciole*—still slowly simmered on the woodstove. The pounded steaks, which Adolfo had bought from the butcher the evening before, was traditional for l'cingule. They were spooned from the pot onto a small plate and set on the table.

Tutto sistemato. Concetta had it all perfectly timed. This middle-of-the-week lunch, as much as it was a common midday ritual for the whole community here, was nevertheless cathartic for me. It was a special treat, an experience I felt I sorely missed out on not having had my grandmother cook for me the way Concetta was doing now. It was the first meal that Concetta and I sat down to alone; I was humbled to be invited to partake in this ritual with her. By this, and by how much devotion and craft had been distilled to fewer than forty minutes of preparation.

When l'cingule were done, Concetta took down the macaroni by pouring them into the tin colander that waited in the small porcelain sink. A thick column of steam rose up, blanketing the glass on the front door. The plump and slippery 'cingule were transferred to a large porcelain serving bowl lined with sauce. Then a few generous handfuls of grated pecorino and another ladle or two of sauce were mixed in before they were ladled onto our waiting plates. Finally, each serving was topped with a last ladle of sauce and more grated cheese and then set at our places on the table. With steam still rising from the heat of the macaroni, on a cold February day, those bowls were a gorgeous and inviting sight. Concetta then turned from the stove, unhooked the embroidered curtain from the nail on the door, and let it fall across the glass. Her action was fluid and purposeful. It seemed to convey that in her home it was now lunch hour and she did not wish to be disturbed. At last she took her seat and we began our meal.

Buon appetito.

Winter in the Old Village 97

Wood Stoves in Winter

❦

When not walking around the village with my camera I was kept occupied by my cousin Adolfo and his mother, Angelina Cicoira, and zia Concetta. There were lunches cooked on wood stoves and dinners with their families. Adolfo and I would drive around most days in his faded red Fiat in the cold and snow for hours. The car had a thin paint job, but a great heater! It snowed every day that February. It was the grayest, coldest winter on record in Italy. It even snowed in Sicily that year. The mountain towns we drove to were desolate at best, earthquake damaged, nearly abandoned, situated on high mountain cliffs like Calitri, but even higher, teetering over an endless expanse of fog and snow, the Apennines a dark imposing backdrop in the distance. After a while, I thought I must have been crazy to leave beautiful sunny Los Angeles with irises blooming in my yard for this.

Adolfo, who would be handsome if not for his thick glasses, was not always the best company though. Often brooding and too politely quiet, he was annoyingly noncommittal about everything, anything.

Once we visited the house of Graziella, a friend of zia Angelina's who lived in a deep, grotto-type lair near the very top of the Centro Storico. Zia Angelina had invited me along one freezing morning to do a bit of visiting with her in her part of the old village. As always, Adolfo was in tow. We climbed a tight curve in the lane just above Angelina's house on via Posterla to a small cul-de-sac off a forgotten vicolo tucked away from the rest of the neighborhood below. We finally reached the old iron front door, a perfectly framed view of the godlike volcano Mount Vulture visible from the stone landing.

Graziella lived there, behind that door. Her small private *terrazza* off vicolo San Nicola was shared with only one other neighbor who came and went to her own deep grotto-cantina perhaps once or twice a week. Zia Angelina knocked on the old woman's door to see if she was about. We were in luck. A moment later she pulled open the heavy door and greeted us with a squint of her eyes and raspy toadish voice.

Graziella was dressed as most of the other residents were this February to ward off the deep mountain cold that seeped into just about every nook and cranny of the old village. Petite and hunched over, she wore three or four layers of wool jumpers, aprons, and sweaters with two wool wraps layered around her head, like an Italian Bedouin, making her seem even more compact. Inside, her hilltop lair was completely dark save for the light from the covered glass in the door we had just walked through. There was only one other light source, a lonely naked bulb hanging from a wire in the vaulted ceiling. It seemed like another world. I had never been inside a Calitri cave dwelling before.

It was an ancient jumble of a room—deep, high, and narrow separated by a curtained arch about halfway. The back room looked to be a storage area or her cantina. Cords of wood and kindling were piled high, and rugged garden boots and shoes caked in mud were slung from poles in the rafters. Empty green demijohns for the *vendemmia* and tall tin cans for the olive pressing stacked in rows. The rounded wall in the back was exposed rock, raw *tufo*, the color a wet mustard yellow, just the same as it probably was when it was cut into centuries ago. The bleak dampness was barely vanquished by the smoldering embers at our feet.

In the front room where we stood courteously waiting, an old, understuffed sofa draped with layers of hand-woven wool blankets was wedged between two makeshift cabinets. It sat directly across from a white-tiled wood fire cantina stove, a fornacella. Just like the one in zia Angelina's kitchen, I thought. The one she used every day to cook meals. And like in Angelina's kitchen, there was a smoldering fire spilling out from its base.

A fornacella is a large, waist-high, ceramic-tiled, wood-burning firebox stove. All the houses in the old village here had them. Three or more deep round openings up top hold hand-hewn copper pots set above the fire burning below at floor level. One main fire for all the openings. Winter or summer. Rich or poor. To heat or cook. Yet nothing was being simmered in the cooking cavities above Graziella's fornacella. Instead, the stove was piled high with what looked like a lifetime's worth of clutter: spent votive candles and plastic saint figurines, empty ceramic cups, various rusted tools and utensils, and old newspapers to light the fire. The walls above it were layered with out-of-date calendars, color reproductions of the Madonna, Padre Pio, and a few family photos from various years of celebration. Tucked below was another faded picture of the Madonna in its own small alcove in the wall, as a sort of altar with various offerings laid in front of her. An old cracked plate held collected stones, a dried cob of yellow corn, small talismans and coins and other quasi-devotional objects. Not unlike an alchemist's den, it seemed like the natural and supernatural were given equal placement here among her everyday implements.

Like most of the other elders I had visited in the Centro Storico, the contents of her household—actually, the household itself—seem to be out of time. It was almost as if a parallel universe existed up here above la ripa, and the Ofanto Valley, unfettered by modernity, save for the occasional black-and-white television set. Still, some houses were set apart, even from what could be expected, given the type of community I was in.

Graziella's hospitality was without peer as she ushered us all in to sit on small woodrush chairs in front of the fornacella, while she chatted away in the local language to zia Angelina. Adolfo and I were silent as we waited for her to include us. She was busy shuffling this way and that in the cramped space, disappearing into the main part of the house to bring what she would offer by way of a visitor's welcome. It was still relatively early, no later than eleven o'clock, yet she reappeared with a bottle of homemade *nocino*, the local walnut liquor, and some freshly baked soft biscotti to soak up the strong, dark, sweet alcohol. I was curious about the nocino and was told that one started to make it on the previous June 24th, on the feast of San Giovanni, so it can be drunk in the wintertime.

Once again I was grateful for a warm place to sit and converse, or actually just absorb, as I didn't yet understand their dialect. Would I ever? Every now and then Adolfo stepped in to translate so softly that I could barely follow him. Once in awhile I entreated him with a helpless glance, though these were ignored. Together we quietly drank and ate what was offered. Graziella added a stick or two to the fire at the floor of the cantina stove, arranging them just so, then blew through a long narrow pipe, *a soffiatoio*, to coax the embers once again to flame.

She was a curious character. Fiercely independent, she had lived way up here alone for dozens of years through freezing winters, her husband long passed, her children long emigrated. She seemed visibly envious of my visit to her friend Angelina, younger than her by some twenty years. She had a son and grandchildren somewhere in the U.S. who hadn't been back to see her in years. I felt a bit self-indulgent. After all, I had the freedom to travel and wander. I chose to return to the town and explore this ancient village culture.

Yet Graziella was primarily concerned with me. That I was alone, unmarried.

"*Stai sola?*"

Then she got right to the point.

"*Quanti anni hai?*"

Many of the women here, I noticed, looked old for their years, so I hesitated about revealing my age to all in the room. I finally said, with a little help, "*Una quarantina...*"

She was visibly shocked, then quickly offered her advice that I should not wait too long. A theme that seemed to follow me around in Calitri.

Marriage.

Over my brief time here, I had been asked by family members and complete strangers, women and men alike, often with the probing insistence of the *carabinieri*.

"You are alone?"

"*Sì.*"

"Where is your husband?"

Pause. "*Sono sola.*"

Surprised or confused and not without a few askance looks, they then asked, "Why aren't you married?"

And so on.

One day, when Adolfo and I drove out to the countryside, I strolled further up the barren road alone with my OM1. I spied another homestead up a slight grade in the distance and realized I was near the Zarrilli's farm, which I had visited two years before. I wondered if Giuseppe Zarrilli, The Handsome Man from Macchiursi knew I was near. I had thought about him time and again. After I returned home to L.A., I had sent Adolfo a few photos of that visit in the mail to give to Giuseppe—in his field clothes, some oversized waxy pigs, the Irpinia fields flowing by. Adolfo never mentioned it. I wondered now if he had received them.

On our return to the town in the faded red Fiat I watched as a winter white owl followed us from the tall pine trees all the way down the road. He flew from power pole to power pole alongside us. Traveling alone here I often felt like that lone bird flying solo, yet always reaching for others.

"Look!" I said. "That beautiful bird is following us." In this bleak and mysterious place it seemed an omen, a good sign.

※

Then one day near the end of the month, a week or so before I was to fly back home, Adolfo mentioned an invitation came to drive out to the Zarrilli farmhouse.

"Really?"

"*Sì.*"

"When?"

"Today, this afternoon."

My heart jumped.

We were instructed to arrive around 6pm. The dark winter ride out to the farm was an almost otherworldly experience. Certainly not the wistful drive we had taken in summer, blazing through tall fields of golden grain as cicadas whirred in the grasses. That memory was now looping its way around my heart.

We pulled into their yard. It was jet black. Deep country black, with a bite to the air and a light dusting of snow still on the ground. When Adolfo cut the engine, not a sound could be heard. Only a deep-space silence, dazzling me with millions of stars from above. I knew the great Pleistocene form of Mount Vulture loomed before us on the horizon, yet we were floating in a sea of darkness.

Angelo, Michele Zarrilli's younger son, met us with a half smile of complicity as he rounded the outside corner of the farmhouse. Once inside, we gathered around the wood stove before everyone else came home from work. We all seemed to be waiting for something, someone. Soon, Rosa and Michele joined us. I was encouraged to nestle up to the fire's heat on a low rush chair. I was more than a little relieved. I had spent the major part of my month's vacation trying to stay warm. Their wood stove roared fierce, thawing the chill in my bones. All interest was on me, Adolfo's cousin from America who had come to visit again, albeit in February.

Moments later, heavy boot steps were heard and a tall figure stooped first to look in the living room window a moment before the front door opened. I feigned a glance in the other direction long enough for Giuseppe to cross the room and arrive right in front of our circle.

"*Buonasera,*" There was a softened boom to his voice. He was undeniably the most handsome man I had ever seen.

"*Ciao!*" I chirped. "Do you remember me?"

"*Sì.*" Conviction in his voice. He stood stock still without another word, then glanced at Adolfo.

"Did you get the photos I sent?"

"*Quale foto?*" And shook his head no. Then I glared at Adolfo, who only shrugged.

Giuseppe removed his coat, hung it on a peg, and sat himself down at the long wood table in the center of the room. I followed, by some will of force, and found myself planted right across from him. Michele took a seat at the table's head. He was the first to speak.

"Do you like Calitri?" he asked me.

"Of course, I like Calitri." I said. "Though February is very cold. I'm not exactly used to it." I didn't elaborate on the first cold house in the Centro.

Quickly after, he asked, "*A chi apartieni?*" His two questions, I had come to learn, were standard-issue opening queries for any traveler to their village.

"My relatives? They are Paolantonio and Cicoira. Adolfo's mother and my father *sono cugini*."

Giuseppe kept his cool, leaning into the table, his strong, round hands resting cupped together. We looked straight at each other. Deep amber eyes. I was more than struck. This man is gorgeous, my heart thought. And the first thing I blurted out to him was, "My God, why aren't you married?"

"*PIANO, PIANO!*" he boomed, startling everyone to attention, then looked very pleased with a smoldering glint in his eyes.

Michele continued, "What does your father do?"

"My father?" I looked over to Adolfo for help. "Well, he is retired now. But he was a mechanical illustrator at Ford Instruments and later, Grumman."

"Your mother?" he asked.

"She's a housewife." Michele was interviewing me! I fielded a few other questions until he got to, "So, how old are you?"

I paused. Deflected. My gaze still resting on Giuseppe's eyes, soft crows' feet peeking around their edges. His powerful arms, foreshortened. His shoulders seemed strong enough to pull a sleigh. Tall and rugged, shyly handsome with a hint of brooding. Was it just his eyes that held me so tight? That glint? His father's eyes had it too, even more strongly than Giuseppe's. He was a man of almost sixty with the youth in his eyes of a twenty-year-old.

"Oh, around forty," I finally said, reluctant to reveal the truth.

And then I heard, "Giuseppe turns thirty tomorrow!" And suddenly we were thrust into an "I Love Lucy" episode.

"Oh?" I glanced at the calendar on the wall to note the date. Then directly to the soon-to-be birthday boy I smiled and said, coyly, "So, will there be cake? Presents?"

The Handsome Man from Macchiursi demurred with a masculine shrug. And with that Michele got up from the table to move back to the woodstove.

Giuseppe leaned in to ask where in the U.S. I lived.

"Los Angeles."

"Where is Los Angeles? Is it near New York?" Angelo asked.

"California. Los Angeles is in Southern California. It's across the country on the West Coast. New York is on the East."

With his family as witnesses, Giuseppe quietly asked me to write him, and we exchanged addresses. Later he walked us out to the car. A sad contentedness overwhelmed my exhaustion and took root in my bones. I couldn't decide if it was torture or folly. All I could do was stare up at the sky, so black and beautiful and romantic.

"So many stars," I finally breathed out.

Giuseppe feigned perplexity. He made a quip to Adolfo though he stared directly at me. Adolfo dutifully translated, " 'Don't they have stars in Los Angeles'?"

"Yes, of course," I said. "But nothing like you see here, reaching down to the earth. In Los Angeles there are too many city lights."

When we finally pulled away from their farm, Adolfo quietly murmured, "You like Giuseppe, I think." Without any prompting from me, except of course maybe the sensual energy pouring out of me like gold.

Adolfo and I drove out to the Zarrilli farm once more before I flew home. I wanted to bring Giuseppe the photos I had mailed to Adolfo last year.

When we pulled up, it was still light. Giuseppe peered out from a bedroom balcony while his brother Angelo greeted us at the door. His parents were nowhere to be seen. We sat in the farmhouse with the warmth of the wood stove pulling me in. I gave Giuseppe the three photos from the summer we had first met and he proudly showed me some old family snapshots pulled from a drawer in their rustic sideboard. He knew I was a photographer, with a few artful portfolios of images I had taken around the town. Seemed he wanted to engage me in something I knew.

One of the two photos that struck me was of Giuseppe in a grade school play with other students. He was standing, taller than the rest, beaming proudly, with a gold crown on his head. Whatever play it was, he was the king. The other photo was of Giuseppe as a drop-dead gorgeous twenty-something palling around with his friends at a local wedding.

He got up to retrieve an armload of firewood outside, dropped it John Wayne-style in a heap next to the stove near my feet.

"*Che dice?*"

I sighed. "*Niente.*"

He sat down in front of me with his woodfire-bold knee lightly grazing mine. I drew in a slow, controlled breath.

"Why don't you stay?"

"I have to return to work."

"Can't you call in sick?"

Two days later, it was the night before I left town.

Adolfo roused me out of much-needed nap with the insistent ring of the apartment bell four stories below. We had arranged earlier that day for him to collect me around 6pm to drive me around the town for my final round of goodbyes to my parenti. I would be flying home to the U.S. very early the next morning.

I reluctantly dragged myself from bed, tumbled down the four-story stairwell, and hopped into Adolfo's faded Fiat waiting down at the curb just outside the door. I knew this was the official beginning of the long and uncomfortable journey from this remote mountain village back home to Los Angeles, and I wasn't looking forward to it. Not only that, but this was the second time Giuseppe and I had come in fleeting contact with one another—sparks flying, me leaving. And now every synapse in my body was fighting the overwhelming crush I felt for this handsome rancher's son, with little success.

After that last visit in the Zarrilli farmhouse without his parents, it seemed clear that we were more than just curious about each other. With modest, shy gentility we exchanged addresses with promises to write, across the expanse of miles and vastly different lives. I then spent the following two nights sleepless as I tossed and turned the nearly impossible idea in my head. Should I begin a long-distance romance with a man from a culture, a world, apart?

It was a mild, first-of-March evening. The weather had finally turned on my last day in town. The streets were congested with cars, teenagers, townspeople all crossing this way and that as they attended to their last-minute errands. Adolfo and I slowly climbed the switchback road until we rounded the corner of via Francesco De Sanctis and the fruttivendolo store. Our first stop was the elettrodomestici shop belonging to Vito Cestone, who had been my first emissary in the town just two years earlier.

When Adolfo pulled up to the curb, I was startled to spy Giuseppe double-parked in front of the bar-pasticceria. Like an addled schoolgirl, I quickly averted my glance.

I leaned into the passenger door and with one smooth gesture I was out of the car and onto the sidewalk, about to head in the opposite direction. Adolfo firmly called out to me, "Stop. Giuseppe is in his car just across from us."

I wheeled around in time to witness Giuseppe unfold himself from the front seat. He paused there and seemed to fill the entire frame before me as I felt my heart swoon.

How was I going to resolve this? I was leaving at dawn tomorrow for who knew how long. My life and career were several light years away from this town, this culture, and this man. For a fleeting moment, I thought I heard my father—my grandfather—saying, "Leave the village behind."

Giuseppe's face held a slight fear of rejection caused by my evasiveness a moment ago. I suppose he thought I was about to ditch him. I stepped off the curb and walked the few steps over to meet him waiting in the middle of the street. The two of us stood close enough to sense each other's heartbeats.

"*Buon viaggio*," he said.

"*Grazie.*"

"*Torni presto.*"

"I'll try to come back soon."

"*Scriviamo.*"

"Yes, I will write."

I felt my hand nestled in his. I had vowed in vain not to return home trailing this crush behind me. Not daring to look each other in the eye, we stood silently in the street, neither of us wanting to break the spell.

The flight home was bittersweet. I was now leaving too much behind. I had embedded myself into a seemingly lost world high on a mountain ridge in Alta Irpinia. I longed to stay but I needed to go.

Now I was about to embark on an old-fashioned written courtship with all the longing and suspense that that evoked. I hadn't exchanged letters with a distant lover in years, probably since early college. Out of all my previous travels elsewhere and my months living in Italy, from the very beginning, there were flirtations with Italian men—a cosmopolitan artist, or a local naturalist, even a vineyard millionaire. But Giuseppe Zarrilli, the rancher's son from Macchiursi, was the only one who closed the deal on my heart.

Le neve e 'alla montagna
L'inverno s'avvicina
Bellissima Nerina
Che mai sarà di me?
I giorni brevi e rigidi

Le notte aspre e lunghissime
Come potrò mai vivere
Cara lontana da te?

- JACOPONE DI TODI

Snow is on the mountain
Winter is approaching
My beautiful Nerina
What will become of me?
The days are short and hard
The night's bitter and long
How will I ever live
Dear, far away from you?

- JACOPONE DI TODI

Five Letters,
The Road to Macchiursi

❦

Between February and June I sent Giuseppe five postcards and letters. I heard nothing in return. My American girlfriends were all doubtful. Their expectations of Italian men were quite low in the loyalty department, but I wasn't willing or ready to write him off to that stereotype. All I knew was, he had asked me to write so I did. It just felt right.

My Los Angeles life went on as usual. Getting caught in the frayed emotions of my photographers and designers as I tended to their businesses and mine and the demanding competitive relationships with our clients. My parents and siblings never asked how my February trip went. One month in the town of our family ancestry, exploring the ghostly streets of the old village, visiting our distant relatives, and no curiosity. If I kept returning, would they get it?

Fresh California daffodils on tables and counter-tops, everything in its place, poised for my next adventure. I knew I wanted to return to explore romance in the village where my grandparents were born. But I will admit, after five letters and no response, come June, I began to think—well, this was just not good.

Then, out of the blue, an email came from Adolfo in early July.

"Giuseppe wants to know if you received his letters?"

"What letters? No. I haven't received any letters. When did he send them? Did he receive mine?" No further response. I would have to wait until my next visit to learn the answer.

I was to return to Calitri in September that year. I hadn't secured myself a place to stay in advance. I just alerted a few members of my Calitri family of my arrival date. I wanted to attend the town's *festa* for the Madonna for the first time, as was suggested by zia Concetta. And I wanted to see Giuseppe.

Late on a Thursday afternoon in September, I arrived from Naples by Pullman. The long journey inland from the airport by local bus routes left me more than a little jetlagged and dearly concerned for my errant belongings. My luggage had not made it all the way through. Berardino, Giuseppina's son, drove me across town on my first round of greetings to various relatives. Last stop was the Paolantonio palazzo where zia Dorina, Franco's wife Raffaela, and Dorina and Franco's mother nonna Migliorina were waiting at the curb. It had been decided that I would sleep in the upstairs loft apartment belonging to nonna Migliorina. We alighted—me without any luggage—to their warm smiles and hearty welcome. Dorina slowly described, with economical pride, the comfortable quarters four stories above: large, quiet, private, and "within earshot of the rest of the family on the floors below," she hinted, then added, "So don't think you'll get away with bringing a man around."

Once I realized what was implied and in front of a male cousin, I quickly responded, "*Ma, zia con chi? Sono sempre sola.*"

"*Eh, sì,*" she said, feigning complicity.

Berardino gently shook his head, bid us *buon riposo*, and drove off.

I was simply exhausted, and thankfully, left alone to sleep for the rest of that first evening.

The next morning I met zia Dorina's daughter Lucia, who was down for the summer from Florence where she attended university. This was the first time we had met. She insisted that come evening, luggage, or not, I should attend the passeggiata in the upper town and take my chances of meeting up with Giuseppe.

Lucia was more than a little intrigued to meet the Handsome Man from Macchiursi. I had briefly summed up my fleeting second-chance meeting last February at his family farmhouse, and confessed to her the lost letters and my anticipation of seeing him again.

"*Chi è questo ragazzo?*" She quizzed with concern in her voice, "*È di Calitri?*"

"He's not a boy." I replied. "He's a man. A robust, handsome man." I wasn't used to the local vernacular of calling an unmarried man, whatever his age, *un ragazzo*.

Dorina too, upon hearing the story, was wildly curious. "A virgin love affair?" she only half-happily declared. "Involving one of our own *parente lontana? L'Americana?*" And, in her own hometown to boot. I winced.

"*Chi è questo ragazzo?*" she continued. I think she was rather disappointed that she wasn't in on the news earlier.

"He's just a local guy," I said. "I don't know yet who he is, really."

"*Come una volpe!*"

Did she just call me a sly fox?

She seemed only half joking.

"I am not a fox!" Which I construed as somehow sneaky. "And

yes, I know what that word means."

"*Non è una cosa cattiva*," she quickly retorted. "*Sei furba.*" I was smart, for finding him, a younger man, and all on my own. Lucia now didn't know what to think.

After lunch with Franco and Raffaela and their family—who made no such inquiries as to my foxiness—and a long and well-needed afternoon nap, I called down to Lucia that I was refreshed and ready to take that passeggiata along the Corso. Casually adding, as if I needed an excuse, that perhaps we could get a gelato together, my treat. It was clear to her though what our mission was, and that I was nervous as hell. So, with Dorina seeing us off from the second story balcony, Lucia, her fiancé Stefano, and I piled into her trusty red Fiat at around 9 p.m. and drove away from the Paolantonio homestead.

We climbed up the switchback road via Circumvallazione, then parked on a side street just behind the new Duomo, the Cathedral to San Canio, patron Saint of the town. In a moment we emerged onto Corso Garibaldi to find the town alive with a throng of residents celebrating the start of the most important weekend of the year, the Festa for the Madonna. Everyone strolled arm in arm: husbands and wives, friends and relatives, all randomly crossing and commanding the romantically lit and carless main street. The scene held me in awe. I had never experienced anything like it. It was certainly not an American sensibility, to stroll along within a crowd with one's family in mid-evening, expecting to brush up with everyone in town. Here everyone from near or far—*nei vestiti delle feste*—walked in couplets or groups stopping often to exchange double kisses, or a singular nod of recognition, and then they moved on. It seemed the world populated the Corso of Calitri. Families and relatives from all over Italy, and the world, came to participate in this centuries-old religious festival with neighboring townsmen and their kin. And apparently, they really knew how to throw a party.

In just the few minutes' walk from the car to Bar Jolly, where

I offered both Lucia and Stefano a celebratory gelato, we caught up with cousins from my grandmother's side walking in a large group. They were all surprised, then elated to see me.

"Angela!" Rosetta's voice sailed above the crowd. "*Che sorpresa! Quando sei venuta?*" She air-kissed me on both cheeks.

"Ciao, Rosetta. Nice to see you. I arrived just last night."

She turned to her husband Vincenzo, zia Maria's son, on the sidewalk. "*Vedi, Vincenzo, è Angela! È tornata.*"

"Ciao, Angela. Sei tornata?" He too air-kissed me on both cheeks. "Nice to see you again. Come stai? E i tuoi genitori?"

"Ciao, Vincenzo. Everyone's fine, thank you," I said. "What an incredible night!" I motioned toward the crowd whirling around us. We were stopped in what looked like the epicenter of the action.

"*Sei venuta per le festa?*" Rosetta gushed. "*Hai fatto bene. Meglio dell'inverno, eh?*"

They were all especially pleased that I was in town again in warmer days—after my solo Siberian adventure in February—and congratulated me on my being in town to attend the Festa for the Madonna.

Young friends and schoolmates Teodolinda and Federica, ironically representing both sides of my grandparents' lineage, ran up to greet me, gently air-kissed my cheeks, and complimented my journey back. "*Bentornata!*" said Teodolinda.

"*Per quanto tempo resti?*" Federica asked. "*Dopo le feste?*"

Teodolinda was the daughter of Michele, Dorina's son and Lucia's brother. Her mother Gerardina and others in their party offered me greetings, with promises for us to see each other in the days to come. With all these warm welcomes in the middle of the town, I felt like the errant debutante in *Il Gattopardo* arriving at the Pantaleone Ball. (Perhaps soon to meet up with her handsome Tancredi?)

After all greetings were made and information dispensed as to how long I was staying in town, with more air kisses, Rosetta declared, "*Allora, buon proseguimento.*" A sign-off equal to "have a good time."

Gelatos in hand, Lucia, Stefano and I continued strolling slowly toward the tumult in the center of the Corso, while I scanned one side to the other, looking for signs of the Handsome Man from Macchiursi. I secretly worried whether I would recognize him, or him me. Seven long months had passed without receiving a word in the mail and I wondered if he too would welcome my arrival.

Lucia and Stefano sidetracked me as best they could. They introduced me to their friends gathered in small groups on the street, occasionally scanning my face two see whether I had spotted him. Without any sign, we agreed to rest briefly along a stone wall set back off the wide sidewalk to finish our cups of gelato. The crowd swelled and dispersed in waves, an organic mass moving between one gathering point to the next. Our brief pause seemed like an eternity while the young and old celebrated in escalating merriment all around us.

Soon we headed down the broad street again as we cautiously made our way among the crowd. With barely room to move on the ground, my eyes searched the open spaces above. Wide, graceful arches of festival lights spanned the black dome high overhead, throwing a carnival of color across the crowd. Further up the street, the front of the Duomo of San Canio was framed too, in tiny white lampadine. The famously breathtaking panoramas that sliced between buildings and side streets during golden daylight had fallen black. The amber light of street lamps permeated only so far, as deep shadows and young teens played between doorways and stone benches. The festival street vendors had not yet set up their overstuffed and brightly lit stalls; they would arrive the next day to further crowd the Corso. This night, all the town's residents and their gaiety seemed suspended in the evening's romantic half-darkness. Nothing distracted them from themselves nor their long-awaited enjoyment.

Wandering away from the group, I found myself standing alone in another crowd. I focused for what seemed only a moment and there, just a few paces from the entrance to a popular bar, nestled among another crowd, I spied a long, leonine figure moodily draped over a chair outside the doorway.

Could it be...?

All those months ago holding hands on the street tumbled in waves through my heart. Now, not quite trusting my first glance, I checked again. I turned my focus on the jumbled group in constant movement outside the bar. There he sat in a cafe chair against the outside wall, with a young woman close by his side. I casually shifted my eyes in her direction, then briefly nodded to gain her compliance. In that brief moment though, I felt my knees buckle. I knew this was not what the universe had in store for Giuseppe and me. For I had held fast the belief since that winter evening that his heart was with me until I returned.

One last time I looked over my shoulder toward Lucia. I hoped to alert her and Stefano of my find. They were still there, standing a few paces away from me, embedded in another group in the middle of the street, but they hadn't noticed my gesture. I would have to go it alone.

I bucked up and stepped into view from around the large sycamore tree that straddled the sidewalk, then stood still for a moment with my eyes and smile firmly fixed on the brooding figure in the cafe chair. It took but another second for him to register my presence.

He leapt up and out of his seat, bounded the few steps over to me, and reached for my hand. Gently double air-kissing my cheeks he inquired in close rapid succession, *"Come stai?"* *"Come andata?"* and *"Quando sei arrivato?"*

"I'm fine, thank you." I smiled. "My flight was fine, I arrived just last night."

From that moment seven months of waiting fell away. We

stood fast, surrounded by the crowds of young townspeople, their excited voices muffled in our sudden void; the air beamed electric and in the trees, a warm wind whispered our amorous hosanna as the evening and my ardor were forever transformed.

"*E le mie cartoline?*" He looked concerned, his tanned cheeks flushed warm in the lamplight.

"No, no letters came," I answered. "I'm sorry. Did you get mine?"

"*Sì, sì.*"

I answered his questions and added a few of my own until we were left silent, gauging each other's heartbeats. Then, as if on cue, the young woman who had been seated next to him appeared in front of us. We barely took notice. She leaned up to offer some words to him in his ear and then moved off into the crowd, only to return a few moments later with his brother in tow.

"*Ciao, Angelo!*" I remembered Giuseppe's brother from last February on their ranch.

"Ciao, Angela, come va?"

"*Bene, bene.* You look great!"

And handsome he was too, standing six-foot-three in a bright Italian-pink button down, his long legs in jeans, with a thick sweater casually thrown over his shoulder—he was dressed for the Festa. Angelo introduced the young woman at his side,

"This is my girlfriend, Michela."

"*Piacera.* And you must be Angela, Giuseppe's friend from America," she said.

She seemed more relieved than I was. Her voice was cheerful, bright, and feminine, and she seemed genuinely eager to meet me, and to set the situation straight.

Though nearly forgotten in the time warp of my first moments with Giuseppe, Lucia entered the scene from the left, and quipped,

"*Allora, l'hai trovato?*" She was not smiling, and didn't wait for a response. First she secured an introduction to the Handsome

Man from Macchiursi. "*Salve, Sono Lucia Cestone. Angela è cugina della mia mamma. Lo sai?*"

Giuseppe shook his head that he did not know how we were related. And then she asked him—well, nearly commanded—would he now take over for the rest of the evening? "*Allora, si accompagnare tu?*"

Giuseppe solemnly nodded yes. I was beaming. Lucia next offered a brief introduction to Stefano and then a casual *ci vediamo*, and they were gone.

Those few moments—nay, the entire romantic evening—were now forever etched in my heart as the first of many, accompanied by the tall and ruggedly handsome Man from Macchiursi, as we went for our first passeggiata and more through the town.

The first thing he wanted to clear up were the missing letters, which he produced from the glove box of his car. There they were, the five postcards and letters from me and then his envelopes that had been returned. Why? I turned one envelope over for a clue and saw that he had mistaken the seven I wrote for a one. Westerners don't slash their sevens. Here, I was learning, they still do. There was no 6150 Mulholland Drive, that much I knew. I was annoyed the Hollywood postal service apparently couldn't make the leap.

We slowly went through our cards and letters. Among them, I had sent a postcard of the Hollywood Hills with an aerial view of the Hollywood sign and a hand-drawn arrow to mark where I lived on Mulholland Drive. And he had sent me a pastel-colored Lamb of God Easter card enclosed with snapshots of the spring green hills of Macchiursi with his grazing flock of sheep.

He looked at the Hollywood postcard, then at me, and asked poker-faced, "Aren't there any sheep in those hills?"

"Not really." I knew he was kidding. Or wait, was he?

Later when he drove me down the hill I chastely ended our evening with a peck on his cheek and he promised to see me again the following evening.

Camera Matrimoniale
(Marriage Bedroom)

⁂

The next morning I was startled awake by cannon fire and the September sun blazing through the fourth-story window. Three rounds of deafening ka-booms echoed around the valley, penetrating the very bed where I lay. Bleary eyed, I thought, it couldn't be more than 7 a.m. I had only returned to the apartment a few hours before, having spent my first evening's passeggiata and solo drive afterward with the Handsome Man from Macchiursi. It was a Saturday morning, and save for these sudden explosions, not another sound could be heard outside the window.

I rose out of nonna Migliorina's bed, opened the double windows wider to the day, and soon heard in the near distance what sounded like a tin band playing somewhere below. Scanning the soccer field toward the ridge of the Apennine mountains in the east, my eyes did not immediately find what my ears were alerted to. A kind of Fellini overture was wafting through the summer air and I couldn't locate it anywhere. First canon fire and now trumpet music; was I in some old Italian movie?

I strained my way farther out the window just in time to glimpse four brass banders in crisp white shirts, dark trousers, and gold-braided hats as they slowly made their way up an old back road that led straight up the steep hillside to the town.

They played a sort of call-to-arms folk music with trumpets, *organetto*, and hand-held percussion instruments, and their spirited sounds faded in and out as they made their way up the barely paved road. Eager to follow the music they were making, I went around to the front of the apartment to the kitchen and opened the windows wide there to see the small band stopped, though still playing, in front of a house across via Circumvallazione.

They continued to play this way; walking slowly, stopping occasionally, on street corners and across from houses, for a few bars or so, then would seemingly, reluctantly, move on. Once in awhile someone would come out to greet them and make some sort of offering. Then they would move on again up the road.

The morning was otherwise peaceful. The air blue-bright and warm; no other sound or cars seemed to override the music of the tin band. I stayed for a long while at that front window with its perfect view of the hillside of ancient Calitri and listened to them still playing off in the distance as they made their way through the country back roads of the town and up toward their goal. What I was hearing and witnessing for the first time was the centuries-old tradition of *la Banda* and the accompanying canon fire that shook the town on the first morning of the weekend of the festa.

Alone at the window with their fading musical accompaniment, I thought of the one photo of my grandparents found in a credenza drawer all those years ago. My heart wanted to conjure up some conversation with them, to tell them that my adventures here in Calitri were deepening. That here in my emotional body reminiscence bloomed, announcing this was where life began for them some one hundred years ago, and that I felt I belonged here at this very window with the music of *la Banda* wafting around their hillside.

Upon my arrival in town two days ago when this upstairs loft apartment was offered to me, Dorina, Raffaela, and nonna Migliorina assumed that I would sleep in the small single bed nestled tightly against the wall in the spare front bedroom. It was to this room that I was first escorted after they walked me through the spacious apartment that afternoon. I glanced at the lone bed. The three Paolantonio women smiled their warm welcome. Did I approve?

I supposed that since I wasn't married, and remembering Dorina's remark about not bringing anyone up, it seemed, to them, unnecessary for me to sleep alone in the more comfortably furnished master bedroom across the hall. A form of infantilizing, as seemed to be the norm here. I guess they deemed that even an adult woman should be consigned to sleep in a too-narrow bed unless and until she had successfully tied the conjugal knot.

Why would an otherwise unattached woman need a double bed to herself if not to share with a husband?

The trio of two aunts and nonna were duly thrown when I casually walked into the master bedroom and settled my one bag there, clearly unchallenged by their surprised looks, uninitiated to their deeply ingrained propriety or rationale.

I slept under a large painting of Jesus in the former *camera matrimoniale* of nonna Migliorina and her long-gone husband, Vito Paolantonio, Sr. Jesus sat in the foreground on a hillside overlooking a small rural town in the near distance. Deep blue and green hues lent a pastoral quietness to the simple composition, reminding me of a 1930s Maxfield Parrish painting. A large wooden crucifix draped with a modest rosary of gray seeds hung on the opposite wall to his right.

On either side of the master bed and in the drawers of the bedside tables were devotional books and prayer cards to Sant'Antonio, Santa Lucia, San Canio, and San Vito, all patron saints of the town. Feeling very well protected, I assumed that my dreams and daily ministrations, meditations, and prayers would be safe in their provenance.

Nonna Migliorina too was available whenever I needed an extra blanket or to change over the sheets. She would insist on slowly, carefully, climbing the two flights from the apartment below to help me locate what I needed from inside her large wooden corredo and to assist me in dressing the bed. I was more than grateful for her generosity, for allowing me not only a place to sleep for my extended stay but trusting me with free rein in an apartment that she once intimately shared with her husband.

Nonna Migliorina now lived two floors below these loft rooms with Dorina in her empty-nest apartment. Her husband Vito had been the master *sarto* of Calitri, known for his skill in tailoring clothes. He was the eldest son of my grandfather Nicola's oldest brother, Francesco Paolantonio, Sr. Francesco, Sr., was the eldest of the four brothers including my grandfather who emigrated. Then he later returned to Calitri from New York to work this land and raise his family.

This was also the apartment where I had bid goodbye to nonna Migliorina on my first departure from Calitri, now almost three years ago to the month. That day, she had offered me a beautiful studio portrait of her husband, a still young Vito, Sr., to take with me. As I stalled to leave, I had spied the Paolantonio stemma on the wall just inside her front door. Now I thought I would have a chance to live with the coat of arms, slowly fully examine it, and perhaps uncover some new facts about our distant family heritage.

But when I crossed the room to look for it, it wasn't there anymore.

When my luggage arrived that afternoon—with the help of Lucia; she made one phone call to Naples and within a few hours the courier was at the door—I began to open the armoires in the two bedrooms, looking for places to hang my clothes. In the master bedroom the oversized *guardaroba* was still hung with vintage black wool gabardine coats, silk ties, and a few male odds and ends, all expertly hand sewn. Apart from his tailor trade, Vito Paolantonio, Sr. owned a successful Singer sewing machine business on the Piazza della Repubblica in the upper town.

In the second bedroom was the narrow single bed nestled against one wall. On the opposite wall a series of armoires hung with Migliorina's hand-sewn dresses and dressing gowns. A cast iron, black 1920s-era Singer sewing machine was on the far side of the room under the window. It was the same model that my mother's mother used in East New York to earn enough to feed her growing family in the early 1920s and 30s, the same one I learned to sew on in my early teens.

I wandered over to the tall *cristalliere* in the living room. On the shelves inside were photos of Migliorina and Vito, very young and newly married; a portrait of his father, Francesco, Sr., my grandfather's older brother' several sets of vintage aperitif glassware and a collection of petite crystal *bomboniere*, those Italian wedding keepsakes, from her family and friends. Fueled by a forager's curiosity, I allowed myself to delve deeper into their lives and into the two drawers nestled at the bottom of the cabinet. I sat on the floor in front of the drawers and meditated for a moment on the intrusion I was about to commit, then slowly began to explore their contents.

I opened the left drawer first. It contained a few old cleaned ashtrays, a small box of Singer machine parts, and other masculine artifacts of a bygone era; wrapped and tucked away for posterity. In the right-hand drawer, beneath two more carefully tissue-wrapped wedding photos of Migliorina and Vito, was a simple 1940s-era color illustration of the Last Supper. It was bound between glass with red cloth tape and on the back was a scrap of cardboard on which the year 1959 was printed boldly in black. A wave flooded over me. It was the only thing printed on the scrap of cardboard and it happened to be the year I was born and the year of my grandfather's death. I sat for a moment, silent at this find, and thought back to my formative years growing up without my grandparents and wondered when the last time my grandfather might have visited Calitri.

Cerca trova, I thought, and kept lifting the layers.

Through a stack of more glass and tape-framed reproductions from the early 1950s—the Duomo in Milan, a tree-lined park in Torino, until I uncovered a gray-textured photographic studio folder typical of the 1940s and 50s. I carefully opened the folder and was stunned for a moment, then understood my providence. It felt like I had found a sacred document or shared secret. Inside the folder was an 8"x10" black-and-white studio portrait of my grandfather, Nicola Paolantonio.

I sat for a long time. As I looked at his image, I felt that my presence here in Calitri not only fostered a deep transition in my life's longing to find and connect with the ghosts of my grandparents, but that indeed I felt guided by them. And too, it seemed to bridge the years and lost memories from a drawer in my childhood home in New York to another half a world away. His gaze was strong, self-possessed, though just a little off to the distance. He had an unmistakable powerful sense of self, I thought. The look of a commanding officer. While fixed on his image, I began to wonder about what his life experiences were like growing up here one hundred years ago as a young boy and then bravely leaving in his late teens for America, to embark on a whole other life.

As a contemporary of this village he would have worked the land with his father and brothers on the very lot that this apartment building stood on. The casa di campagna behind it would have been where he slept in summer with his family with his mother Mariantonia and father, Vito, Sr. I was immediately struck too by the providence of finding his image reverently saved for years in this drawer by my extended family here in Calitri. I had heard that my grandfather was a formidable presence in real life—a former sergeant in the King's cavalry during World War I. A man of nearly six feet, barrel-chested and casually, powerfully, strong—not unlike the Handsome Man from Macchiursi—well remembered and well respected for his choices and successes. My own father, though he didn't speak of him often, would always refer first to his father's physical countenance.

"You wouldn't mess with him. Nobody messed with him," he once said. "But he was easy with the ladies." As if to be clear, he added, "My father had girlfriends, you know." After he lost his wife. But he seemed to call this up in private reverie from somewhere else.

"In New York, he owned a bar in the decade before the second World War," my father continued. "In those days we called it a saloon." He didn't laugh. "It was a beer hall, on the Kings and Queens county border, in Germantown. It was during Prohibition. But don't kid yourself, there were still plenty of drinkers."

Indeed, even in the black-and-white photo, after some forty years, Nicola seemed to be fueling the myth that surrounded his identity for me, for so long.

Since my first visit here, back in the fall of 2000, my relatives had treated me as their special ambassador. I had arrived unannounced with a direct, albeit naïve, link to the one man they held in most high esteem. I remembered Franco's first words to me about my grandfather Nicola being "a very great man." Apart from Franco's impeccable Southern Italian politeness and protocol back then, those words seem to truly resonate with me now.

A young son, one of their own, who emigrated all those years ago, who then returned in the autumn of his life as a widower bearing gifts and stories of experiences none of them could have imagined. The father and grandfather of Americans.

Then I thought of how Giuseppe mirrored my grandfather's myth now in so many ways. Mostly in physical strength and stature. Though his inherent connection and devotion to this land stand out as characteristics all of their own. I supposed they were felt and projected by my grandfather too. Could be Giuseppe was the man my grandfather guided me to meet here under these august skies?

Later that evening Giuseppe and I met up in the town. We had no specific plan and there was no phone call, we were just to meet up on the Corso. As an American tethered to her cell phone I wondered how this could work. But there he was in front of the Bar Poldos where a gazillion other people were milling about. Seemed this was how it was done in small-town Italy. We said our cordial greetings, then soon set out up the Corso. We ended up at the top of the hill well above the old Piazza where they had recently finished restoring parts of the Langobard Castle. The view from up there was a kind of illuminated miniature of the view of the Hollywood basin from the ranch on Mulholland Drive, complete with the trailing headlamps and taillights winding through the town below. When I expressed this to Giuseppe he looked at me askance. We even found a temporary gallery of art and a pizzeria up there open for the evening. We sat down for a well deserved beer and he pulled out his cell phone to exchange phone numbers.

Now things were getting serious.

Camera Matrimoniale (Marriage Bedroom) 131

Sacred & Profane

Lucia invited me to go with her to follow the first procession of the weekend, the Sunday afternoon Procession for San Vito.

San Vito, whose cult is widespread in Campania and Basilicata, and from Rome to Prague, was among the fourteen Holy Helpers. Patron saint of hunters, woodsmen, and travelers, he is depicted with two faithful dogs at his feet. The events of his life are not well-known, though his martyrdom is remembered and celebrated throughout Lucania where villages honor him as their Patron Saint and many, many sons are named Vito. Like my father.

On the walls of the map room in the Vatican Museum, back in the 1400's, Calitri was once included as part of Basilicata or old Lucania. Like the two mythic California's and the oft-rifts between San Francisco and Los Angeles over water, culture, and other consequential things, many Calitrani would like to secede from the region of Campania and rejoin Basilicata—better to benefit from Basilicata's hefty regional funds and *lascia perdere*, the corrupt spending in Napoli that never reaches the eastern regions of Irpinia, no doubt, but that is another story.

A large congregation from young boys to grown men headed the Procession, robed in what I thought was the patron saint's favorite color, sky blue. Turns out it is the Madonna's preferred color and the Confraternity of Fratelli, three hundred strong, wear it in observance of her. From a distance the shimmering folds of their *mantelle* played softly against the breeze as they waited in the street outside San Canio. Several elder statesmen held the sixteenth century statue aloft on his large dais; a carved and gilded Rococo platform adorned with evergreen garlands and blood-red acanthus flowers. The handsome young saint gazed up just off into the distance, walking staff and cross in hand as if expecting to encounter a traveler in the wood, with two German shepherds dancing playfully around his ankles.

By the looks of the crowd, the village was very proud of San Vito's representation as one of their minor patrons. Nearly all of the attendants that lined the street in front of the Duomo were townsmen from Calitri and her neighboring villages. What better way than to honor my father by participating in a procession for his patron saint in the town where his own father was born?

As for Nicola, he too would be proud, I thought, to know that one of his own was attending one of his town's most beloved festas almost a century after his emigration to America and decades after he passed. Along the Adriatic Coast there are many early churches dedicated to San Nicola, patron saint of sailors and the sea. Well placed for the crusades, the duomos are often built right on or up to the beach. Bari, Trani; beautiful places. And a very good name for a boy. Though no church celebrates him in Calitri, Nicola's granddaughter would soon unwittingly celebrate his name day, San Nicola di Bari, parked in the woods in the back seat of a silver Renault.

With the crowd in the street swelling, the marching band tuning up, and the young boys growing a bit restless, final preparations were tightened up for the procession to begin. Young Francesco, the elder son of Lucia's brother Vito, draped in robin's egg blue, waited with the other young boys his age at the very front of the group to lead the procession.

We heard an announcement or invocation in the silence that had suddenly gathered in the crowd. Just as the band struck up their first chord, the large group began to move down the street. First the robed young boys and men began in double file as the standard bearer led well out in front. They were followed by the dais with the handsome young saint held aloft by strong elders, then the priest and his attendants, the brass band, and finally the crowd of gathered congregants who slowly filled in behind.

As it was a seemingly all-male affair, an intense and somber masculine energy hovered over the crowd. The scene felt charged too with the excitement and expectations of the weekend celebrations to come. Was the Handsome Man from Macchiursi near? Lucia and I fell into the procession, sandwiched between groups of older contadini with just a few of their wives in accompaniment. Though we were not very tall women, we had a definite height advantage over the crowd before us. A sea of shorter black and gray heads advanced down the broad street in their slow and rhythmless country gait.

We made our way down via Francesco de Sanctis. Up ahead, the street opened out on our right to wide panoramic views southeast toward Basilicata. The proud sharp lines of the Apennines glowered in the near distance against a pale blue sky. Not a cloud to be seen. Footsteps and gentle murmurings were all that were heard as we slowly moved on toward the Chiesa dell'Immacolata on the southeastern edge of the town. Her broad yellow facade tucked down a steep slope, waiting for her devoted congregants. The procession paused there. A few rapid gun rounds and fireworks were set off as the band played a bit livelier, suddenly filling the windswept piazza with all the noises of a carnival in motion.

We set off again down the main narrow street that led deep into the Centro Storico, as the crowd condensed and filled the roadway wall to wall. It felt like we were descending into a windowless maze. Slowly, deliberately, footsteps shuffled and scraped along cobblestone. Deep shadows fell where the sun could not reach. In the middle distance there was chanting and dirgeful singing, and in between their voices brass cymbals and wind instruments brightened their atonal prayers. We climbed and wound up and around vias and vicolos as the crowd lifted en masse, until we reached the main Piazza della Repubblica. Here the band played a long repast.

The procession ended back at the steps of the Duomo. Lucia staked out a great vantage point for us just beneath the high double balustrades of the Church of San Canio. Here the priests performed a short solemn ceremony with prayers, dedications, and *canti* in Saint Vito's honor. After it was over the crowd erupted into sustained applause amid more cannon fire. Saint Vito was returned to his resting place inside the church as the villagers mingled in tight groups around the base of the steps.

It was nearly evening now and though the sky was still light we returned to our houses for supper. Later, the whole town would slowly turn out again in the streets for the first official party of the weekend.

Around 9:30 p.m. Lucia and Stefano took me up to the Corso and again we walked the crowded festive streets now complete with *le bancarelle* selling everything under the colorful festival lights: toys, sparkling costume jewelry next to Italian rodeo garb, cotton candy and roasted ears of corn, and then I spied a booth offering fake coats of arms. It wasn't too long before the Handsome Man from Macchiursi lit upon us, his head well above the crowd, and as I got closer I saw that this evening he was wearing a well-cut suit. He stood stock straight in the middle of the street, cocked his head slightly to one side, and waited for me to reach him.

"*Buonasera.*" Serious gaze.

"Hi." Big grin.

"*Vuoi prendere qualcosa?*" He wasted no time. I liked that.

"Okay." I tossed a wink and a wave to Lucia as we walked back down the Corso toward the bar.

"*Cosa prendi?*" he asked as we sat down at a table outside Bar Jolly.

I had learned from friends in Naples a cordial response.

"*Cosa ti prendi tu,*" I said.

The evening was a bit chillier than last night so he ordered us warmed brandy in snifters and soon I was firmly in his charge. Before we knew it we were surrounded by the curious. He seemed nervous but pleased. Yet as soon as our drinks were finished he rose to lead us down the Corso.

Slowly we walked the entire length of Corso Garibaldi, then turned right up a darker, less-populated street, passing his friends sitting outside a dark men's bar until we reached the Piazza della Repubblica at the top of the town. Someone called out my name.

"Angela!" It was young Teodolinda with her family—her father Michele, mother Gerardina, and others. They were all pleased to see me and meet Giuseppe. Greetings and smiles were passed all around, then they politely left us to our evening.

He walked us down to his car parked behind Bar Poldos where we first met. He drove a new silver Renault Quattro GT and told me proudly that it was the millennial version of his father Michele's 1970s Quattro wagon, a classic Euro-country workhorse of car. Like father like son, I thought. We hopped in. He leaned across me to pop open the glove box and pulled out the lost letters again and handed them to me to fondle.

Then without saying a word, he pulled out of the parking lot heading away from the Corso, down the switchback road toward the Paolantonio palazzo and continued farther to the very bottom of the hill. He hesitated there, then turned left onto the Ofantina and drove on into the dark.

I had no idea really where we were going. The Handsome Man from Macchiursi commanded the road, the car, and me. Effortlessly. We swung off an exit to the right, climbing up into a deeper darkness on a narrow country road dense with trees and brush. The road did not open up but wound and climbed and veered for quite a while. I put my hand on his knee. He gently clasped my slender forearm with his big hand and jingled the silver bracelets on my wrist.

"*Non porto anelli*," he said. "*Né un orologio.*"

"I wear these, a few at a time. I'm never without them."

The sensual urge between us was palpable. He drove us slowly around the rim road of what looked like a lake surrounded by mountains. Oh! I suddenly realized we were in the crater lake park of Monticchio. These were the double caldera lakes of the massive volcano Mount Vulture that loomed in the distance from his fields and between slices of buildings all around the town. The only light was from the full moon rippling on the lake. He pulled up close to the water and parked.

"Can we go for a walk?" I asked.

We got out of the car and after a few steps he took me by the hand and pulled me closer. I wrapped my arms around his muscular waist and looked up toward his bold, innocent face. You could feel the pull of moon on the dark water, the powerful Pleistocene energy of the volcano under our feet.

"Kiss me," I willed with my eyes.

He held my eyes for a long moment then leaned down, kissed

me softly, tentatively, and then let his weight go.

I melted into his mouth, into his chest. He pulled me over to a high rock wall facing the lake and the shining moon on the water. It was stunning. It felt stunning.

"Oh, my. The moon is huge," I said. He responded by gripping my hips.

Then, far across the lake, suspended high on the caldera's chestnut forest-covered wall, a huge white mass glowed several stories tall.

"What is that?"

He kept me pinned to the wall.

"*Abbazia di San Michele.*" And kissed me harder.

This was a tenth century Benedictine monastery and chapel built upon a Paleolithic settlement, dug deep into a grotto of the volcanic *tufa*, dedicated to Archangel Michele, slayer of dragons. The cult of San Michele was brought to the south of Italy by the Langobards in the fifth century.

According to legend, the Archangel Michele had appeared there on several occasions.

He pulled my thin skirt up.

"Wait."

"*Cosa?*"

"Won't someone see us?" My head on a swivel, turning to see if anyone was near. He held me in place effortlessly, waiting.

"*Non c'è nessuno,*" I said.

"*Eh, sì, non c'è nessuno,*" he confirmed.

Then he took me under the shining harvest moon.

⁂

The next day was Monday, September 8th, the Festa for the Madonna. Cousin Lucia and I did not attend the Mass, though she wanted to arrive early enough in order to be among the gathering crowd to witness the exact moment of the emergence of the Madonna and her attendants from the Chiesa dell'Immacolata. She came to call for me in her grandmother's apartment at 5:45 p.m. We drove together to the upper town and parked again behind the Duomo on the main Corso. From there we walked down the hill a short way to the end of via de Sanctis to hold our place outside the church.

The plaza in front of the church was calm, not its usual wind-gusty place. Even though we were quite early, a small crowd of people were already milling about the steep grade and adjacent steps of via San Vito. Many were townsmen who waited outside for their mothers or wives undoubtedly inside attending the High Mass. Lucia and I chose our spot to wait directly across from the immense and highly polished double wood doors and leaned against the high stone wall that supported the end of via Concezione above. There was a hush about the crowd and even Lucia, who was normally quite vociferous and conversationally challenging for me, was reverently silent.

We waited.

I was alone in my thoughts about the evening before and in expectation of the events to come. Studying the gilded pavement that stretched out before me I thought it odd that a large pentagram enclosed in a magic circle, an ancient pagan symbol and barrier against evil forces, was the central mosaic motif of this inlaid stone plaza dedicated to the Madonna. The wide expanse of the façade of the church was painted a golden yellow and in the setting sunlight, a warm glow reflected on the gray stone houses all around it. I scanned the growing crowd, recognizing few. I secretly hoped to spy the Handsome Man from Macchiursi. Seeing his tall broad frame in the crowd would have given me the sense of carnal balance I felt I needed here. The spiritual excitement demanded more than I could muster. So many months of anticipation and waiting to see him had been consummated the night before and I had exhausted all emotional reserves in the process.

Lucia briefly wandered over to a small group of friends. My mind wandered to Venezia. I recalled how a few years ago, alone on my fortieth birthday, I had attended Mass in Saint Mark's Square for the Feast of the Annunciation on March 25th, asking in earnest meditation if the Madonna di Nicopeia would help me win a handsome new lover. A deep wave of warmth swelled in my hips. Now would be the perfect time to thank her.

An hour or so went by. Congregants from inside the church began to exit. Women of all ages filled the plaza with low voices, greeting their husbands and relatives already gathered there. The wind picked up too. It grazed the piazza with a sun-setting drop in temperature, as followers shifted their positions to shelter themselves from the advancing chill. It would be another several minutes before the Madonna herself appeared from the church doors. A lovingly rendered papier-mâché effigy some three hundred years old, she would soon be borne down the aisle of the Chiesa. We all waited patiently for the first sight of her.

When all at once she appeared from the candle-lit *chiesa*, the crowd called out in awe. In the sudden rush of emotion that swept through the piazza I was surprised to be caught by tears. A regal figure emerged, draped in sapphire blue, with a halo of twelve stars encircling her head. Underneath the celestial cloth, a white robe embroidered with pale pink roses. She stood barefoot on a cloud. Garlands of fresh flowers, roses, gladioli, and lilies graced the floor of her dais. Around her neck and adorning her breast were several thick ropes of gold chain, suspended with glinting medallions, and upon her wrists were layers of gold bracelets. From under the cloud at her feet, three cherubim gazed up to her as her right foot rested on the head of a serpent. The angels were all but singing. Her expression was not sorrowful nor supplicant but modest, compassionate, and peaceful, her hands held demurely close to her heart. As she was maneuvered toward the center of the plaza, several rounds of gunfire, then cannon fire, were set off echoing down the valley. Her attendants paused with her just over the pentagram, assembled themselves, and with more rounds of cannon fire to signal her departure from the church, the procession slowly began.

We found ourselves walking along behind the mayor of the town in a bright red sash and three petite women with matching gray braided buns set at the napes of their necks, a traditional design of the elder women of the region, as Lucia explained. Zia Concetta's hair had once been braided in this bun design too, although I noticed her hair sheared short this autumn. I admired the festive lights and decorations that arched over the street and how they contrasted with the earthquake-crumbled buildings that lined the road and the breathtaking, still-bright Apennine vista off to the left that was created in their absence. I panned from left to right, wide eyed, and took a few photos. Lucia gathered in among a few of her friends on my left.

Slowly we were advancing down via Matteotti under the spell of the crowd when I noticed by a brief glance over my left shoulder Giuseppe standing against a wall. I quickly checked myself as I began to raise my hand in a generous wave of recognition and instead pulled back with just a nod. Somehow I knew it was more respectful. He nodded too and a sweet rush took me back to the evening before when we parked together under the full moon inside the crater of Mount Vulture, beside shining reflections in the caldera's lake.

The procession once again ended back at the steps of the Duomo where the priests performed a longer ceremony with prayers, dedications, and canti for the Madonna. After it was over the crowd again erupted in applause amid more cannon fire. The Madonna was then walked back to the Immacolata with fewer processioners and met by brief fireworks, though by then Lucia and I had already driven down the hill.

The evening fell soft and quiet, early September in the mountains. The night air warm and soothing, a fragrant balmy blend of freshly rolled hay, turned earth, and old stone. The Apennines were a strong outline of deep violet blues and grays against the fading rose embers of the last light of day. Soon the bats would begin flight, fluttering wildly against the street lamp below my windows. Nine bells were tolled from the Immacolata at 7 p.m. Three sets of three. The sky fell a deeper shade of cobalt, and in the distance following the ridge of the mountain line the lights of other towns across the valley begin to flicker deep gold, yellow, and white.

Back home, the landline phone on Migliorina's antique dresser began to ring.

"Hello?"

Pause.

"*Vuoi uscire?*"

There was nothing sexier than the sound of his baritone voice over the phone; my knees went soft.

"*Sì, volentieri.*" Of course I wanted to go out.

⁂

The Sunday evening passeggiata is a centuries-old ritual very much alive in contemporary small-town Calitri. And of all the small mountain villages nearby, Calitri's is the most frequented. Townspeople begin or end their week, depending on how you frame it, with the time-honored tradition of slowly passing the evening on the Corso with their family or spouse or *innamorata*. Families greet other families as they treat their young ones to gelato or a dolce. Teenagers jockey amongst themselves in bold displays of superiority. For a regional culture that didn't have home phones until at least the mid 1980s—making or receiving the rare telephone call from the closest *tabaccheria* was until then the norm—the passeggiata was and is still how they kept up or met up with one another.

Everyone strolls the main street of the town. Up, then reversing down again and again, the pace becoming progressively social as the evening wears on. Couples seen for the first few times together, and who may or may not be falling in love, are greeted or cajoled by friends or registered in the memories of the elders, who record their spied coupling for posterity or the next morning's discussion on a bench in front of the post office.

Body language is a powerful communicator, an open curtain onto the stage of which the relationship is viewed. All protocol visible or implied is taken very seriously and is metered out in very specific increments of intent and public announcement. In a traditional small Southern town like Calitri, everyone is *sotto l'occhio*. Under watch.

It used to be that throughout Italy, to be arm in arm with a man meant that you two were already married or at the very least engaged. More than likely this public display took years of patience and proper attention by the family of the strolling couple. Not that Italians didn't condone consensual sex; everyone knew everyone was secretly doing it, and with whom. (Fathers even seemed especially proud that their sons knew how to use their equipment.) But that the couple was not opposed to communicating this to the town with or without a pending spousal contract. Italy is a fairly open society now but would never have allowed such behavior even so early as twenty years ago.

Southern Italy is another story.

In Southern Italy a man and a woman alone together anywhere are indeed seen as a couple. It is entirely up to the gentleman to initiate and monitor this very public display of affection toward— even ownership of—the woman he is keeping company with. If he is mature enough to acknowledge the politics of the situation and its potential for exaggeration in the imaginations of the community, he will protect his date by accompanying her accordingly. Moreover, in a remote mountain town such as Calitri, a couple seen twice together for passeggiata immediately sparks a round of gossip that by various implications might mean you'll be married within the year, and soon after start a family.

Experiencing this for the first time in a town filled with your relatives and cousins concerned with your every move while you may or may not be falling in love, is to say the very least, socially taxing and at its height emotionally thrilling. There is no mistaking the ritual and its progression and, at times, the tender trials of a very visible love affair.

Accompanied by the Handsome Man from Macchiursi for the first time on a Sunday passeggiata, I felt the ingénue.

Giuseppe walked tall and proudly just a slight half step or so ahead of me with his arms firmly folded high across his chest or relaxed behind his back. He led me up, then down, the entire Corso, slowly and with intent. He often looked straight ahead while he paid close attention to the needs or whims of his date. Friends gave him the space to stroll along, respecting his privacy, though they were surely gossiping *sotto voce*.

That evening, feeling triumphant and free and still innocent of these morals and rules—novice was maybe a better word for how I was in the beginning—I had unwittingly wandered ahead of him more than a few paces when I suddenly heard a sharp whistle from behind my shoulder. Twice. Since I was not used to this form of call, I had no idea it was Giuseppe who had whistled to stop me. He had stopped in front of a bar, invited in by a friend for a drink.

When we three walked in I was transported back to Brooklyn. The early 1960s Brooklyn I briefly knew as a young girl visiting my parents' older siblings and their extended families for Sunday dinners. Parked cars on black street pavement, steep stoops of the rows of gated brownstones, and one dog-eared, wallet-sized photo of nonno Nicola in an overcoat and gray fedora, on a wide bluestone-paved sidewalk.

In Stewart Manor, up on the main avenue in town, not unlike the Corso here, were a series of mom-and-pop stores that serviced the neighborhood.

One of those was Jack's candy store. Popular with most of the neighborhood kids and teens, I didn't spend too much time in there alone. It was as dark and foreboding just inside its cluttered bay-window storefront, as were the empty phone booths way in back, and to my child's impressionable eye, these seemed like more adult surroundings. The smells too of fresh newsprint and tobacco, mingled with dusty supply boxes, root beer, and Beems gum were for adults, adult men. It was, oddly, Stewart Manor's equivalent of an old Brooklyn soda fountain complete with long, polished-wood bar and red swivel stools, tin ceilings and deep brown naugahyde leather booths that seemed able to swallow a thin-framed girl like me in one slide over.

Jack was always found hunched behind the cash register; his two sons filled in after school as soda jerks. The entire family lived in back of the store, creating a daily scene straight out of central casting from the 1930s. It was gone now some thirty years, maybe more. My father used to tell me his father's first job in the new world, in New York, was as a soda jerk in Colletti's Ice Cream Parlor in Brooklyn. Whenever we walked into Jack's I would feel his wistful nostalgia clasping my hand.

"*Grappa e una birra*," Giuseppe ordered for himself, then looked at me.

"*Campari soda.*" I said.

We stayed only as long as it took to finish our drinks, spending our time in the narrow space that was between the bar and the wall with his friend, making small talk. Brooklyn. New York. Now California. Poldo's was populated by men. I was the only woman and I held fast to my man. Giuseppe soon closed the scene by acknowledging his friend with a quick nod, thanked the bartender, and we moved on.

By midnight or so in the middle of the still very-crowded evening he walked us back to his car and drove us slowly down to the bottom of the hill, over the narrow bridge of the river *Ofanto*, and up a back road to a wide clearing with a perfect view of the rising hill of Calitri. We parked and he first alighted to pee. The evening was late-summer warm. I rolled down my window, and in that moment the first thump and boom went off over the town, quickly followed by a burst of flame-red fireworks, huge triple chrysanthemums in the sky.

Wide-eyed and elated, I turned to him and gushed like a schoolgirl, "*AMO fuochi!*" Just as he grabbed me and kissed me. And another boom and another triple spray—over and over they rocketed—flowers and fountains of colorful light brightening the jet-black sky, the hill town lit brilliantly so near. It was all so near. I was in awe. And I was thrilled to be alone by his side. He pulled me in and kissed me again, just as thrilled it seemed to be there with me. It seemed to go on forever. After the fireworks display we drove to a more secluded back road and made more bold outdoor love.

By the following Sunday his friends, cousins, and coworkers had begun to acknowledge him with me within the town's specific male social order and treated him accordingly. He was popular, well respected, and cordially greeted by his fellow townsman, young or old during the weekend passeggiata. It said a lot about his status within their community.

He was a man's man. An alpha male in a pack of hopefuls.

Though they may have wanted to acknowledge the woman he was with, they would not speak directly to her. They waited out of respect for him until he made the introduction and then greeted her in kind. In our case, since I was the visiting American woman from the big city, and he a local farmer's first son, there was more than enough curiosity about our union. I could only assume that the bets were on as to when how and where we would consummate our relationship, with sex, or marriage.

Piano, piano.

Fireworks & Lucciole
(Fireflies)

He wore a marine blue turtle neck that knocked me dead as he stopped by the side of the road to pick wild quince in the blooming dark, their branches hanging high on a stone wall above us. The fruit of lovers.

Told me of their wonderful fragrance when you set them in a bowl. How they filled the room with their sweet aroma or when reduced to a rosy, sugary syrup taken for fevers and colds in winter. How can you top that? Another night he brought the car to a sudden halt along a back road to pick wild peaches as small as walnuts. We ate them on the spot, licking our fingers of their bright pink juices.

We drove headlong one night through the grain fields to a forest of old olive trees, this became my favorite place to make love. In the moonlight the silvery leaves took on a soft glow. Their one-hundred-year old branches thick and gnarled in a *Wizard of Oz* sort of way, I half expected the Tin Man to appear and ask for our hearts. In the distance the lights of the village flickered on the hillside like a Neapolitan *presepe*.

Sulla strada a Macchiursi...

On our third night together he parked us at the bottom of the main switchback road that leads up from the river into the town for a spectacular view of the fireworks from below. It was the grand finale to the weekend-long festa to the Madonna, and only my fourth night in town. The fireworks worked their magic on my heart piercing it blow after blow with dazzling sprays of color and force. I've always loved the 4th of July and have craved that dual sensation of joy and fright for years as an adult, never finding even an approximate likeness from my childhood. But here, in the deep black interior of the Italian countryside, they held their grip on me for over forty minutes. I leaned far out the window of the car to get a better view and every few minutes or so he would grab me, pull me back in, and kiss me with as much intent and force.

We spent nearly every evening together; Giuseppe picking me up in the driveway to the Paolantonio palazzo. (I supposed all my parenti were wildly curious. But only Dorina had the temerity to ask. And boy, did she—nearly every morning, over strong coffee.) His headlamps would slowly pull into the drive from the road; I'd hop in, Dorina sometimes waving from the balcony. We would silently continue down the hill, sharp switchbacks to the bridge over the river, away from the prying eyes of the villagers and on out of town.

We drove every evening, exploring between the nearly abandoned towns and villages that dotted the surrounding hilltop landscape of eastern Irpinia. Here, towns are few and far between, and her *contrade* occupy wide swaths of endless space. Not too long ago, it would have taken a rider the better part of a day to reach one or another of these towns on the back of a rickety donkey—if he had to get there. Seasonal *transumanza* herds have crossed its terrain from the north for millennia, bringing cowboys and shepherds and hunters and their teams.

Brigands on horseback roamed these parts well before us. Clothed in rugged canvas capes, their rucksacks filled with peasants bread and wine. Many evenings we too roamed the countryside searching for a place for dinner, safely tucked in against the complete blackness that fell away just outside the reach of the headlamps of his car.

Ninco Nanco was the illustrious Southern Italian brigand who, legend had it, rode wild in the Irpinian countryside in the middle of the nineteenth century accompanied by his beautiful raven-haired maiden and a formidable band of cohorts at his side. Townsmen and contadini peasants alike sang their praises and sorrow after he was finally gunned down during a well-publicized government manhunt. Even zia Angelina once sang of him in this Irpinia poem:

Ninghe Nanghe, pecce si muerte?
Pane e vino, nun t'e' mancat
Ninghe Nanghe, pecce si muerte?
La'nzalate stia all'verte
Ninghe Nanghe, pecce si muerte?

It is an ancient land too where the geographic regions of Basilicata, Puglia, and Campania all converge, offering striking contrasts in all directions on the horizon. Rising and falling in great peaks, Basilicata casts its dark forested shadows across the sweet hills of Campania. Puglia lays out flat until the eastern coast of the Adriatic, offering miles of rich olive groves and endless fields of sensual grasses.

We drove with our hearts *sulla strada a Macchiursi.*

Macchiursi, "the place of wild bears," is old Germanic, therefore Langobard in origin and is a reference to the constellation Ursa Major. The Greeks marked this area of Irpinia on their quest to traverse and populate this far eastern region on their way from Neapolis toward Puglia and the Adriatic Sea. It was a place without electric lights or cooking gas until the late 1980s. They lived on ninety hectares, with one hundred sheep to graze, a dozen or so milking cows, several pigs, various chickens cats and dogs. My breasts were milked hard with hands so firm and round and strong from his honest repetitious work, lusted for like teats. His caressing lips were soft and sweet, then devouring. With each suckling kiss I grew weak.

He knew every wood and back road, every season and its planting, the turn of the road where native cyclamen bloomed, the waxing or waning of the moon and its cycle of life on the farm. Yet he was a warm and gentle soul. Once, he pointed out a family of mud tracks in the one-lane road between fields,

"*Cinghiale.*" Wild boar.

Red fox and gray wolves roam the roadsides as darkness approaches the countryside. In the lamplight of our passing car farm cats hugged the grasses at the pavement's edge hunting smaller prey. Snow-white owls took sudden flight across our windshield as our vehicle approached under their perch. I felt as an intruder on their early evening's dance in the wold.

Wind and rain ruled the skies and hamlet villages this late October, whipping and drenching in sudden gusts and bursts. Returning late one evening with me behind the wheel, a great wind scattered autumn leaves like dervishes across the two-lane blacktop. Under a dark canopy of tall swaying trees, their small bright spears of reds, yellows, and greens whirled in front of the beams of the car. We were alone on the narrow road; two souls traveling headlong in the empty night.

Calling out in excited awe at the dancing leaves before me, I startled alert the rugged handsome man dozing in the seat beside me. "*Guarda! che bella, é bellissima!*"

Aroused from half-sleep Giuseppe calmly looked up, nodded in agreement, and intoned, "*Sì, sì, molto bello.*"

Then he firmly grasped my right arm to keep me from steering into an oncoming truck suddenly bearing down in the other lane. The huge semitrailer passed us with great force, creating a powerful vacuum; leaves and twigs again taking flight all around us.

I continued to drive in a sort of trance, knocked back by the wake of the truck, trying hard to concentrate and ignore the sudden well of fear that rose up and through me from the seat of the car. Blackness fell around us again. At well past midnight, my imagination sensed that brigands or goblins at any moment could leap from the shadows in front of the car.

Giuseppe paid attention for a few moments further and then relaxed again, leaving the helm to me. Luckily, a few minutes later the road opened up on both sides, allowing a clear view of the hilltop lights of Calitri. A mellowed fog and mist enveloped the town just a few miles ahead. At last we had emerged from the interior mountain road that entwined down and around the dense local foothills of the Southern Apennines of Basilicata. Approaching a now-familiar landscape I could see a clear line of lights delineating the settlement that graced the hillside and the cemetery lamps that clustered along the left side of the town. Driving briefly parallel now to the Ofanto river, I would soon turn right and cross the two-lane stone bridge over the narrow waterway, and begin the switchback climb up to the base of the village. It was a small consolation but it was the only civilization for miles around, and I was happy to be in its confines again.

As always at the end of our evenings I would be dropped off at the modern palazzo of my Paolantonio relatives at the base of the hill, given a forceful kiss goodnight, and watched as I entered the building. Every evening we spent together ended this way. Out of an innate sense of respect for our collective families and largely cultural taboos we could not, nor would attempt to pass the whole night together, though we both held private places in which to do so.

After recovering from his kiss, I would leave the car and his warm sensual presence for yet another evening to sleep alone in the camera matrimoniale upstairs in nonna Migliorina's loft apartment, dreading the approach to the double wood doors at the street level entrance. Once outside the car the silence of the town fell around me. The ancient hillside rose directly in front of me, lit with street lamps pulled out of focus in the dampness of a coming early winter's chill. At that hour, nearly 3 a.m., the whole town and surrounding countryside was completely void of sound or activity. One errant move would set the dogs to barking.

I put my key in the lock and entered the cavernous hallway as smoothly and quietly as possible. Until the heavy wooden door snagged against the marble floor. Each night it's stubbornness would take me by surprise. After a while, I learned to lift the whole door just slightly to avoid the ominous scraping that I was sure would wake everyone in the building if not the whole town. Once inside, the challenge was not over. I had to then struggle to close the door noiselessly, securing the building for the night without disturbing my parenti, who I assumed were sleeping soundly in the two apartments above. No matter how hard I tried, the door would not easily close nor the lock latch smoothly. It took great effort, yet the careening echoes rose up the marble stairwell as I vainly leaned on the heavy door again and again to get it to engage.

In the end it seemed comic to me and it was all I could do not to cry out in frustration or laughter. Finally successful, I would gingerly remove my shoes and climb the four flights of marble to the top floor, enter, and cross the cold apartment tiles to the bedroom. It was not until I had climbed between the smooth white sheets that those echoing noises and the pounding in my heart fell silent again and I could drift into the netherworld of sleep.

Sleep. It was the only escape I had from the nervous fear of revealing our new and what I hoped was still a clandestine love affair.

⁂

But there was Dorina.

Zia Dorina had my best interest in mind, really. It became a sort of game for her to greet me as I descended the apartment stairs every morning and indulge her with the comings and goings of my new romance with Giuseppe. Each morning she wanted the update first as if it were her own private telenovela. And in fact it seemed to be, as I was more than swept along the current of her endless gossipy curiosity.

At once cajoling and intimidating she had a grand solution for every non-event of our budding romance. First she declared she wanted us married by end of my stay. Two months.

Then she laid claim that,

"If he doesn't ask you over to his parents by the end of the week, it's clear he is using you." For sexual favor and fodder and will soon gladly see you off, with a resounding—*"Va via, Americana!"*

This was of course, she guessed, after I'd allowed him to have his way with me.

Very early on I was duly warned of her forceful meddling and advised, ominously, by her eldest son that I shared way too much with her. Gradually I learned to treat her insistent and repetitive prodding with reverse rancor as she immediately laid claim to each day's news. It soon seemed her declarations and behaviors were just a vehicle to assuage her boredom. Years of widowhood and raising a family alone in a small Southern Italian town on wit and spunk can do that to you. Life could do that to you. And it seemed life in Calitri was an unending melodrama of her own design.

One morning I was able to distract her and talk about the one thing she and I seemed to have in common. Sitting in her spare bedroom was a 1970s era sewing machine, the best Singer had to offer from that time period, and one that I myself owned. I shared with her this fact and without a bit of surprise she countered that in her prime she was a *sarta* and sewing teacher for young women coming up in the town. It was quite a common need in her time for young girls of a certain class to take sewing lessons, as it would have been part of a finishing school for them; to learn to sew and embroider not only the numerous sets of slips, sheets, and linens, expected for their corredo, a requirement for any young woman as part of her dowry, but clothing for their children and kitchen linens for their home once they were settled in marriage.

I admitted to her that I learned to sew not from my mother but from her older sister, my Aunt Grace, an expert tailor in her own right who learned at her mother's skirt. And expressed that to this day I appreciated the skill she imparted to me at a very impressionable age.

Intrigued, Dorina said she too learned her home trade as a young apprentice but from her father, Vito Paolantonio, Sr., who was a true maestro. She recounted that in all the years growing up as a young woman in this rural village—prone to hours of *zitella*, or solitude—before marriage and family gave way to other responsibilities, she sat in front of a Singer sewing machine on the other side of a large picture window in her father's atelier, positioned at a prime street front address on Calitri's then highly trafficked and popular Piazza della Repubblica.

Calitri boasted the most populated and prosperous town of Alta Irpinia in that era, a virtual satellite in a constellation of smaller poorer villages. Dorina continued with her tales of sewing and teaching. Not only learning her father's trade well and earning a living herself, but also watching the comings and goings of the townspeople young and old out for their daily errands and in the evenings for their passeggiata.

Dorina just couldn't help herself. She was a natural at small-town gossip and cunning premarital undercover work. Back then she could keep track of who was strolling with whom outside the window of her father's shop, perhaps inventing secret stories of romantic intrigue in her head. It was all sotto voce of course. Only for her and perhaps a confidante friend or cousin or two. So now years later when her prized parente lontana, who arrived all the way from the sprawling metropolis of Los Angeles, began to keep company with one of her own townsman's adult sons, it flung her back to her youthful folly—cunningly harvesting first-hand news and sightings of young lovers in town.

Of course her advantage with me was that I was conveniently sleeping right upstairs from her in her mother's former apartment. So each morning as I left for errands or walks I naturally had to descend the flight of stairs and pass her door. In the first few days of my stay her apartment door seemed casually left open. As I came down she would call out to me at the moment I reached her landing. In the beginning, I innocently responded to her invitation in for a morning greeting and a second caffé.

"*Come i gatti e i topi.*" Like cats and mice. Giuseppe leveled this response one evening when I told him my problem. And as the days wore on it became necessary for me to invent increasingly creative excuses to keep our budding affair to myself, lest I be taken *farti far fesso*—played for her fool.

And if I playfully dodged her prodding?

"*Cattiva!*" she would say.

"*No, non sono cattiva,*" I countered, having for the moment skillfully side-stepped her questioning.

Even the previous February when I had spent nearly the entire winter month driving around the neighboring towns in the cold and the snow with my younger cousin Adolfo, zia Dorina alone concluded that he and I must secretly be lovers. That everyone else knew we were merely touring the small cities and towns around the countryside to pass the day seemed to escape her. Or did her folly with me escape me? One evening she had me cornered. While we waited together for Adolfo to swing by and pick me up, she insisted on teasing me with what to her seemed untoward behavior.

"*Un'amicizia particolare,*" she said to me. A kind of Italian friends with benefits—was what she concluded of the time I spent with my otherwise single and chaste, at least with me, cousin.

"Zia! Don't be ridiculous."

"Well, do you have a man?" She pressed on until Adolfo arrived, which then only further fueled her suspicions.

Now with a real romance under way, and right under her nose, Dorina could not contain her appetite for first-hand gossip for her personal mill. Whatever details I may have first offered her were a big mistake as they soon swelled, gaining momentum with her with each passing day. Even her sons and daughters-in-law were dispatched to engage in information subterfuge; all of whom, luckily for me, carefully respected my privacy, or at least pretended to.

To make matters worse, in this first month of my two-month stay a family festa was planned for Dorina's grandson for his Catholic confirmation. I was invited to attend the church ceremony and formal pranzo afterwards along with the entire family. The Sunday mass was held at 11 a.m. and the large modern church was packed with what seemed like the entire town. Parents, children, and godparents were all in attendance for the high mass in the Duomo of San Canio on the main Corso. It was a beautiful fall day and all the families were turned out in their finery.

Zia Dorina specifically entreated her son Vito, father of the celebrant, to invite Giuseppe. Thinking it a generous gesture to include him, I innocently agreed to extend their invitation to him, confident that he would accept. So one evening a few days before the event, while we headed out for our usual evening drive, I broached the subject.

"My family has invited me to Francesco's confirmation."

Giuseppe kept his eyes on the switchbacks.

"There'll be the church, and then the pranzo. They invited us both," I continued. He calmly glanced at me without a word. "You'll come with me, no?"

To my surprise, Giuseppe refused.

I protested at first. It seemed a harmless inclusion.

But he was adamant and we continued down along the switchback road away from the town in silence. The road was sparsely populated. Few cars climbed or descended in the usual meager flow of twilight activity. The harvest moon was rising in the east and the towns that dotted the hillsides high across the valley twinkled romantic trails of amber and yellow lights. All I could do was glance out the car window and wait.

When at last we reached the bottom of the hill, he pulled the car to a full stop on the side of the road and gave me, and the matter, his full attention.

He turned to me and began, "*Sono molto contento di uscire ogni sera con te, al cinema, a cena, oppure una passeggiata al Corso.*" He reassured me, "*Ma è troppo presto per questo invito.*"

Being a neophyte in all matters of small-town Italian subterfuge, I was confused at first, and felt just a bit slighted that he would not reconsider and attend the cresima with me.

"Look what pressure I would be under," I reasoned. "Attending a large family festa—my first!—in a crowded public restaurant without you."

Still he strongly refused. He explained again slowly and patiently. "*La nostra vita privata sarebbe annullata.*"

His handsome face so close to mine looked for solidarity. I looked him straight in the eye. And in the next moment he pulled me to him and kissed me with ardent force.

With this convincing persuasion I had no choice but to acquiesce.

The next morning when I brought back the news of Giuseppe's decline, my relatives were duly astonished. Declarations of their disapproval immediately rang through the apartment.

First Dorina: "But how could he refuse our invitation?"

Then nonna Migliorina: "And to reject his masculine duty!"

And finally Lucia: "You better keep both feet on the ground with this one."

I stood in the hallway, surrounded and stunned by their continuous volley. And it was repeated later with a fresh assault by Vito and his wife, the parents of the soon-to-be confirmed eldest son.

I realized much later that this show of force was as much for their benefit as mine, *una bella figura* so to speak. They simply had to protest his decline of their invitation for the simple fact that as long as I was a visitor to their town and a guest in their apartment house, I was in their charge and the recipient, whether I liked it or not, needed it or not, of their just and unconditional solidarity in all matters great or small.

But Giuseppe was wise to this and so deflected their advances with me as much as he could and sternly suggested that I do the same. So, no, he would not accompany his *fidanzata*, L'Americana, to the Sunday festa of her parenti lontani.

With another month or more to go in this self-imposed residency, was I in for a long and bumpy ride.

Tramandare
(To Hand Down)

~·~

We arrived Saturday morning in the faded red Fiat, me holding a tin of cookies bought for the occasion at a local women's bar on the Corso. Giuseppe heard Adolfo's car trundle up to their *massaria* and ducked his head out the door to be the first to greet us. Early-risers, he and his father Michele have been inside their cantina since daybreak distilling the year's grape harvest, the vendemmia. Rosa his mother and brother Angelo I noticed, were nowhere in sight.

It was coming on late September. I had been in town nearly a month and firmly in the arms of their eldest son since the Festa for the Madonna, that first weekend of my arrival. Hard as we tried to shield our new romance from the piazza, the news was out. The handsome son of a local rancher and L'Americana were an item. Concerned relatives pressed. It was time to Meet The Parents. Luckily, I was allowed the quick and decisive response when the coached question was posed of when a good time would be to pay this new visit to the family farm and officially greet his parents.

"*Quando vuoi.*"

Emboldened by the passionate tumult of our budding relationship, it wasn't a matter of nerve. I had met Giuseppe's parents twice before this visit. True, it was 2003 and not 1953; nevertheless the significance was equal to none. In terms of the systematic and ancient protocol of the dating culture of Southern Italy—*piano, piano*—this formal venture into the lives of Giuseppe's parents was in a wholly other stratosphere of implied intentions.

An American woman makes few leaps in her life equivalent to the adventure and reverence of paying forward to the parents of her *fidanzato* in a small provincial town deep in the wilds of Irpinia. Still, I did not realize Giuseppe would not be the one to accompany me; that is, personally drive me out to their farm and present me to his parents. I was duly informed I would need to be chaperoned by a family member—usually an older brother, as is the custom—as if on a simple visit out to the country albeit, with a previously specified appointment.

I was petrified.

I made a slow pan around the large room that sat directly under their farmhouse. This was my first time in their cantina. A well-worn country table held court in the center of the room. Wood rush chairs hung from the wall on one side. A large upright cristalliere painted a dark, glossy brown set against the other. Various harvest tools lining the room's perimeter were stored on nails in the walls and along a system of poles crisscrossing from rings suspended from the high ceiling hung herbs and dried branches of *cecci*, strings of onions, garlic, and long bright peppers.

Red embers glowed from an early morning fire at the floor level opening of their cantina stove, a fornacella.

The cantina's backroom was windowless, small, and dark. The room's aroma heady with the smell of grape must and wine-soaked chestnut and oak woods. Two wide-mouth barrels held the fresh pressed nectar—deep crimson, sultry, and sugary to taste. *Aglianico.* Cultivated here since the days of Pliny the Elder. Giuseppe and his father's hands were black as they scraped and packed the crush from a smaller barrel into the press. Later Giuseppe explained, ink-black hands meant a successful harvest of sweet grapes that would ferment to a very good strong wine in the year ahead.

Wine for men, as my women friends in Verona had declared.

And it was true. Because to drink any local table wine here was more akin to drinking an ancient nectar of the gods than some well-publicized vintage sold for a king's ransom in urban *enoteche*. Country wine is consumed the year it is made and preferred in its native surroundings. Many farmers in Calitri still drink wine in winter with their first meal of the day to fortify themselves before heading out to the fields for the long day's work. Since my first visit I had tasted very good homemade wines, at the tables of zio Giovanni and Vincenzo and too, one cold morning last February while navigating the narrow vias and vicolos of the town's Centro Storico on my way to lunch with zia Concetta.

That morning, I paused to greet an old woman whom I met near a small corner chapel that I had admired yet never been inside. She happened to be the widow of the keeper of Chiesetta Sant'Antuono, and, naturally, had the key to the church on an iron ring just inside her front door. After the tour of the one-room *chiesetta* she invited me across the lane to her deep and rough-hewn cavern for a glass of wine. It was not yet 11 a.m.

Inside, her grotto was musty and damp and crowded with tools for the vendemmia. Handmade utensils and instruments and coiled black hoses hung on stone walls. Wine-stained barrels and green glass demijohns of assorted shapes and sizes and a large wooden winepress were tucked in a far corner. A single bare bulb hung from a wire. Her middle-aged son climbed down from the loft on a hand-tied ladder as we three gathered in a small damp space between the artifacts and, from the three *barriques* stored deep in the back of their cantina, we tasted his wine.

Back in Macchiursi, a bit flummoxed by Adolfo and I idly watching as he and his son worked the press, Giuseppe's father turned to me and teased, "Not too long ago this job of extracting the juice from the fruit was done by the young women *contadine* stamping the grapes with their feet."

I stole a wide-eyed glance toward Giuseppe. The classic "I Love Lucy" episode looped in my head. He stood just a few inches away—with the countenance of a choirboy—rhythmically clicking the heavy metal arm of the press back and forth with ease, nodding in solemn confirmation as the young wine trickled down the spout. Lucy and Ethel tramping as peasant locals, costumes above their knees, stamping the grapes in open barrels exactly like these here—the hapless and contorted looks on their faces priceless.

The wood winepress was a simple apparatus. This fall I noticed nearly every household in the village had one. I had spotted them drying outside cantina doors on my walks all around the town and the one stored in the modern garage of zio Giovanni. Michele presided over mixing the elixir in two open barrels standing on risers on the floor. First the grapes with their skins were scraped from the sides of the fermenting barrels with a large and neatly tied bunch of fragrant and prickly branches freshly gathered from field shrubs, then packed by hand into the top of the press. Thick wood spacers were stacked on top to hold down the swelling fruit and the crank set in place. As the press cranked, the crimson must slowly drizzled a fine line down the spout into a bucket awaiting at its base.

I heard Rosa and Angelo return from their morning in town. And as if on cue I broke away from the men and tamely made my way over to offer Rosa my latent greeting and present my tin of biscotti. Rosa quietly nodded her thanks, then motioned for Giuseppe to retrieve a bottle of nocino from the sideboard. It was just after 11 a.m. So far so good. And even though the days in the town were still warm this late September, we gathered around the smoldering fire and wood smoke of their fornacella, drinking their wine.

Later in the afternoon, after I had returned home, Giuseppe picked me up for an early drive to Avellino to take me on what I would come to know was a time-honored post-family visit outing along the main Corso in that much larger town. I hadn't been back to Avellino since my evening with the Freda's though I recognized the main boulevard all the same. Giuseppe and I shared a gelato as we talked gamely about the future; the family farm vs. the U.S.

"Where would we live in Calitri?" I asked him out of the blue, just for fun. "In the town or in campagna?"

"*Campagna*," he said with conviction.

"With your parents? Or in a house of our own?"

"*Solo noi.*"

"With a shower? Washing machine?"

"*Sì.*"

"What about a dishwasher?"

Without missing a beat he said, *"Eh, moh lavastoviglie, no."*

"E perché?" What was it with men and dishwashers?

He concluded this verbal volley with an alpha-male stance.

"Troppa tecnologia."

And that was it. I had to laugh. It was all in good fun. Yet we laid out our living arrangements—*"Dopo sposati!"*—according to what I thought was possible way out there in his god's country. But he had his limits. He wanted to put his foot down somewhere. Okay. No dishwasher. He could take me in front of the sink?

Then I ventured with, "Do you think you could live in the U.S.A?" Knowing what a leap that was.

The 1980s anarchic sentiments of a young populace no longer willing to leave their villages—*'Non vogliamo emigrare'*—graffiti was scrawled on a wall in the Centro Storico some years after the 1980 earthquake. Most young town's-men here were very loyal to their tribe. Even Rosetta, Vincenzo's wife, made it pretty clear to me recently that young people today don't want to have to emigrate to find work like so many generations before them. Not that Giuseppe had ever had any problem with employment. He held a full-time job and worked on the family ranch. I supposed in small town Irpinia if your family owned and worked the land, there really was no reason to leave unless you've found a reason to follow your heart.

The Handsome Man from Macchiursi did not reply. Maybe it was too soon to ask.

He was genuinely so reserved he hardly uttered a word. Conversations were mainly carried by me. He radiated strength and confidence naturally, a kind of man I went for, though he was nothing like the men I knew in the U.S. With empathic intuition I felt my way through the depth of his deep-country masculinity. If I faltered, or he disagreed, he immediately set me straight. But we were easy with one another.

"Whatever it is you want to do," I remember saying often to him. He was my dashing Country Joe, a chop-your-own-wood kind of guy. Indiana Jones to my Marion Ravenwood. Or were those roles reversed? Still I felt he was increasingly curious about my life in the U.S.

When we returned not too late he pulled up to his family's city house down a back street in Calitri. It was modest, with one floor for each of the sons when they married. His aging grandmother Angela was safely stowed in the street-level apartment.

"Can't she hear us?"

"Chi?"

"Your grandmother."

"*Nah, è sorda.*" He winked.

We climbed the stairs and entered his family's apartment. Stalling, he brought out his parents' wedding album circa early 1970s and set it on the bed. Time capsule photos: black-and-white images of his mother and father's church ceremony; walking soon after down Corso Garibaldi to the *Casa del ExEca*; family, friends, and well wishers following for their post-nuptial communal wedding-hall pranzo; home-cooked large copper pans of macaroni, demijohns of local wine, and traditional desserts, all brought over from houses nearby, carried on the heads of the village women who prepared them. Tucked among those photos—was a 5"x7" Kodachrome of a young, beaming Giuseppe.

In one hand he is grasping a branch of lilacs like he would the teat of a milking cow. Wearing a dark blue suit and bow tie, standing as tall and as proud as a seven-year-old might with an adorable squint and grin across his knowing face. The earth beneath him is bare and turned. A lilac bush towers above and behind him and a cluster of early blooming snowdrops spread at his feet. Other spring flowers pop up around as sunlight dazzles through pale emerald leaves. It is his first Communion portrait, and to look at it melts my heart. What boy would have such mischief and resolve in his eyes that speak of someday owning the heart and soul of this land? Who he is gazing at is a nearly impossibly lucky soul. Bathed in the light of those auburn eyes now some twenty-three years later, I can't help grinning too, knowing what I know of his adulthood, his integrity, and his charms.

There were two copies of this photo, one a bit faded and folded than the other.

I glanced at him and he knew.

Putting the 5"x7" away, our shared secret, I sometimes covet it and hold it near, then hide it away, only to retrieve it again and again when moved and not yet filled with regret.

We then made long and uninhibited love until very late evening in his parents' city bed, his ancient grandmother quietly tucked in below. The raw wool-stuffed mattress and pillows, probably sheared from their own herd, yielding to his passionate force with muffled warmth and strength, before he drove me home.

San Nicola,
Falling Far from Home

I was falling far from home.

Amore?

With no house or car stereo nor guitar to sooth my soul or even a portable radio - no playlist to go with this new out-of-all-time-and-place love story, an interior soundtrack cued up songs in my heart. Some I used to play and sing and some I used to cue up myself long ago, as a young college radio DJ (The Nightbird)—drifting in and out of my waking dreams and sleep.

On top of Migliorina's dresser was a small framed wedding photo of Franco and Raffaela holding each other close on the dance floor, gazing dreamily into each other's eyes. It was the only other framed image in the room save for the Jesus painting. Each morning when I awoke and every evening while dressing to meet the Handsome Man from Macchiursi, the two images guided my heart and mind from silent wonder and meditation to dreams of conjugal love. Their wedding day photo recalled another nuptial portrait, that of my parents on the wall in their bedroom and seemed too, to remind me once again of my own lost place in the world of love and marriage.

Giuseppe came to pick me up to take me out each night without fail. He would call me and formally, tentatively, ask me.

"*Vuoi uscire?*"

"*Sì, volentieri.*"

I would dress in the master bedroom with the wedding portrait of Franco and Raffaela and the Maxfield Parrish Jesus on the wall and then wait in the darkened front bedroom with the vintage Singer sewing machine and the single bed, mingling memories from the past with the present until I saw the lights of his car pull into the driveway three stories below. I had never known this kind of old-country chivalry. Giuseppe was the closest I had come to having a man all to myself since my first lover in college, some twenty five years ago. And like that long-ago first lover, there was no worry in me that he might be with someone else some other evening. We were sailing.

The craving between us evolved into deep passion. My hips grew full and swayed like Greek amphorae lolling about the bottom of the Mediterranean Sea, the sea and current that was Giuseppe. If only we were on some siren's island, then the world might leave us our solitude and contentment. For I didn't know what anyone here really knew save my cousin Lucia and the few friends I called back home, but I did know that the whole of my body had blossomed into a fluid and sensual vessel open to the rhythm and waves of amore, and the pull of his arms.

Some evenings we happened upon some fairly serious pillow

talk, mostly revolving around his confusing desire to break away from life on the farm in a small rural town in Campania. This desire however was strongly countered with his deep family affection and his love for the ancestral earth beneath his feet. In his clear eyes, the glow of his skin, in the heft of his weight at once both lithe and powerful, I saw and felt his connection with this land. Sure of himself and mature beyond his youth, he was a commanding and naturally gallant man. Pragmatism and sensuality, two qualities to look for in a mate; Giuseppe had both in spades.

One night we broke silence and talked about our age difference.

"*Quanti anni hai?*" We were in his parents' bed where I had coaxed him to bring me more often rather than making love like teenagers in his car or outdoors. He knew I was older, yet it seemed by this question that he wasn't quite sure by how much.

Hadn't he been there when his father asked me back in February? I asked.

He was over me now, held me with his eyes and shook his head yes, but said, "*Ma non lo ricordo.*" Timid now, I flashed four fingers of one hand twice. Giuseppe grimaced. And I turned my head to the wall, retreating inward.

"*Non trentaquattro?*" he asked hopefully, grasping my chin with his oversized hand, gently pulling my face to meet his. I shook my head no. He had just turned thirty in February.

"*Se fossero stati trentaquattro, farei la mia valigia e volare stasera con te in California.*"

Here the traditional average age difference between husband and wife was still eight to ten years, in the man's favor. Tears welled in my eyes. Again I turned my head away. And again he pulled me back with loving force.

"For now, you are still mine."

Since then our bond and commitment to each other grew deeper, yet no closer to the necessary resolve that surely stood before us.

I looked for a sign, some guidance, in the hope that both he and I would be delivered from the heartache that would surely follow my departure. Some simplicity, understanding, or faith.

⁂

One night Giuseppe told me he was sad. And then, as if he had read my mind, he asked with sweet curiosity about possible pregnancy, since he had been coming inside me. I assured him I would not easily get pregnant. Still he lay beside me, naïvely thinking out loud, *"Se nascesse negli Stati Uniti sarebbe ancora italiano?"*

From first passeggiata to pregnancy in two beautiful months? I could be carrying a child. It might be too early to tell, though my body was giving some signs of life there. I'd had only one period since arriving in Calitri, my first since early June and very light, after having recovered from nearly losing my life. In the months between March and September, home in Los Angeles writing postcards and artful letters to Giuseppe, I was felled a second time by severe hemorrhaging from insidious intrauterine fibroids.

It was not worse than the first episode, a few years ago; no, not nearly as frightening. That time, the fibroids had slowly, methodically begun to create swells of blood clots deep in my womb, dropping them like slippery and silent bombs again and again one evening as I sat down to pee. Gravity.

Over the course of only a couple of hours, just after having gone to dinner and a movie with a friend, my uterus swelled with an impacted heat, producing an enormous amount of blood and then just as slowly released it—clot by clot—leaving me weak beyond imagine. When at last I could get up no more, I picked up the bedside phone in a fog and hit the redial button. My friend Heba on the other end of the line heard my weakened distress and immediately, intelligently, said, "Hang up. Dial 911 and I'll be right over."

I lay back in my bed waiting, drifting further, the room and my consciousness getting darker. I didn't realize I was slowly fading into a coma. Paramedics roared up the driveway, red lights blaring through the double windows above my head. Four beefy men charged into my bedroom and found me half lucid in a fetal position under the duvet. My two cats fled from the room.

One of the paramedics straddled the bed and took quick action. Not finding a vein in my arm, he jammed an IV needle the size of a crochet hook into the top of my hand. The saline liquid burned, bloomed across my hand, up my arm. Heba arrived. Another big form hovered over me with a clipboard. A few questions were asked. I don't remember my responses, as I was in another dimension. They hoisted me to the stretcher, unfolding my legs, but I felt my knees drawing back up to my chest. They ratcheted-up speed, raising the risers and wheeling me out of the house into the cool late April night. My cul-du-sac neighbors were milling about the back door of the truck. Heba followed to the Studio City emergency room. Cold, bright. Too bright. My world was still dark.

"You'll need a transfusion," the on-duty doctor told me. "You've lost five pints of blood."

I did a weak calculation in my head and then faded out. He ordered a D&C in the morning. I barely survived this. My family reeling, my father characteristically mute, standing with my mother and my sister out in the hall of my hospital room. I was thirty-nine years old. Months of slow living, weekly acupuncture, and a round of HRTs subdued the fibroids for almost two years.

Yet I continued to travel.

Then the second time, the second episode, four years later. Dark, liver-sized clots, unassuageable blood loss, emergency room, and all the rest. I opted for the uterine artery embolization. At a very young forty four, I was miraculously saved from a full hysterectomy—which I refused outright anyway—by Googling, by calling in by some divine manifestation, in the eleventh hour, the handsome consummate UCLA research gynecologist-cum-surfer in wingtips and a bowtie—Dr. Bruce McLucas. Who deadpanned in the operating room while about to save my entire *Women Who Run with the Wolves* womanhood; my intuitively creative second chakra and selfhood.

"You're going to love this procedure," he said.

I didn't blink so much as breathe.

Fading under the blue glare of surgical lamps, my doctor seemed a bespoke vision of Tom Wolfe but better looking, sans the fedora. I gave him a wide-eyed, my-life-is-in-your-hands look as I went under. Because I believed in the law of the chakras. The first is for survival, with the second you create.

Three months later I would be on a plane to Italy to consummate my love with the Handsome Man from Macchiursi—two, three times an evening—and so, yes, I thank god for science. My doctor, with whom I fell madly in crush for saving my life, knew of my adventures in Italy and my first bus ride to Calitri, and gave me the thumbs up.

One last question, I said to him, "Am I now predisposed to other diseases?" Pause. "Cancer?"

"No." he said. "You're going to be fine. You can even still conceive, have children. You're a healthy woman, in great shape."

In the few weeks of my home recovery I felt the pull of my father's past.

Just before I was born, my grandfather Nicola was admitted to a Brooklyn hospital suffering an early heart attack, at age 69, and never made it home again. Back then there were not nearly the heroic procedures to save people's lives there are today. My father had also long ago lost most of the women in his family. He was actually the last of his family from quite early on. He was petrified of hospitals and what might befall those dear to him once admitted to them. His mother was confined to one at a very early age over and over, again and again. He was very young as she fell headlong into a darkness from which she would never really emerge.

Shuffled off in summer to relatives as a young teen, it was well out of his or anyone's control or reach back then. Sanatoriums and secrecy, possible lobotomies; some very sad and terrible memories, though he never spoke of them. He never spoke of her.

And now here I was, nearly as old as my grandmother was when she was left to finally expire, nearly losing my life. Twice.

༺༻

My two months were nearly up.

I began to make advance plans for the necessary rounds of *salutare* to the few new friends I had made, and those *parenti* on either side of my family tree. Staying so long in town I had made new bonds not only with the adult children of relatives but with one or two other locals in the village. By now I knew it was ritual. My new relationship with Giuseppe's family added to my growing list, making it necessary for me to start ever earlier in the week before my departure.

Giuseppe and I made an appointment for a Saturday night on the final weekend of my stay, driven and accompanied of course by Adolfo. It was *Tutti Santi*, All Saints Day. An Italian national holiday that honors all the Saints of Christianity. And my name day, though I didn't know it at the time.

The afternoon before my appointment I was busy shopping around town for parting gifts and stopped in at a local *bibite* shop to pick up something to bring to the Zarrilli's. With the help of the shop girl I decided on a bottle of *spumanti*, the South's compliment to a dry, northern *prosecco*, and something my father always bought for birthdays or other occasions. With it I selected sugar dusted Camporelli Biscottini, perfectly simple and delicate cookies to go with the sweet and sparkling wine. I was quite nervous about this particular salutare and wanted to bring something special.

As we had arranged, Adolfo came to collect me around 6pm at

the Paolantonio palazzo on via Circumvallazione. A late autumn sky still glowed with crimson light from the evening's lingering sunset. From the balcony of her apartment zia Dorina waved and called greetings as we got in the car. Slowly driving off, Adolfo climbed the switchback road up to the town, then turned left at Incroce'Cola onto Corso Garibaldi heading out toward Bisaccia. At the very edge of the community we turned northeast toward the expanse of turned wheat fields in the upper valleys and drove far out into the Macchiursi countryside.

Early evening was mildly cold now. The autumn season in the Irpinia mountains had begun its transition to early winter though the solstice was more than a month away. Exposed to the landscape on all sides, the raw night air out there at a higher elevation was a marked temperature change from the village up on the hill. Scanning the horizon I spied a red-tailed fox and two gray wolves darting after it through the fields ahead of the road. A weather front too was visible just behind the ancient and dormant Mount Vulture, a dark mass of clouds glooming further across the valley. As we approached the Zarrilli massaria the last of the evening light faded to violet. In the distance the backdrop of Apennines was a solid curtain of deeper blue-black. We rattled up the rocky drive in the old red Fiat where a barking sheepdog betrayed our presence.

Giuseppe emerged from the angled darkness between the barn-corral and the main house, meeting us out in the driveway. We greeted each other with silent glances. Now that I knew of his commanding masculine self-assurance, it immediately put me at ease. A moment later though I sensed that he was far more nervous than I was.

Spumanti and *biscottini* in hand, Giuseppe took the lead as we walked the low grade up to the house, climbed onto the covered porch, and went inside. His father Michele appeared first, beaming at me as he grasped my hand in greeting. I could tell he was proud and happy to have his eldest son entertaining a girlfriend.

This particular woman, of course, was the one he greeted from atop his tractor nearly three years ago, when he asked Adolfo conspiratorially if I had met his son. Now here we were all here again in more advanced circumstances.

Rosa entered the room carrying a basket of warm out-of-the-oven cookies and sweet cakes. She set them down and sat herself at the head of the table. She motioned to Giuseppe to pull a bottle of nocino from the sideboard. Rosa poured generously and the evening's conversation began.

"*Ti piace stare a Calitri?*" asked Rosa.

"Yes, of course, my stay in Calitri has been wonderful," I said with a smile. It seemed this was the first time I had been directly addressed by her.

Michele sat opposite his wife at the other end of the table with me nearer the middle. He seemed very eager to engage in conversation with L'Americana too, curious of my adventures and conclusions on how I found life for two months in Calitri.

"The town and the countryside are beautiful!" I told them. "And this was my first time here for the Festa for the Madonna." Mentioning the Madonna was always a good thing. Notwithstanding the lighted Madonna and Child watching over Giuseppe and I as we made love every night in their townhouse bed or that I adored the handsome rancher like a novice in her habit.

We then exchanged news of my parents in the U.S. and current events, which meant the aftermath of 9/11. During my second trip to Calitri, I'd left Italy that late August 2001, only a few days before.

"And your family? Why don't they come with you?" Michele asked.

"I would love for my father to experience Calitri and meet everyone, all his relatives." It was a polite digression. Though I was hopeful, I knew it might never happen.

Through most of the conversation Adolfo and Giuseppe

remained quietly drinking at the other end of the room. I glanced at them from time to time for help but they seemed content to listen to we three, struggling as we were with their dialect and my limited understanding of it. We continued on this way for a half an hour or so, eating the sweets and drinking the strong liquor, until Rosa got up to go to the kitchen.

Evening had arrived. It was black outside now and colder inside, as the night air seemed to settle into the main room of the farmhouse. Attracted by the warmth, I wandered into the kitchen to sit with Rosa stoking a small fire in the fornacella stove at the other end of the small square room. Adolfo, Giuseppe, and Michele stayed in the living room discussing travel and someone's military duty in Verona, as well as their curiosity about California and other destinations outside of Calitri. Someone produced an atlas and they were soon bent over it with more drinks.

Within a minute or two Giuseppe joined Rosa and me in the warmed kitchen. The three of us gathered silently on low wood rush chairs around the base of the stove. To our right I spied a large basket of fresh *castagne*, or chestnuts, set on the floor tiles and a small wooden bowl of what looked like locally foraged chanterelles.

On Rosa's cue, Giuseppe gathered the mushrooms in his large hands, gingerly dusted them off, and sprinkled them with salt. Rosa then tossed them directly into the fire to roast, deftly turning them with a fire stick. An intoxicating aroma wafted up as they softly hissed and sputtered. She left them there for only a few moments before lifting them out one by one with the stick, almost as in a ritual.

Blowing on them to cool, she offered the first one to me then another to Giuseppe before helping herself. She continued this way until all the chanterelles were grilled and our *antipasto del bosco* was slowly, appreciatively, consumed.

Though we sat closely around the fire there was no conversation.

Giuseppe, who seemed sustained in a state of nervous charisma, remained quiet, and I simply hadn't the skill to start, much less carry on, a conversation alone in dialect with his mother. It was nice though. A reverent and comfortable warmth settled in the room.

Rosa eventually began preparing dinner for the table. All of this was a great surprise to me, as I hadn't any idea that Giuseppe and I were having dinner with his family. I was under the impression that we were only arriving for *un aperitivo* and a visit *di salutare*. This would be the first meal I was to share in the Zarrilli farmhouse. It was not without its implications of course, as I was counseled later on. I was glad the nocino had relaxed my nerves.

Giuseppe disappeared momentarily as I helped with setting the table. A plain cloth, tableware, and glasses set all around. He arrived back in the room with a small round of spiced pancetta and set it with a thud on the tile counter near his mother. She produced a large round *panella* of bread from a cupboard. Michele and Adolfo entered the room with a double-liter bottle of homemade wine, claret-red and slightly chilled; Aglianico from their vines.

Dinner was now ready and we all took our places around the small kitchen table. Rosa had prepared an ancient regional dish typical to her roots as a contadina in the countryside—*baccalà* simmered in thick broth laced with fresh olive oil and flavored with local *peperoni*, round deep red peppers soaked in vinegar with sun dried long sweet red peppers cracked and crumbled in. Baccalà, or dried codfish, is well known throughout the Mediterranean region as it was and still is a staple in most Southern Italian mountain communities. But this was my first time. Rosa's dish was deeply flavorful and satisfying with chunks of fresh bread. Michele's wine flowed and everyone ate heartily.

Afterward came the roasted chestnuts. They had been cooking in the kitchen fire at the base of the fornacella stove while we were eating dinner. Charred and steaming, they were tumbled on to the center of the table for all to share. Rosa, sitting next to me, made sure to shell enough of the sweetmeats for me to enjoy. Her hands were dusted black. We washed it all down with more glasses of their homemade red wine.

Giuseppe and I then left the dinner table together for our last night out around the town. Before leaving, his mother Rosa offered me a parting gift, a large jar of fresh summer honey from their local fields. Often gentle in his observations, Giuseppe seemed to have remembered me eyeing a smaller jar of rare eucalyptus honey one evening while at a *sagra* together in one of the neighboring towns.

Completely surprised, I accepted this prized gift as I glanced over to Giuseppe, doe-eyed in appreciation. The honey's color was soft creamy yellow and had a sun-warmed aroma of fresh summer hay. Once back home, when I opened the jar in my own kitchen, I felt transported as on an Irpinian breeze back to the rolling fields that surround Giuseppe's homestead.

❦

Zia Giuseppina invited me over the next morning for what I thought would be a last private moment, just the two of us, to say our farewells; a mutual salutare. It was now All Souls Day, November 2nd. The second of the consecutive national holidays that weekend, the one that honors all the dead.

I walked from the Corso by way of the cemetery to Giuseppina's apartment on the far side of town. There were plenty of people milling about the gated entrance and the florist shop; entering, exiting, double-kissing greetings, and making the signs of the cross. Nearly all the residents of the town came from near or far to honor their interned family members. They left carnations or mums at their gravesites as was the custom. I hadn't been to a cemetery to pay familial respects since I was a child. And then only to visit my mother's mother way out on Long Island. I was not sure who, if any one, of my direct relatives were buried here in Calitri. Certainly not anyone close enough yet to matter. I didn't even know where my father's parents were buried.

When I arrived, I found Giuseppina in an unusual mood.

"Permesso?" I called down the hallway.

This new word—the permission to enter someone's home—I had gleaned from her, inferred from her 1930s fascist upbringing; a very hardscrabble, rigid, and correct way of life.

"AVANTI."

Her voice abrupt, terse, as if she were waiting to pounce. And pounce she did. Generally she met me at the door, with a broad smile. This time I rounded the corner to her kitchen to find her back to the entrance. She turned and began without a moment's hesitation, a prickly rasp to her voice.

"Angela, what do you mean staying as long as you have? Don't you have work? What about your parents? What do they have to say? And you left your house for this long in the U.S.?" She barely took a moment to breathe, then continued.

"And Raffaela. Don't you realize what you have done?"

She continued to bully me with a string of dialect words that I could barely make out. Her fierce energy however was unmistakable, as was how it made me feel. My neck and face inflamed, I felt like an abject sinner. But for what cause?

"Don't you have anything to say?"

My self-esteem had fallen well below its already humble outsiderness. Its L'Americana-in-remote-hill-town-foreign-ness. My fledgling wild-driven Alta Irpinia love story now reduced almost to shambles, and just about any other amorous joy I felt for this ancestral place these past two months. I felt splintered, supplanted by gutless fear.

I rose and began to back out of the room.

"Go then, and goodbye!"

No longer an adult in full command of herself, I stammered as I reached for the door,

"I don't know what to say. I'm sorry."

I retreated down the four flights of stairs. If anyone saw me or ran into me, I might easily crumble. Not two steps out into the street, I spied zio Giovanni walking up. My heart reeled. He was in perfect gospel Sunday dress, the deep crown of his 1940s fedora shading his weathered face. He was never so elegant. Was he coming from the cemetery?

"*Tste, mi dispiace,*" was all he could offer.

I flushed completely.

So he knew. I was furiously confused. I barely uttered a word, then choked back tears walking all the way home to the Paolantonio palazzo and throughout the rest of the day. What had I done? I honestly didn't know. But it felt like certain betrayal. I felt unbeloved.

I did not rouse myself for lunch, with anyone.

Later, Raffaela and Franco went over to zia Giuseppina's for an explanation. When they returned, they had me come down to their apartment that evening for our salutare.

"Would you like a *camomilla*?" Raffaela asked.

I feebly nodded. "*Sì, grazie.*"

Franco remained pensive, smoking.

Raffaela delivered the hot *tisana*, then gently spoke, "We will always be here for you. We hope you will return."

What a beautiful thing to say. It calmed me. I then presented her with a thank-you gift that I had bought the previous morning. I had already brought them a gift from the U.S. But when I saw these I bought them too. "A small token of my thanks for letting me stay, taking such good care of me."

"Oh! How lovely." I was happy Raffaela was pleased. "Look Francesco, a set of demitasse cups for the apartment."

Franco quietly nodded his approval. I was learning though

this was an awkward reversal of the gentility of the South. Here, they gave the parting gifts.

Early in the evening Giuseppe came to pick me up for a last turn in his car, a last chance to be together. Dorina did not see me off from the balcony. When he saw that I had been crying and heard what had happened, he was furious.

But I didn't want to say. I knew how I felt about him. But what now would become of my relationship with my relatives, or with the town? It was our last evening together, and though my heart seemed ruined, I was determined to keep this newly learned *timore* to myself.

Giuseppe and I said our farewells amid tears and desperate kisses at the airport in Naples the next morning, bringing to a close my two months' residency in the town. On the early morning drive down the Ofantina we were both wordless, until I broke the ice.

"You rock," I said.

"*Io pietra?*"

I laughed. And he did too. We both relaxed and he took my hand.

Then, in the terminal, he held my blue American passport, scrutinizing my photo and data as he began to crumble into tears, and all but begged, *"Come andare via?"*

"I'm sorry love, I don't want to go," I said. It was a strange reversal of all my relationships that had come before. But this was different. We were in agreement. We had fallen hard for each other.

He shook his head, remained unconvinced. We were outside now, against a wall, getting some air. Giuseppe continued to let his tears fall. I tried to sooth him but was helpless. I had cried all my tears the previous day.

"Can't you come visit me?"

"Non lo so."

He walked me to the gate crowded with Neapolitani businessmen forcing themselves to the front of the line.

"*Va bu. Salutiamo.*" He kissed me hard one more time and then turned and waved and was gone.

Another long flight alone ahead of me. After a few minutes he called me from the road. He had pulled over. He was in tears, sobbing.

After fourteen hours, the plane was finally circling the basin of Los Angeles. We banked left and I looked out my window to the velvet horizon covered in the lights of the city, seeming so many sequins on black. Instead of the gazillion stars above in Macchiursi, they were below on dry land, glimmering white yellow and pink.

As we approached, the plane slowly circled the red ribbon of taillights along boulevards stretching for miles, and I realized the contrast between my life in Los Angeles and the two months I had in the Southern Italian hill town. The Hollywood sign, the Hollywood Bowl, the Capitol Building with its murals of Sinatra and the Beatles. My drives home along the crest line of Mulholland and how they compared to the soulful flickering lights of the arc of the hillside village that was Calitri—the vantage point at night from the top of the Langobard *castello* as it overlooked the lights of the town, a sort of an illuminated miniature, on many levels, of what I had here on Mulholland Drive.

On the first night back in my own bed in Los Angeles, I had a vivid dream of my grandfather Nicola. His face suddenly looming large, I held my breath with my eyes closed. I stayed as calm as I could, absorbing his presence for as long as I could. I had never dreamt of my grandfather before. What did he have to tell me? Was he unhappy with me too?

I called out to him in haste and awe, "Wait!" as his strong countenance began to waver, then he was gone.

When Giuseppe called me the next day to see if I had arrived safely, he was just as reverent as I was at this sort of visitation, given all that we had felt and done that autumn. He was the only one who knew I had found Nicola's portrait in Migliorina's cristalliere. He had no reservations that Nicola had come to me in a dream. After all, he appeared to me just after All Souls Day. The Handsome Man from Macchiursi knew it was a sign, an omen.

"*Cosa ha detto?*" His strong baritone voice nearly sotto voce. He wanted to know what my grandfather might have said to me or imparted.

So, even as he made love to me over hill and dale while protecting me from intrusion from my earthly family in Calitri, Giuseppe wanted, would have welcomed, my grandfather's elder, if ghostly, approval. Seemed the wall between our world and the spirit realm had really begun to fall.

Head of an Italian Girl

☙

In early spring of 2004 I returned to Calitri to reclaim in my loins what still beat in my heart from the day I left last November. Six long months of standing Saturday phone calls and artfully composed letters fanned our amorous flames.

The small house I rented was midway up one of the oldest streets in the village. Via Torre, aptly named, led from the flat main Corso in town up to the early Langobard Castle and its one remaining tower—*la Torre di Nanno*—that dominated the top of the hill of ancient Aletrium until the late sixteenth century. Via Torre was a long and steep grade, a difficult climb home on any day, in any century. This spring I was easily the youngest resident on the block. And in this neighborhood, la straniera, was a curiosity for all to wonder and talk about.

Giuseppe, who seemed excited to see me and at the same time equally confounded by my return, didn't understand why I was staying solo in a rented house instead of with my family. My first night in, after we made urgent, hip-crushing love, he demanded,

"*Quanto costa questo casa?*"

"It didn't cost that much," I replied. It was too much by village standards, I found out. The novice once again, I was actually being taken advantage of. Or was it a kind of *omertà*?

"*E dove mangiare pranzo?*"

"I thought I would cook."

"*Hai comprato vino in bottiglia e questi asparagi?*" He indicated my purchases, a bottle of white wine and asparagus that were a gorgeous, deep brilliant green, plump and very fresh.

"Yes, I went to the market today! It was fun. Everything is so fresh, just like in California." Trying to bring him around.

"*Vino di Calitri è molto buono.*" He scoffed. "*E so io trovarti nel bosco asparagi selvatici.*"

Wild asparagus was better? "Maybe you could bring me some the next time you come over." I didn't realize you could collect wild asparagus around here, or anywhere.

"I was merely hoping to have a cozy place to invite you in for one of my own home cooked meals." I explained. Girlfriend like.

Unfortunately, I found there were few utensils and cooking implements to inspire much of a feast. I would need to improvise rather quickly. There was just one dented pasta pot and a very small dirty skillet, a gaggle of mismatched spoons and rusty knives, and one lonely fork.

"*Non ti preoccupare, porto proprio io una forchetta.*" Giuseppe was always quick with a great and sometimes leveling response, but with whom was he so displeased?

Zia Dorina too was genuinely upset when I insisted on

finding my own place, instead of staying above her again in nonna Migliorina's apartment.

"Where no one knows you or can properly look out for you?" she tried to reason. But I was wary. Finally, she made the arrangement in the neighborhood for a place for me to rent.

Lucia and I went to view the house on via Torre in the late afternoon's half light. Again a house on the dark side of the hill. Not wanting to waste time, I took it. Try as she did, Lucia could not convince me otherwise. Though later I was more than chagrined at its abject shabbiness. The town seemed not used to renting houses short-term to tourists, or the likes of me, a fledgling parente lontano, as there were no tourists. Everyone else was *sotto l'occhio*.

To my surprise, zia Giuseppina was urgently apologetic this visit after the way she had lashed out at me on the final day of my two-month stay last November.

Now it seemed she was only concerned that I had a working TV and *riscaldamento* in the rented house. I could only guess that her anger had something to do with the fact that it was All Souls Day and Franco and Raffaela had tragically lost their only daughter not that long ago.

Maybe Giuseppina felt I had intruded on their private mourning, was insensitive to their great personal loss. I knew she wouldn't understand my freelance professional life; my own mother didn't know what these things meant.

Never having met their daughter, and further, fully distracted by the love I was falling in, it didn't occur to me at the time that it could have been a grave miscalculation. It was the main reason for my determination this spring to rent a house on my own to stay as I had that last February. And it seemed everyone in my Calitri family circle felt this in my adamant decision to stay alone.

"Ah, you come only for carnal passion," Franco said.

Raffaela, always the most level-headed of the group, gently and firmly insisted that I was welcome to stay upstairs in nonna

Migliorina's apartment any time I returned to town. Or she may have been her husband Franco's spokesperson. She extended this dispensation soon after I arrived at lunch one day; we dined alone, an event that until that moment had no precedent.

I was learning by trial and error there was no manual for navigating these delicate shifts of protocol, whether reading the heart and mind of an ardent Italian lover, or steering around the generational and cultural expectations of Italian relatives. There seemed a clear cultural gap that is the very core of Italian gentility: their peerless hospitality and generosity, particularly with relatives and visitors from out of town.

Spigolare. It goes well beyond the caffè offered in every kitchen to a guest. My relatives opened their hearts wide as they offered meals and beds to sleep in again and again on my various short trips to the South. And when these visits began to expand in length from two days to a week in summer then for a month in the dead of winter, and then finally this past September with my two-month sojourn into their daily lives and culture, falling deeper in love with the town, there was finally a certain responsibility felt toward me and I toward them. Each carefully assuring the other respect and privacy, though not without a measured concern for protocol and appearances; for there is nothing more concrete in Southern Italian society than that of strict social etiquette and a carefully cultivated public image.

Even as an adult I was in their charge. And on their turf—so they felt it was their duty to keep me from any untoward comments or assumptions about my behavior, no matter how publicly chaste. For as always, as much as I could, I followed their lead—after all, when in Rome.

But Rome was relative until I discovered Southern Italy.

On short trips I happily stayed in their empty nest apartments. They wouldn't have it any other way. And because I was an unmarried woman traveling alone, they would insist that someone accompany me on mornings or errands around town; it being unseemly here for a woman to walk about on her own. As an American I barely gave it a thought. But I was learning.

⁓

On one of my first mornings on via Torre I met an old woman severely bent over, feebly climbing the steep grade, struggling with heavy plastic shopping sacks tangled in gnarled and twisted hands. I left the key in my door, walked down to meet her, and offered my help. She thanked me first, then quizzed me in the local dialect through thick bifocals who I was and to whom I belonged.

"*A chi appartieni?*" It was difficult to understand her, though by now after these many visits I had grown accustomed to the standard questions-cum-greetings in the streets of the town by the elders I met. As we slowly advanced up the street to her house I answered with who I was, that is, that I had relatives here and was renting the house for a short period while visiting them, and that I wouldn't be any trouble.

"*Stai sola?*"

I wondered if she had already spied Giuseppe.

"*Sì. Sono sola.*"

It turned out the old woman was a childhood friend of nonna Migliorina's, who had lived not far from via Torre as a young girl. So she was already aware of all the facts and of my attendance on the street she had lived her whole life. She was just confirming for herself, and with that I supposed my character had been approved and clearance granted with the rest of the few residents who lived on the block.

When I returned, I spent the next few hours rearranging the meager furnishings in the house, assessing the sparsely equipped kitchen cupboards and sweeping the cobwebs from the corners of the bedroom. Seemed the house hadn't been occupied for some time, and in daylight I could see there had been little cleaning done before my occupancy. True, I had confirmed the rental at first viewing and within only a few hours or so of my arrival. It seemed now a hasty attempt to secure a place to assure my privacy and minimize the responsibility and concern for my care by my relatives.

Once I was settled in, the other elders of the lane one by one approached my door with gifts of welcome for my kitchen and curiosity, no doubt, for their circle. An old woman gave me a sprig of basil, though it was still quite early April in these cold mountains, not nearly sunny nor time enough for seed to sprout; I didn't know how she could have grown something so fragrant. An old gentleman across the way gave me a firm bulb of garlic.

And my relatives helped out too.

Zia Giuseppina offered a small bottle of her peerless olive oil.

Zia Dorina gave me a few small eggs from her hens, which she quickly admitted with a shrug were insufficient for her daily recipes.

"*Queste uova sono troppo piccole. Porti tu...*"

I thanked her for the fresh brown eggs, carried them carefully wrapped in newspaper to my kitchen, and looked forward to how I would put them to use. And so I had the beginnings of a fine meal and presumably a new chapter in the town.

On the first Sunday morning after my arrival, but before the first entanglement of invitations for lunch with various *parenti*, Adolfo offered to take me out for a country drive. It was a gloriously bright spring day. The surrounding hills were awash in young silky green grass. Billowy dark clouds like ominous fortresses threatened in the distance. If we hurried, we could make the morning outing last before the spring rainfall and the call to his mother's for lunch.

We chose to drive down the single winding road visible from the north balcony of his parents' house. They had in my opinion, one of the most spectacular and unobstructed views of the countryside from their side of Calitri's crest. And in any time of year, it was an excellent vantage point for weather watching. Standing on the narrow balcony facing the cold northeast there below was an ancient back road gracefully following the undulating grades of farm-lands and silver stands of olive trees up into the Apennine foothills, pushing further to the ancient and massive volcanic caldera of Mount Vulture. Lago di Monticchio, a local summer destination for picnics, boating and general family fun, where Giuseppe first took me last fall.

One evening Giuseppe and I explored the circumference roads of the caldera of Mount Vulture, after a particularly hard rain. The dense fog was quite low to the ground in the higher altitudes surrounding the lake when he slowed the car and opened his driver side door to scan the side of the road. A moment later he leaned out and picked something up off the road and held it in the lamplight of the car for me to see. A small glistening frog blinked at me from the palm of his hand. When he cut the engine to listen, we heard their lakeside mating calls. Another night down a particularly darkly wooded area we collected castagne that had freshly fallen from their majestic laden trees. These mountains are covered in forests of chestnut trees. It was a local vocation to go out collecting. Later I put the smooth-skinned chestnuts in a crystal bowl on the table in nonna Migliorina's kitchen. Their dark silken patina contrasted with the cheerful buttery texture of the quince. The fragrance of both *bosco* and fruited *fiori* filled the room.

The volcano's last eruption was some forty thousand years ago, leaving the land below it richly fertile. Over and beyond Monticchio about an hour and half drive out lay the ruins of Paestum, Pompeii and Herculaneum, the teeming metropolis of Naples, and the Tyrrhenian Sea. They say Irpinia is a sea of another kind. An earthen sea. Its windswept undulating masses of spring green sweet hills effortlessly germinated *fieno* or semolina; *il grano*—for Italy's pasta, bread or pizza.

After a short distance Adolfo stopped the car at a cross in the road and parked. We alighted there, leaving the old Fiat along a fairly dry mud ditch and took off strolling down the pavement. On one side was a high stone wall. There planted all along its length were wild flowering quince bushes, their papery pink-and-white blossoms sending a sweet fragrance floating just above our heads. When I recognized them I was struck with the memory of Giuseppe collecting the downy yellow fruit for me one evening last September during one of our drives. I realized it was along this back road that we often returned late from our evening outings, savoring our time together.

On the other side of this road, a bright green field of wild grasses lay fallow for the season. A stand of red poppies waved a bit further down field. There were no other towns in sight on the hills before us, and only the atoll of Calitri silently spreading over the hillside behind.

We meandered slowly, quite content to while away a half hour or so in the mornings deep blue horizon, the clouds still a safe distance away. And I was secretly pleased with myself for finally returning to Calitri in time to witness spring. It had now been four seasons that I had visited this town and its surrounding countryside and still I had yet to drink my fill.

Most of my family seemed steadily curious at my periodic returns, yet at the same time had come to accept L'Americana and her apparent carefree ways. Adolfo too. A young bachelor adrift in this work-deprived environment, he was often in a state of stunned aporia; having had no economic resources to fall back on or build up from most of his adult life.

"This is a country of arrangements," the Prince of Salina remarks in the early pages of *Il Gattopardo*. And none more so than in rural Southern Italy. It had taken me several attempts to understand this intrinsic Irpinian mindset of a habitually underfunded and underdeveloped land. There were many bright young people not merely out of work but with no future prospects on the horizon. Here, or in closely neighboring towns. The answer certainly didn't lie in my upfront curiosity or in any can-do American optimism that I could espouse.

"Life won't wait for you," I told Adolfo. "Go, look for something in some other city."

Adolfo, meekly noncommittal, slowly blinked, then blandly responded, murmuring something about not wanting to leave his mother. Or maybe the piazza, a contained universe, where many such arrangements between men still took place. Sometimes I felt that my visits here were in fact a kind of showing off to them, a lack of empathy for their hard-won and mostly meager advancements. After all, my grandfather left the village behind. Why should I return? What did I want from them? Though nothing could be further from the truth. I returned because I had fallen in love with this place, its country, and townspeople and the wild landscape.

We strolled on.

In the near distance a low and rhythmic tinkling came from down the road. Within a few minutes a magnificent herd of tawny oxen slowly took over our path. Striding in great pairs on the narrow road, wide-faced bulls appeared from around the bend; heads low, their great golden-brown and black horns bobbing in rhythm with their steady stride. The females' hides in softer tones with young calves towing close to their double line. Handsome hand-forged brass bells hung from wide swaths of tanned leather around their necks, the larger the bull it seemed the heavier and more somber the bell.

Tinkling gave way to clanging in varied tones as the bells of the herd closed in on us. Cowboys walked close behind each group with tall wicking shafts, gently prodding their haunches, calling out in tongue clicks and whistles to direct the herd. They hugged the stone wall, moving slowly, steadily toward their destination. I stood by just listening to their hoofs on packed earth, their atonal bells punctuating each stride, grateful not to have been distracted by a camera viewfinder; my eyes naked before the sight.

Instead it was Adolfo who produced a sort of digital instamatic. Bringing it up to his eye, he stood firm to take a picture. At that moment a young herdsman chastised him as he walked by, waving his staff and shouting that he and his herd were not for tourist consumption. I found this objection odd given that we were in the middle of absolute nowhere; deep in a mountain valley in eastern Irpinia, within a silent hollow of overlapping hillsides untrammeled by anyone other than those who tended the land. Never had I seen a tourist other than myself in these parts, even as I explored in the town. I wonder where the herdsman could have gathered such an assumption.

Later that night, when I described what I had seen and heard to Giuseppe, I asked what type of cow had crossed our path. Did they produce milk for *burrata*? Or the soft delicately fragrant ricotta? Or maybe the *fior de latte* that I had recently purchased in the small grocery in the town? They were certainly different from the cows he worked every morning; their muscular and tawny hides a visual contrast to the corpulent and placid dairy cows at the Zarrilli azienda.

Patient with my curiosity, he explained, *"Sono Podoliche. Fanno caciocavallo."*

Part of the seasonal *transumanza* of the herds, these oxen arrived in early spring to graze on new green grasses in the Ofanto Valley. They were a rare and an ancient breed, prized for their wild herb fragrant milk. An aged artisan cheese called caciocavallo was made specifically from their milk in this high mountain region.

❦

The days in April didn't remain bright and sunny. The crisp air of that first Sunday morning turned wet every day after with cold rain and fog and would last for the remainder of my stay on the mountain.

During this time I explored.

Borgo la Cascina, is the small Centro Storico neighborhood that hugged the southeast hillside of the village. It stood just above via Ferrovia that ran the length of the lower hillside that once formed the baseline ridge of the original town, but well below the patrician mansions that reached up to the top of the hill, and the ancient tumble-down ruins of the Langobard castle. Most all the dwellings in la Cascina were houses with ground level rooms or entrances. What the gentry of days ago would have called "al piano terra."

When I asked Franco, "What does *la Cascina* mean?" he responded in English with a gentle *tsk*, "Animal shacks."

I thought he was being facetious.

At the time of my grandmother's birth near the turn of the nineteenth century, and for many decades after, la Cascina was said to be the liveliest neighborhood of the town. There were two back roads that led out from this neighborhood to the distant fields, where for decades many of the townsmen and women went off each morning at daybreak by foot or mule to work, to break the soil. From land-break to harvest season they brought food home to their table and the tables of the wealthy or noble families—feudal barons—that owned the land and managed the town.

This was one of the few Centro Storico neighborhoods to live on after the severe earthquake that struck the central Alta Irpinia region in 1980. Many of the grander village homes, the palazzi near the top of the hill—closer to the ruins of the Castle, where Franco grew up—were abandoned that early morning in November, declared tear-downs, never to be inhabited again. It rendered the upper part of the hill town ghostly, windswept, and neglected, long barren of any human touch.

Not la Cascina. Within its labyrinth of stone arches, steps, vie, and vicoli, it still preserved an ancient and tenacious activity;

a commingling of folklore and spirituality, frugality and productiveness. There was a certain feminine synergy felt within its borders, the populace being nearly all women. At least it seemed that way, as black-clothed and enshrouded women moved silently, diligently, through the quiet lanes in early morning to market and again later in the afternoon on their way to Mass.

Zia Concetta Borea, at over eighty years old, was an original resident of la Cascina. She was a well-revered member of this matriarchal community; still upright and tall, a slender figure rendered entirely in black and fiercely independent. She lived alone self-sufficiently in her two-room stone house at 21 via Fontana, with its rear balcony that looked out over a round patch of land on the opposite hillside. Land that was a sort of hardwood kitchen garden with fruit and olive trees tended by her daughter Maria and Maria's husband Vincenzo. Concetta had steadfastly remained in this house through the years of her marriage and widowhood and would more than likely depart this life in the same bed she gave birth to her children in. As most elders here did.

My grandmother Angela Maria was born in this two-room house on via Fontana, over one hundred years ago. This blazing detail was finally revealed to me as I sat with zia Concetta late one morning passing the time in her kitchen, as she had come to expect from me each time I visited. Of course I had been in her house now a few times, sat and talked with her on small wood rush chairs bedside the *stufa-di-legna* in winter or out on the balcony soaking up the late summer sun. But this morning I had finally put the question directly to her,

"Zia, where was my grandmother born?"

No pause. Just a swift sweep of her hand in the air then it fell firmly striking the wood table, *"Qui! In questa casa!"*

Angela Maria was the third child born to Vincenzo Cicoira and Maria Russo, though she was the first to live past infancy. The oldest of four siblings, she was also the first of her core family to marry and emigrate. A few years later, once established in her new home in Brooklyn with my grandfather, her two younger siblings followed her to a new life in New York.

Though like my grandmother, I never knew of them.

I recalled my first visit in Calitri when zia Concetta arrived, unexpected and unannounced, with her daughter Maria Cicoira. She had brought with her two small black-and-white photos, of herself and one of her husband Pasquale to offer me. I see now how she must have wanted, hoped, to make the connection for me from her life as a young woman, sister-in-law of my grandmother, who stayed behind in their old world neighborhood, as she witnessed my grandmother's emigration with Nicola Paolantonio to America.

Angela Maria and her siblings that followed left behind their brother Pasquale. Seemed someone in the family always stayed behind. And though he was the youngest of the four, I gleaned from Concetta's stories that he proudly took charge of the remaining clan in the lean years that followed.

Pasquale Cicoira and Concetta Borea married, then raised their children in this small stone house in la Cascina. Concetta seemed proud to stay behind in Calitri even though most or all of their immediate family moved on forever. Few of them returned, as did my grandparents. And zia Concetta indeed would have been a destination for their return journeys.

Carved into the keystone above the chestnut wood doors of 21 via Fontana were the initials V.C. 1900—Vincenzo Cicoira, my great grandfather. In 1900 my grandmother Angela Maria was just five years old. Twenty years later she married Nicola Paolantonio and embarked on her life's journey far from the small hillside village of la Cascina to the teaming ethnic neighborhoods of Manhattan and Brooklyn where I was born. Below the door across the threshold was a well-worn single slab of softly marbled stone, worn down by the boots of my grandmother's family for over a century.

Cera Una Volta
(Once Upon a Time)

Amid all the drama of renting the house on via Torre—paying too much for what essentially was a hole in the wall—and weathering, literally, Giuseppe's cool, curious reception in an even colder early April, my checking account had been hacked in Los Angeles. I made the discovery when, by my third ATM withdrawal, my account was mysteriously blocked. The bank could send me a new ATM card by FedEx, but I couldn't file a claim until I was back in Los Angeles. I considered my situation and changed my return flight that same day.

Everyone in Calitri was up in arms. Intrigued to see me back in town again so soon, they were now just as incredulous that I made the choice to leave early. I paid the *padrona* of the house in cash for half my stay. La padrona was not pleased. Generous I thought, as I had had to clean it before sleeping or showering in it.

I wondered how Giuseppe would take the news. He seemed reluctant to return to our previous romance. I was confused why. This seemed a good reason to go and not come back for a while, maybe even good reason for him to get on a plane to visit me in the U.S.

Over pizza late one evening in a very out-of-the-way town, I remembered zia Dorina's opaque inquiry "Don't we have pizzeria's in Calitri?"

I broke the news. "I have to leave for Los Angeles."

"*MO'h?*" he said, rather taken aback yet with the sharp timber in his voice of, "Hey, I'm in charge here."

I returned his use of the dialect. "Yes, *mo'h*."

Then for internal moral support, I added, "I called my father today." Pause. "He made it very clear I should return home immediately."

Giuseppe had no choice then but to acquiesce. He was trumped. I could see it on his face. No Italian male would dare go against the wishes of his girlfriend's father, anyone's father. I flew home three days later, three weeks early.

He called me as soon as I landed to tell me he put in for his passport, his first, and was planning a trip to see me in August that same year.

When he arrived I picked him up at LAX in my red, sun-roofed Audi A6. It was 2:55 p.m.; the southwestern sun still high in the sky and little traffic at that hour. We drove the scenic route along the crinoline ridge of Mulholland Drive, exiting off the 405 freeway just before the Sepulveda Pass to reach the cul-de-sac property of the Luciani ranch, with its unobstructed view of the Hollywood sign and other tony landmarks of the City of Angels spread out below. The Handsome Man from Macchiursi was clearly impressed and amazed, and then later quite pleased with himself when he offered my father his strong hand and said,

"*Come va?*" It was an Italian greeting in the familiar form.

Without missing a beat, my father casually and illogically answered, "*Non c'è male.*"

My father was smiling, clearly amused with this new-found memory of his. It was a very typical Calitran response, in dialect! And again I was struck with incredulity. Giuseppe just turned to me and grinned. He had at last triumphed.

We drove up the scenic coastal route of California through rolling Paso Robles to coastal Big Sur, through San Francisco to Napa Valley, Sebastopol and Santa Rosa, stopping along the way to stay in small prim hotels and drink what to him was a strange and foreign libation, California wine. Sitting down to dinner one evening we ordered a bottle of red, a Pinot Noir or Cabernet, what they call in Alta Irpinia, *vino nero.* As the waiter poured our selection, Giuseppe immediately recoiled, saying that it was too warm, and to my surprise, asked the waiter to put it on ice for a while. When the waiter retreated to correct the temperature of the wine, Giuseppe shared a colloquial saying of his fellow shepherd countrymen,

"*Vino caldo è come l'acqua per i maccheroni.*" Warm wine is like water for boiling macaroni. And that was that.

I knew my mother always liked to put ice cubes in her red wine. She said she got that from her Sicilian father. Wine made and stored in cool grottos. Now I realized where this anomaly came from. It was the equivalent of keeping wine or milk on Brooklyn balconies in winter, as she occasionally liked to recall, sometimes culling fond, wistful memories of her childhood from the bleak: sleeping four or more to a bed, lacking hot water in her family's early New York cold-water flat, or my favorite, having to clean out the coal burner in her wedding gown.

When my mother first met Giuseppe, she burst out with, "Wow, Angela! He's gorgeous!" Giuseppe's proverbial lion's tail proudly flicked this way and that, as mine stood straight out. It wasn't the first time she had unsubtly put me on the boyfriend spot.

Then she floored me with her usual, "You're not going to marry him are you?"

Giuseppe's second visit seven months later was a bonus. I planned a surprise drive to the Grand Canyon, an international favorite, I knew, and the sixth of seven wonders I hadn't been to myself. We drove the Audi out along Route 66 to the canyon's south rim playing two compilation CDs of Neapolitan songs that someone back home in Calitri made for him. Caruso crooned *"O'Sole Mio"* from the loudspeakers as landlocked Riverside incongruently sped by. I booked a lucky romantic cabin for two at the rim's edge. An early April snow fell our first night in. We took long solo hikes at sunrise or sunset to Hermit's Rest and along the Hermit Trail to Lookout Point. The Handsome Man from Macchiursi now seemed in his element, though still duly impressed and amazingly pleased, getting a kick out of urbanites setting up on the canyon's mule trails, but by then I could tell the U.S. wouldn't be his life.

We gamely tried to recreate our falling in love from the fall of 2003, almost two years earlier, but it just wasn't the same as in the wilds of Irpinia.

❧

Two months after he returned to Calitri, Giuseppe had called to inform me that the town had discovered a tomb while paving a new parking lot for the business school just across from the Paolantonio palazzo. It was pre-Etruscan or Samnite, dating from at least 2500 years ago, and the archeologists who were called in said the figure inside, laden with gold-and-jewel-bedecked robes and artifacts for the afterlife attested to her royalty—a princess.

When I heard the news I was stunned and delighted.

I had slept in the Paolantonio loft apartment with its perfect view facing the arching crest of the ancient hill town in autumn 2003—la Banda playing the morning of the Festa. On my first journey to Calitri, while having lunch with Franco and Raffaela in their kitchen, Franco teased me about not being married, calling me a *principessa*, as he pointed out the window toward the castle to find my prince. He had essentially pointed across the site of her tomb buried beneath the lot of the business school that he attended as a youth.

So there she was all along—the Princess in the story. Pointed out the very first time I set foot in the town. Seemed I was guided directly to her—but by whom? Certainly Franco, Giuseppe, and others play important roles. Or was it that Calitri itself was a thin place? It seemed now that from the moment I arrived everything opened up from the heavens: these earthly clues, my relatives' unconditional love, the spirit of my ancestors, everything I had been missing. And I just kept following, saying yes and returning, again and again, until finally it grounded me. Italian fairy dust pulling me in.

But I never imagined this.

༺༻

C'era una volta un Re, seduto su un sofà. Che disse alla sua dama, 'Raccontami una fiaba'. E la dama incominciò.

Impiccherà Jordi con una corda d'oro, è un privilegio raro. Rubare sei cervi nel parco del Re, vendendoli per denaro. Mentre la maga Circe dopo aver trasformato i valorosi guerrieri di Attila a maiali, disse loro: Porcellini voi siete dei porcelli. E mentre radio Tirana trasmette musiche Balcaniche Vulcaniche danzatori Bulgari a piedi nudi sui carboni ardenti, il lupo lanciava un grido sotto l'ombra della luna, anunciando l'imminente ed inevitabile, arrivo delle streghe.

Once upon a time there was a king, sitting on his throne.

And he asked his lady to tell him a story. And she began to spin a fairytale about a princely warrior. The story of a brave *paladino* in love.

It came over in lengthy texts from an old school friend of Giuseppe's who now lived in Turin. No less than two kings, a Greek goddess, and a witch are summoned in the telling, and along the way there is clever thievery, wild fiery music, and brigand adventure. I was reminded of Italo Calvino, Umberto Eco and some centuries-old Italian children's fables collected in a volume that I kept by my bed.

It was the beginning of September 2005 and I was back in Calitri. Giuseppe and I sat in his car as he patiently transcribed each line from the tiny cellphone screen onto a slip of paper. He translated what he could literally as I tried to decipher figuratively what sage advice was being handed down.

It was a poem about a princess and a king.

As Giuseppe and I began our drive down from the top of the town, down along the ancient and steep back road that led out of the village, we began to talk about the history of who first built the castle at the top of the hill. Did he know what people built it, and who the ruling families were who presided over the town? I had been collecting some history of the Langobards since exploring Verona in 2001, when I uncovered the story of a daughter of a king and queen of the Langobards—*Authari* and *Teodolinda*—that is, a princess. I remembered reading that Authari and Teodolinda were married around the year 570 in a field outside of Verona. And that their granddaughter *Aldeperga*, the last Princess of the Langobards, reigned over the region of Benevento.

On my very first trip to Calitri—the side trip that I took during my three-week vacation in Rome, Sorrento and Verona—several coincidences happened. First, the Angel of Brescia—that gorgeous athletic guy with the amazing thighs whom I sat next to on the plane from Naples to Verona. He pointed out an article in the in-flight magazine about a landmark Langobard art and artifacts exhibit in his hometown of Brescia, where I first read the story of Authari and Teodolinda.

Little over a year earlier, just days before my fortieth birthday vacation in Venice, while in a Los Angeles public library, I had searched in the stacks for ideas on the region. I ended up pulling out *The History of the Langobards* by Paolo Diacono, or Paul the Deacon. I read a few paragraphs and decided to check out the book. Paolo Diacono was a contemporary of the Langobards; born to their noble line, their trusted chronicler. He later retired as a monk and lived out the end of his life in a Benedictine abbey in Monte Cassino, near Benevento only, fifty miles from Calitri.

As I read his book that evening in bed, I was transfixed by the Langobards ancient history and influence: barbarians sacking then ruling Milan, Brescia, and Verona in Northern Italy; then Benevento, Salerno, and Sorrento in Southern Italy. And by the strange tingling feelings I was getting. Something about what I was reading rang very true, like I knew the story and the people in it. It was tangible.

The first time I was called a princess was quite innocent of any portent. I digested it within the context of the moment and the current events of my life and just as quickly forgot about it. As I had once heard, it was important to consider the source. The source this first time was an older hippie chick girlfriend. We were life-drawing classmates at Southampton College on the east end of Long Island.

I was suffering through the first of many breakups with a certain boyfriend, who was a master surfer, and a bit of a rake. And as we sat together in the dark Chinese restaurant where we both waitressed off season, the hippie chick nonchalantly said, "Well, sure you are confused. You have a very complicated connection with him. You share a past life."

"Oh?" I knew I was sensitive to ghosts, but this was different.

"He was a warrior and you were the king's daughter. A princess. You were lovers. Though I'm afraid to say, fatally."

"Wait. What?"

Ridiculous as it seemed at the time—a princess and a warrior!—I so wanted to wallow in this prophecy for as long as I could. I never felt like a princess before. It made me feel better. Like a Neil Young parable. And of course, in my willing innocence, I allowed his philandering for a few more semesters to come.

Seven years later, this boyfriend tracked me down through mutual friends and initiated a call. I was cautious but curious. Yet made the unwise decision of taking his bait. After several months of phone dating and a few visits back and forth came his proposal for marriage. Oh! The awful bumbling proposal! And I agreed to follow him. I left my job as a temp at Scribner's in New York under the baleful warning of the senior editor I typed for, "You're going where?" Texas. "Are you sure? Who is this guy?" Funny, or maybe not, I never heard anything from my father. He wordlessly handed me a twenty on the day I was leaving and left it at that.

With the repurposed engagement ring, our rekindled relationship quickly tumbled downhill. Was he just trying to be honest? One day I ran into the only new friend I had, his brother's girlfriend. After shopping together at the new Whole Foods market, she and her friend offered me a car ride back to our apartment. Her friend just happened to be a new-age chakra therapist and crystal healer back when those types weren't so ubiquitously spread like humus on a hillside. Upon hearing and sensing my emotional turmoil—living with him away from friends and family, having left my roots in New York for godforsaken Houston—she said in the car, "It makes perfect sense to hear you're unhappy. You two shared a complicated past life."

I turned my head—

"In an ancient time he was a warrior and you were a princess."

—and immediately went blank. She had left out "fatally." But still, it felt like I was shot through the heart by an archer. Then I admitted that it was the second time I had heard this past life story, and now, well, I didn't know, seemed I should be a little concerned about it. She calmly told me that all I needed to do was listen and act from the heart. Pause. And, "That if you are really that unhappy you should get the hell out of there."

Well, now that made sense.

Within a week I was gone. But for a long time, my still very splintered open heart felt it was a spectacular defeat.

Over the years I came to reconcile that the princess and the warrior was a pretty cool fable, even if I wasn't quite convinced of its truth, or maybe it was just truth for that ex-boyfriend and me. With time it was eventually stored away in the corners of my fractured, happily-ever-after love life.

Some years later, I was sitting in the office of a Korean doctor of internal medicine, practicing acupuncturist and Buddhist priest in Los Angeles, after treatment. His office assistant teased me about a particular male patient that had walked in. Being two women in our late thirties brimming with confident sexuality, we had been joking with one another about finding a new lover, maybe even a good life mate. This male patient innocently walked in and she took the opportunity to ask me, "Do you think he is attractive?" In other words, "Would you do him?"

I casually glanced over to survey his mild countenance and meek frame and faked a grimace. She concurred.

At the same moment, the doctor entered the room and overheard us. After the patient was out of earshot he said something in Korean, for he knew no English. His assistant translated. "'Of course you don't find him virile. He was a geisha in a previous life.'"

And just like that, he had laid out this man's effeminate past and subsequently his inability to attract me as his lover. Fascinated, I asked the assistant to convey the following question,

"What was I in a past life?"

Without missing a beat, he replied, "You are the daughter of royalty."

A princess. Present tense.

Okay, now I was listening. And for the first time I wanted to be filled in on the details, but the doctor would not comply.

No, the details were not to be freely handed out like sweets from a grandfather. I had to do the soul work myself. I had to continue on just as I had in my otherwise contemporary non-royal skin in this current life and see what unfolded.

The following year I would turn forty. I had decided to treat myself to a second trip to Italy. I researched and planned a solo vacation that would somehow not be too depressing. Just enough adventure and relaxation so as not to feel like a new forty-year-old on the make in Italy on her birthday. Rather than tour Tuscany as I had a few years ago, I decided on one city for my entire birthday retreat—Venice.

Yes. I had decided to spend ten days celebrating a milestone birthday in *la Serenissima*—a city of sensual excesses and the ardent carnal pleasures of Casanova and Carnivale. With most of my friends as well wishers—my mother and father sulked that I wouldn't spend my fortieth with them—I was off. Discovering Calitri was more than a year away, a still unconscious dream.

I arrived in Venice by public boat from the airport, as most do. The Alilaguna pilot deftly cruised past the empty *Zitelle* stop as no one was there to get on, and no one got off. I had come as a young maiden alone with a couple of Holgas and my OM1. Before long, I found myself sitting in front of the Madonna Nicopeia di San Marco where she has held court in the left transept capella of the Basilica since the early thirteenth century. It was March 25th, the Feast of the Annunciation, and my birthday. I had wandered in through the nobles' north entrance, with a couple of hours to spare before braving dinner alone. Saturday night. Six o'clock Mass. The Basilica was full to capacity with the devout, honoring the Virgin on the day that beholds all the mysteries of Christianity.

At that moment what I longed for was simple. A new lover,

a companion to celebrate this birthday's evening with me. Hands clasped in prayers for deliverance, did I think the Mother of God could help me?

A Byzantine relic from the first century, angels, saints and prophets, martyrs, apostles, and bishops, surrounded her gold-and-jewel embellished frame. The Madonna Nicopeia was hailed as an indomitable Empress, Princess of Venezia. Byzantine soldiers held the Virgin icon aloft like Nike on the front lines of every crusade battle. In her presence they knew miraculous episodes abounded.

So, there I was, meditating for some carnal desire in front of Venezia's Virgin on the holiest day of the liturgical calendar. My mother always reminded me of the significance of this day whenever I blew out the candles. Nevertheless, I might have been on to something. In just a few hours I would meet a handsome young lover who would accompany me for the rest of the weekend. Immediately, incredibly, fulfilling my wish—powerful stuff those Byzantine icons—or was it me?

These thoughts of the princess and the warrior came back to me as Giuseppe and I drove down the switchback road leading out of the town, with the castle above us and the twinkling lights of the hillside trailing down. I asked him, in the best Italian I could come up with, "Do you believe in previous lives?"

He probably just nodded out of kindness or to keep me going. I continued with the King and Queen, and how Benevento and the area surrounding Calitri and the castle up top of her hill was in their charge some centuries ago, and that I believed I may have been their granddaughter. A princess. And that maybe he had once been my prince.

Giuseppe slowly, silently, navigated the switchbacks. I could feel the heat of his tanned chest under his dark linen shirt. I leaned into him then, and kissed him, and said, "Past life or not. You are my prince." He liked that a lot. He pulled over along the side of the road and kissed me very hard.

Sense & Sensibility in the Old Village

"*Fegato*, for a strong heart," he said, "for breakfast in winter." Sautéed with red onions and olive oil with warm fresh ricotta or pecorino from the herd, on thick, fresh slices of home-baked bread, all washed down with vino nero, before heading out to the fields. At 5:30 in the morning, under cover of darkness, the work begins in the great fields surrounding Macchiursi. There is a marked difference between the men and women who work the fields with those who haven't. It's in the composition of their bodies and the confidence in their stride. A quiet reserve of how backbreaking the work is can be read on their faces. Their hearts seem light. Their lives, though hard, are mostly wholly content.

From September to November the earth is turned and prepared for seed. *Fieno, avena*, and *grano* that will sprout bright green in late February or early March. It is honest and exhausting work. Machine-turned in teams of two or three. One man drives the tractor while another walks behind to collect the stones as the field releases them. Ranging in size from softballs to prize-winning pumpkins, they are hand tossed into a waiting camion, then piled into large cairns near the roadside or dumped into a local ravine. And so they are returned to the earth to appear some millennia in the future in some other farmer's field.

"Why don't you build stone walls?" I asked Giuseppe once, knowing those crisscrossing the northeastern American landscape or in the Lessinia hills above Verona.

"*Chi ha tempo non aspetti tempo.*"

And, when he saw that I didn't quite understand, he simplified it. "*I nostri nonni hanno fatto prima di noi.*" Like our grandparents.

There is a certain beauty of a lone pear tree or cherry tree far out in a freshly turned volcanic black field, its narrow base piled high with stones from the earth. A kind of beacon on the horizon, a cairn of a larger sort. And a sweet reward for those who halt work under it. October follows with the vendemmia and in November the olive harvest. And so the circle and customs continue.

The evening of the *lucciole* and every evening on this road before then, seemed a metaphor for my deliverance to this place of wildness in my soul. L'Americana, the Girl Scout in me, the intrepid single adventurer who usually led yet longed to follow in the wake of the masculine king of his world—the Handsome Man from Macchiursi. To ride shotgun through those narrow passes of road, feeling every exhilarating breath in his car, on a path, in the forest, along the lake, anywhere that was him. I would follow him anywhere.

His masculine, king-of-the-wood stance allowed me to follow. *La principessa.* My city woman to his wild man. Aching in and blessedly not acting out within our September-May romance. His deep-country, back-road conservatism reared by Irpinia wildwood parents. Their ranch far out north away from town, under command of a volcanic shadow—these things—kept him slightly in check, but not enough to let go of me. My metropolitan Long Island upbringing—autonomous art school maverick, antiparental guardianship self—kept the flame lit, the fire stoked. Alluring and game, by now it kept the villagers second guessing with—"Why don't you live with your parents?" Or finally, that we should give it up and shut them up, and "Get *married* already."

We could not think of parting.

We could be picking cherries in late May. Their innocent nubile branches snapped in two with a crack, as we enjoyed the fresh hot-pink fruit littering our seats with leaves and twigs just before he took me against the car, with the town aglow on the sunny hillside in front of me. Or savor a slow drive along the road encircling the ancient volcanic crater of Mount Vulture after a rain to watch the moon rise, as he slowly pined me, lifted my skirt, then took me against a stone wall. On the far side of the lake was the white castle-like monastery with its thousand-year-old chapel to San Michele the Archangel—Slayer of Dragons—protecting us with his sword held aloft.

We could be on a Sunday post-pranzo drive along a verdant green, thunderclap-soaked back road and discover a lone hamlet with wisps of wood smoke nestled against a rocky hill, where a shepherd family lived among their grazing flock. We sat in his car beside their wild, idyllic glen dwarfed beneath muscular Michelangelo cloud cover. And the look on Giuseppe's face was of complete acceptance and contentment for the romance of this kind of life. A look not of longing, but belonging and knowing, to be in that house, us living that life. Yet it seemed not very far from his own life—was his life—Joseph and the lambs of god.

I looked over my shoulder to see three handsome black goats

chained to the fence at the roadside eating wildflowers, their bells tinkling, handmade witch charms colorfully dangling from around their necks. He nodded, indulging me, as I set my OM1. Their big soulful eyes eyeing my interruption, sensuously inviting me, knowing this was not who I was but what I naïvely wanted, where I thought I belonged with the Handsome Man from Macchiursi.

And finally one evening in June, as we drove along my favorite back road, graced now with wild delicately flowering quince, we rounded a bend to what seemed to be the darkest part of the road, where you felt you were in a tunnel of hayfields, with concave walls of earth and grasses looming on either side and a dome of clear evening sky above. With no moon in sight, the air warm with the aroma of mature hay smooth as honey, he cut the headlamps. A hundred million lucciole swarmed the hill, the road, the windshield of the car. So many fireflies an audible gasp was released from my soul as they vanquished the stars from the night.

A well-known mystical force of nature in these parts, just before the wheat harvest, when the grain is at its peak maturity, fireflies gather in clouds, floating around the tops of the stalks, or spighe. Fields and fields of golden grain are lit up with tiny beams at dusk or in early evening when the fireflies swarm out to mate. It is a spectacular and mystical sight to behold. Poems have been written about it. Writers wax nostalgic about the near disappearance of this most revered childhood memory, and with it the loss of innocence in rural Italy. Lucciole, as they are known in Italian, is a double entendre; it also means streetwalker in Italian slang.

Little stars of the night.

༺༻

It was my second time in town to attend the September Festas, and our anniversary. The Handsome Man from Macchiursi and I were celebrating those first months of our virgin affair just two years earlier that same week. I had come again for one of my month-long trips, not only to see Giuseppe, I had not seen my relatives in a year and a half.

On the eve of the Festa for the Madonna, we took a warm, still-light evening stroll in the old village just after the town's procession for San Vito.

We walked down the Thursday market street toward the Chiesa della Immacolata where in just a few hours the feast would be celebrated. Strolling together in time honored, man-woman accompaniment, Giuseppe led me away from the crowd. Man leading his woman: proud, strong, in control, in charge. Shades here of the Prince of Salina. We walked not too slowly. Giuseppe was a strapping country guy with long, impatient legs, he naturally liked to get where he needed to go.

Taking just a half step behind me yet somehow steering us along, we sallied down a wide, graded street toward the big yellow church on the windswept precipice, crossed the plaza in front of it, then continued into the lower maze of the town. I had no idea where I was.

The Handsome Man from Macchiursi seemed to like that idea. But soon I remembered I had once been on this particular stretch of the lane. I remembered that along this white wall outside one of these doors was where I had greeted a very elderly couple one summer a few years ago, sitting together for some afternoon sun and fresh air. I had asked them to point me the way to zia Concetta's. Did they know who I meant?

"*Certo! Siamo pure parenti,*" they had replied.

"Follow that woman there, just now carrying her two sacks down the street. Continue straight past the tabaccheria and you will find her on the right."

I took a photo of the woman as she descended the long stone steps, thanked the couple then hurried to catch up with her, offering her a hand. She refused of course, politely pointing me again on my way.

That day, I found zia Concetta's door open with a small rush chair out front on the street. She must have just stepped inside. It was well after lunch, yet the sun was still high in the sky. I walked up to her half open door and called in.

"*Permesso?*" I ventured.

"*O' oh?*" came her soft, assertive voice.

"*Ciao zia*, it's me. I came to find you to visit. And I brought you these fresh plums."

"*Che bella.* You have come to see me? *Entra figliola mia*, and what nice fruit you brought."

She gave me the double cheek kiss so softly as to almost not register; her skin transparent peach, a painterly contrast to her all-black wool widow's dress, even in summer.

I have learned that visiting elder women in this small town is something like a religious commission. It is deeply part of their community life. A reverence paid in this simple way is never forgotten.

Concetta ushered me into her small kitchen then, to her bedroom, and soon out onto the balcony. The full tour. This may have been the first time I was fully in her house, the first time I went alone to the Centro Storico with intentions of strolling into the lower town to find her. It was a moment, a visit that would change everything I thought about her and the old village, everything I knew up to that moment about my grandmother and my life.

It was mid-afternoon in summer. At that hour the balcony was cooled by shadow, a contrast to her front door on the street bathed in strong sunlight. We sat for a while as she reminisced in dialect about the poverty this region had witnessed and its lasting hardships on the families who lived here. We gazed over the balcony toward the circle of land in front of us and the Apennines beyond it, as she talked of her husband Pasquale and their life when they were a young family.

With a baby strapped to her back she would pack out with a good lunch—cooked on a wood fire—to meet him working in their fields, then stayed the afternoon to give a hand. She would then walk back to the village, always ahead of him, to tend to the house, carry water from the fountain nearby, and prepare the evening meal. Season after season; year in, year out. Three children, Pasquale and zia Concetta all living in this small, two-room stone house. The house where Angela Maria was born.

Now Giuseppe directed us down this staired lane that sparked this memory and suddenly I realized I knew where we were.

"Let's go visit zia Concetta," I chirped.

"Do you remember the way?" He didn't so much ask as command.

I faltered for a minute. Still two steps behind, he ushered us by sheer masculine force down the long steps of the narrow street, towered in on both sides with multi-leveled stone houses in various stages of abandonment and disarray, until we emerged onto the wider via Fontana. Though I didn't know it was called that at the time.

We arrived at zia Concetta's door. I saw a light shining from within in the now-near dusk light. I was happy to visit, not alone as always, but with the Handsome Man from Macchiursi accompanying me. Great importance, this—in Southern Italy, to Southern Italians—great tradition, this. Man accompanies woman. He must, to lend respect to her and the family, legitimizing her. It was the first admission from Giuseppe, the first time he would even allow us to be recognized as a couple in the presence of one of my parenti. And not just anyone, zia Concetta.

She welcomed us in with soft peals of delighted approval, clearly pleased to see me and the big guy together. Giuseppe's respect for the elder status of zia Concetta and the traditions of the village showed through. And zia Concetta, who may well have known of our courtship, nonetheless never made direct inquiry. We sat for a while in her small white kitchen. She happily chatted in Calitri dialect. Giuseppe nodding, occasionally asking me if I understood, in his—in contrast to Concetta's soft soprano—ten-octaves-below-sea-level voice. She offered us some glasses of cold Coca Cola. We drank them quietly. Giuseppe's rancher's hands delicately encircling the etched glass with his pinky finger held aloft higher than mine.

We soon said goodbye and silently moved on down the lane toward a house of one of his relatives. Now two village elders would have an opportunity to chat across the lane about hosting the reserved, traditional, local Country Joe and his American girlfriend. I enjoyed the role of ingénue to his court-manly command, in his historic childhood surroundings.

The Handsome Man from Macchiursi then led me out again through the alleys up into the higher levels of the Centro Storico. We strolled along dark cobblestone vie and vicoli with streetlamps darkly unlit as he began a lusty caressing, groping, and kissing. I half expected him to throw me against some abandoned patrician palazzo's noble wooden entryway—worm-eaten yet still majestic—and have his way with me. I squealed and squirmed and gently reproached him for acting the schoolboy, and he laughed in delight. He pinned me then and we embraced. His heat and desire devouring mine. We continued on in the dark, his strong arms commanding my now-love-weakened body forward and ever upward toward the main piazza and the crowded street above, as we silently re-entered the modern life of the town, the Festa, and the passeggiata of the evening.

Just a few days later zia Concetta would be gone.

Questa la Vita
(That's Life)

An altogether different feeling from the vibrant open life of the fields are the dense somber tones when there is a funeral in town. Church bells peal down the stone walls of the village in waves, marking the beginning of the service and then again when the dead leave the church.

So it was for the first funeral I attended in town, which was not only a shock but a pivotal event in my Calitri life.

"Angela." Zia Dorina called my name urgently the moment I stepped into the hall from the street. It was early afternoon. I was coming in from across town and this news was so important to deliver to me that she didn't wait till I reached her door. "*Zia*

Concetta, è morta."

"Zia Concetta?"

I stopped on the stairs. I knew what I heard. But it took a moment to sink in.

"When?"

"*Stamattina.*" Just this morning.

After a moment I finished the climb to her door and stepped inside. She was already making us caffè.

"How did this happen?" I asked. "I just saw her the other day!" I wasn't aware something was wrong.

"And zia Maria?"

I was told she will arrive this afternoon with the hearse.

Apparently zia Concetta had been admitted to a hospital in Naples the day before for a routine procedure and didn't make it through. I was overcome.

Just then my phone rang. It was Giuseppe.

"Dove sei?"

He was glad I wasn't alone, though disappointed that he hadn't reached me in time to give me the news himself. He too was upset to hear zia Concetta had died so soon after our historic visit together.

Zia Dorina then gave me all the particulars about protocol and procedure.

The paying of one's respects, *le condoglianze*, is a deeply felt and tightly reciprocated compulsion in small-town Southern Italy. There would be a lutto this afternoon held in zia Maria's house. Then the Mass at San Canio and then the cemetery. Southern Italians hold their funerals immediately, giving one little time to collect one's feelings, it seemed to me. And they hold them in their own homes, the only homes most of them have ever known. No public funeral parlors here. Old-world Italians leave their houses apparently only upon death.

Dorina waited for me to express what I wanted to do.

"I want to go to the house to pay my respects."

We went over together to sit with the extended family and friends to wait. Dorina explained who I was to the few who didn't know me. After about an hour a grief-stricken zia Maria arrived with her son. She gasped just as she turned into her living room and saw me there. I rose to greet her.

"Angela." And then she broke down in tears.

The attendants were assembled outside their front door where a crowd of people were waiting out in the street. As the hearse slowly began moving away from the house, the mourners gathered, filling in behind. We were headed first to the Duomo of San Canio. About half way there a soft rain began to fall.

After the Mass the cortège again slowly walked behind the hearse to the cemetery on the opposite side of town. Amid the shuffling of shoes I heard zia Dorina defend me, my choice of dress.

"Tutto colorato," someone had said.

I was walking my first and very somber funeral cortège in the town to accompany zia Concetta on her final journey, and they cared what I was wearing? Or was it Dorina's comment?

Everyone was a shapeless, shifting mass of deep gray or black— the thousand or so townsmen and women who came to the chapel in the cemetery to pay homage to zia Concetta. I hadn't thought to pack funeral clothes. Nonetheless I thought I was appropriately dressed in a navy blue dress and Burberry-style raincoat. *Dolcissimo civitas?*

Then, as we finally reached and entered the cemetery chapel, I felt suddenly pulled into the receiving line by zia Angelina. The softly singing, carefree country zia, with her retired *fabro* husband and their meager, meager pension, pulled me next to her into the bereavement line that began slowly enough with the first few but then continued for more than two hours. Those thousand or so townsmen and women, some of whom recognized L'Americana, nodded their condolences, just as their faces betrayed ever so slightly their surprise at seeing me standing there—Angelina proudly showing me off beside her. It was exhausting. Raining outside and hot and humid inside, with hundreds of people in the queue. I stood embarrassed, reserved, apologetic. But I could not extract myself from the line. Even zia Dorina had moved on home without me.

Later, after a long and well-deserved rest, all that walking and collective mourning, Giuseppe called to go out for dinner and a movie. He picked me up at the Paolantonio palazzo as always, zia Dorina incredulous that I would go out the evening of Concetta's funeral.

"*Dove vai?*" She attempted to impose her influence."*Sei in lutto.*"

Giuseppe was not easily convinced. "*Lutto? Eh, moh. Questa è la vita.*" That's life.

I wasn't so sure where I stood.

We drove around the Corso once or twice as I filled him in on the day. I was in a kind of cultural overload from my first funeral in a very long time, in a still fairly foreign place and of someone I held very dear. The ghost of zia Concetta felt near. Our first meeting. Our lunches in winter in the Centro Storico. Our recent visit together. After a year-and-a-half absence, I had felt connected again, and now again lost. These trips back and forth were now wearing me down; the long-ago loss of the house on via Sant'Antuono a buried dream; not feeling grounded in the town.

It became pretty clear to me then that I wanted to look for a house in the old village. I wanted to try again to buy a place of my own in Calitri.

"Will you help me?" I asked Giuseppe. "Find me a house in the old village to buy?"

"*Io?*"

"Could you? You know the village so well. And everyone knows and trusts you."

I thought of our romantic anniversary walk through the Centro Storico, paying a visit to his relatives along with zia Concetta. Giuseppe grew up in those old alleys too, he told me. He walked to his grandparents' for lunch after school and commanded the narrow stone streets with cousins and friends.

But he was noncommittal. We went out to dinner and a movie then he drove me home without much more discussion. The rest of the month did not feel the same between us. It was the second time that I had reason to second guess his affections.

One afternoon I took a walk alone into the Centro Storico to find zia Concetta's house. I entered from the Church of the Immacolata on the eastern precipice, the same route that Giuseppe and I had taken just days before Concetta died. Coming upon her door on via Fontana, I saw that the simple white-washed walls all around it were virtually covered with funeral posters. I was new to these public death announcements around the town. Apart that it was the first time I had someone in the village close to me die, these posters are a very Italian, a very Southern Italian, ritual. Printed in bold black and white they are always present outside the bereaved families homes where the viewings still take place, and posted in strategic places around the walls of the town, announcing for all to read the latest to fall.

Their design is perfunctory. Naming the departed, the family and extended family, the day they died, and the day of the funeral. And they seem to spring up within a few hours of the death. Then there are the printed condolences from friends, neighbors, co-workers, again in black and white, showing support for the family, son or daughter of the dead; a half dozen different condolences could be pasted up for one funeral.

On the facade of her house on via Fontana, I read again and again, in big black, cursive letters, Zia Concetta. Just zia Concetta. And I realized at that moment it was all that was needed. She was a revered epochal matriarch of the village. Pre-earthquake. When everyone in the village was from the Old Village. A well-respected elder. A universal zia. All the women of a certain age here are called zia. It is an endearment and a very old world salutation. Living in a warren of close alleys and narrow streets, everyone is a relative. Everyone knows you, takes care of you.

I stood on the small grade right in front of her door and said a silent goodbye. It seemed like an end of a brief era for me. The end of a connection, the direct link to my grandmother Angela Maria and the house of V.C. 1900. What would happen here now in 21 via Fontana? Would I have reason to return?

I took a few photos of the front door and walls, and turned to go. As I walked up to the dry goods store at the top of the grade, I met a neighbor on the street. She recognized me as zia Concetta's nipote, L'Americana. We exchanged brief greetings and sorrows over her loss—*questa è la vita*—and I moved on down via Concezione toward the Immacolata and further out along the long market road toward the newer town.

At the end of the month, when Giuseppe and I drove again to the airport, he seemed distracted, displeased. He started to express some reasoning that the relationship wasn't working for him.

"*Tu la, io qua.*"

Was he telling me now we lived too far apart?

"Geographically undesirable?" At this late stage? "And after all the good that had happened between us?"

Sure, I often felt guilty about always having to say goodbye, how it seemed a role reversal of sorts. He was an important part of my journey here, a catalyst for so many of my discoveries. Yet he had to know he was not the reason I first came to Calitri, nor the only reason I kept returning. And what of his two recent trips to see me?

It hit me all a little too hard. I had had enough emotion for one vacation. Were these visits just vacations? I knew they were much more than this. When I finally boarded the plane I just let it all go.

I cried all the way home.

When I arrived back in Los Angeles I was exhausted. My phone didn't ring. And I did not call him. We used to have standing Saturday calls, during which, far away in Los Angeles, I would follow the Handsome Man from Macchiursi's whereabouts in the season or about the town. When we talked it would be late evening his time, morning my time, so he would begin our conversations by asking me where I was and then recount his day. In Calitri's late autumn his calls would find him sitting on a heavy sack of olives waiting in the queue for them to be pressed; one of about twenty quintals from their grove, the sound of the massive millstone heard in the background. Later in winter from his car on the rocky road to Macchiursi home to dinner, he cursed the weak line and my carefree driving life on smooth Los Angeles asphalt to his windswept barren country road now barely passable in the snow. Then spring would arrive and there were the one hundred sheep to sheer. From wind-blown piazzas, walking the Saturday Corso or standing in crowded bars, his calls always came in.

This past season it proved all too complicated. I was settling in back home, back at a freelance project, happy to be distracted by work.

Then my parents told me that after twenty years in Los Angeles, they were selling their Ventura County townhouse and preparing to move back east, to Florida. I wanted to buy it but my parents did not want to sell it to me.

Again, my attempt to buy a house had been foiled. For years, I had wanted to buy the Luciani house that I rented on Mulholland Drive—my father encouraging me. But the Lucianis were Southern Italian and never wanted to sell it. *"Chi si vende, scende."* An Italian colloquialism, meaning "He who sells, falls," or fails.

In the summer of 2005 I tried to buy a bit of land outside Los Angeles as an investment, build some equity. I got all the way up to faxing back the signed documents with funds in the bank when the contract inexplicably fell through. Incredulous, I had wanted to secure the purchase before I headed out of the country. The real estate agent offered to show me other properties. But with an upcoming trip to Calitri, it would have to wait. Turned out, not more than a week or so later, she called with the news that the land had burned, been wiped out in a severe brush fire—a classic Los Angeles desert brush fire. It seemed Biblical. Seemed someone was looking out for me and my investments—my dreams—after all.

Then there was 49 Sant'Antuono.

I remembered the day when zia Concetta counseled me, impatiently, after the loss of that house; recounting the sad story of her sister-in-law Angela Maria's last visit to Calitri in the summer of 1935; losing her youngest child Mussolini there in infancy; having to leave him behind in Calitri, before returning to the U.S. with her husband and four remaining children, including my father, three years old at the time. So, 49 via Sant'Antuono was never a family house to buy.

I had always had good housing karma. But these last few attempts seemed to prove illusive, difficult for me to apprehend. I was ready. I wanted to buy a house to secure my future to put down some roots. Yet I was getting snuffed out or refused or not making it in time. As much as I could, I had let all those disappointments go at the time, having no idea what was in store—what, if anything, would replace the loss of these goals.

I had felt grounded again and now once again, uprooted. Something out of the ordinary for me. After my parents moved later that fall, I received a phone call from Giuseppe.

Seemed he had some news to give me about a house in the Centro Storico. He told me to call Adolfo and his father.

"I don't understand, why Adolfo?" I was thrilled he was involved but confused too.

"Loro sapranno, chiamali." He will know.

Within a few minutes I had emailed Adolfo.

"Giuseppe tells me you and your dad can help me find a house in the Centro?" I wrote.

The next day Adolfo's response came in with the news that zia Concetta's house was available and that they would offer it to me first. Italians don't sell houses within the family, that much I knew.

"What about zia Maria? Doesn't she want the house?" After all, it was the house where she was born and raised.

"No, the house is for sale."

"Well, then yes. Of course, I want the house."

It took just a few moments to sink in. Then it hit me—I wasn't about to buy just zia Concetta's house, but the house of my long-lost grandmother; the house where my grandmother was born; with the beautiful view, those chestnut wood doors; kept in the family for generations.

V.C. 1900.

I could hardly believe it.

Zia Concetta. In hindsight, it was almost as if she were making room for me, that her death was the catalyst I needed to end up buying my grandmother's house.

Or was it a gift?

I emailed my brother. Then I called Giuseppe to tell him that I had said yes to the house. Giuseppe seemed pleased though a little hesitant, content in his stoic style. I realized then, that without his alerting me to Adolfo and his father's new vocation of listing vacant houses for sale in the Centro Storico, I might never have made it in time. There was a sustainable tourism project underway in the town, with a rogue real estate team from Rome, sweeping up vacant houses to sell to Northern Europeans in the old village. Zia Concetta's house could easily have been swept up too.

In late spring of 2006 I flew back to Calitri with most of the money to buy my grandmother's house at 21 via Fontana.

Fatta Bene
(Well Done)

~

I woke this morning to the sound of silence.

A summer kind of silence where you know that soon enough there'll be something that will enter and break it. Maybe a rooster or two calling back and forth to each other, or a train whistle in the valley below. And then I heard in the sound distance what I thought were a group of voices. Women's voices. Singing. A sort of mantra really. A Catholic mantra, steady and strong.

I got out of bed and went to the balcony doors, opened them, and stepped outside. Glorious bright mountain daylight flooded the hillside. Directly across in the near distance I spied a long line of people walking along the road that led out to the little church of Santa Lucia. They were led by the priest and his men in blue capes, the Confraternity of Brothers for the Madonna, and they were walking slowly toward the village. I wondered what day it was and why they were out there so early this morning. It took me a moment. Then I remembered it was Thursday. But what Thursday?

I had arrived just a day or so ago and hadn't really tuned into the goings-on in the town. The Handsome Man from Macchiursi would know but he left my bed about an hour before sunrise heading home to his morning work far out on the family ranch. So I turned inside and went to look at a calendar, one of those Italian calendars that lists all the saints' days of the year. Even the vague or obscure ones like San Valeriano or San Giocondo or Ubaldo? Were there really people, saints with those names? And what could they have done to be so canonized? Then, lo and behold, it said in bold—*Ascensione di Nostro Signore*. Jesus. I mean *Jesus*. The Calvario. Not that I knew what it meant. It was just that it meant the people were coming not from Santa Lucia but from the Calvary church at the top of the hill. And they meant business.

I went back out to the balcony, thinking, When was the last time I awoke to the sound of parishioners with men in blue capes singing, processioning along a hill across from my view?

Well, never. I watched them for a bit longer, following the drifting cadence of the women's voices from below to see where they were headed. They continued down the long and gently sloping road, rounded the curve at the gray neglected church of San Bernadino, then reappeared below the bridge near the church of Sant' Antonio. There they paused just before disappearing again into one of the crevices that opened from via Ferrovia into the vias and vicolos above. I realized then, that in not too long they would climb up the triple-arched street of the gypsies, wind around a few tight twists and turns, under another two smaller arches, and walk right by my door.

Not by my door as in out on the street and across from my door.

I mean by my door as in within an inch of it. My new house fronted a very narrow passage of via Fontana. The whole procession of pole bearers and crest carriers, priest and his retinue, dozens of men in blue capes of the brotherhood, and then the little ladies of the lane chanting their Catholic mantras as they atoned for one of the high holy days of the liturgical calendar, would nearly invade my kitchen as they walk by.

I quickly threw on some clothes, grabbed my camera and set it, then unlocked and opened my double wood doors. There was no one else in the street. But by then the chanting was very close, echoing off the narrow stone walls. I stood in the quiet lane watching, thinking that any minute they would round the corner, but the procession was still hidden from my view. I popped back into my kitchen one step down from street level, focused, and waited, OM1 in hand.

The plaintive wail of the lead male's voice came from around the bend. The women's voices answering his incantations were softer, slightly further off. Then the pole-bearers suddenly appeared. Their breathless commands and heavy steps raised and lowered the towering staff that bore the church's standard. Controlling it with fore and aft ropes they guided it around a tight curve, swooping under then free of the low support arch to the right of my door.

I was glued. But they were right there. Beefy young guys in pale blue capes in control of their charge—the standard for Jesus. Through my viewfinder their action then momentarily stopped. Shuffling and chanting came closer. Women's voices. Then the priest in white vestments slowly came into view, his head bowed, crucifix in hand, murmuring prayers. The congregants repetitiously answering. He did not pause in front of my door but just beyond it. Someone set out a simple wood table covered with a brilliant white, exquisitely embroidered cloth. It stood alone in the street. The priest and his entourage took rest at the table, their vestments resplendent against the dirty gray concrete and stone.

Then the pole bearer shouted a command, the plaintive wail took up again, and they were slowly on the move.

I stood where I was and shot frame after frame. Men of various sizes and ages in blue capes were framed by the chestnut wood doors of my home on via Fontana. Oh! There was zio Angelo. He turned to look in my door the moment I pressed the shutter.

I kept shooting till all the men in blue capes filed past and the ladies in black began to bring up the rear. I stepped up on my stone threshold as the chanting dirges continued down the street to my left. One by one, the little ladies of the lane from in and around my street quickly grabbed me or snapped at my leg as they slowly filed by. Nodding and snapping, some giving me that look like, Where were you this morning? I smiled the maybe-next time smile. And they smiled back. No wonder the street was so quiet, so empty before. They were all in attendance up at the Calvary for the Mass, and now in this processional line.

The procession slowly continued on down via Fontana toward the Church of the Immacolata, their singing fading into the distance. I stood alone in my doorway watching until they were around some other bend and out of sight. And I realized then that I was now the keeper of the flame, the new bearer of the torch here in this doorway on via Fontana. That zia Concetta, her daughter Maria, my grandmother, and her mother on down the matriarchal line had stood in this doorway too, watching the procession walk by. That they'd had a box seat to these religious goings on, these processions in the streets of the old town going back years. And now so did I.

How many generations? I didn't exactly know. But I felt something shift in me. Why all the silence all these years? Look what they lost, could have had.

I closed my front door, made some coffee, then went back out to the balcony to sit with my cup. The air was still morning soft. The sky a Della Robbia blue. The only sound now was the occasional distant crowing of a couple of cocksure roosters. But via

Fontana was quiet again.

It was May 28, 2006. Ascension Thursday. The fortieth day of the Easter liturgical calendar. In Italy, in the months of May and June, in the few weeks just following Easter, there are a series of high holy Sundays on the Catholic liturgical calendar: the *Ascensione di Nostro Signore, Pentecoste*, and the season finale, *Corpus Domini*. And they would all march right by my door. A lapsed Catholic, I knew nothing of any of this until I got here, and it really didn't end there, as by June first the *Tredicina di Sant'Antonio* would begin.

⁂

The day I arrived in Calitri was a bit of confusion. Taking as it does at least twenty-four hours of travel door-to-door from Los Angeles, the first and only thing I wanted to do was sleep. Adolfo picked me up at the bus depot in Avellino on prearrangement. I was coming with the down payment for the house, so my Cicoira relatives took the initiative to host me this time. Most all of my other visits were spent almost exclusively with Paolantonio relatives. But this trip I suppose they knew they would have to acquiesce.

I hadn't spent much time with Adolfo's mother, zia Angelina, since the winter of 2003. She welcomed me in with a steaming plate of handmade raviolis smothered in homemade tomato sauce and then sent me to bed. It was early afternoon. I slept for hours. In the meantime, Adolfo was dispatched to inform the other relatives that I had arrived safely. I supposed Giuseppe was in on that too.

Later that evening we drove to zia Maria's for the keys to via Fontana. I would be in town at least a month as always and hadn't made any other sleeping arrangements. I had hoped I could spend my nights in the house. So I gingerly asked zia Maria if she would allow it. And she agreed. But not without vocalizing a certain concern for my well being. After all via Fontana was the deep Centro Storico. Far from everything, and nobody there knew who

I was. Who would look after me? Where would I eat lunch? Some of zia Concetta's old furniture was left for me to use, thankfully. It was a little like camping: how to use the bombola stove in the kitchen, no American shower, but I was in heaven. The original chestnut wood doors alone were enough to be proud of and to covet. I was now a card-carrying resident of the old village.

Still, I wondered, would I fit in?

The little ladies of the lane, the mostly widows in black who lived above, across, and adjacent to 21 via Fontana, soon began stopping by to say hello. They all recognized me of course as zia Concetta's niece, since I had visited so many times and even stayed in an old house on their street that freezing February three years ago. But now I was here to buy her house. Few of them knew this news in advance. When I explained, they would immediately begin their congratulations and formal salutations.

And soon the news spread.

"*Brava, cara.*"

"*Fatta bene.*" Well done.

"*Fatta bene, cara, brava.*" The half-dozen neighbors living of the lane and small *piazzetta* in front of my door—some were widows, some clearly not; some who lived further up or down via Fontana who all knew and revered zia Concetta in age-old matriarchal respect—came in, stopped by, or peered in my door, what was once zia's door, to welcome me and congratulate me and thank me. Most proclaimed individual allegiances or histories with their recently passed Concetta, or her daughter Maria, and some even with Angela Maria, my grandmother. Angela Maria was the eldest of the six siblings who grew up in this house, some one hundred years ago. By their tradition and rights she was the first heir to this property that I was now beginning to live in as L'Americana.

They all remembered the stories of my grandmother as *malata*, unwell. But they preferred the happier one of the second-generation namesake who had come back to the town again and again and was now finally here to buy the house, which would have been sold to stranieri, had I not been informed in time.

They brought gifts, they shared keys, they complimented me on my housekeeping abilities. I was the new keeper of a matriarchal lineage in this largely matriarchal society. I was as welcome and as normal as one of them, immediately. Maybe. Now all I had to do was marry.

Within a few days my new neighbor Michelina quickly made it known that she spied a certain someone's evening comings and goings. She shared her advice, stealthily, that it was the woman's prerogative, and that of her mother's, to not only lure him in, but control when and if marriage happened.

"Really?" I said to Michelina.

"Mom?" I said to myself.

Meaning I suppose, it was my responsibility to keep my reputation intact, and by proxy that of my extended Calitri family. So, out went my privacy. Again. And it seemed I was now opening myself up to a new standard of scrutiny.

Luckily, I felt some of us shared a common bond. As I recorded their names one by one to memory—*Lina, N'glina, Angelina;* it wasn't easy as they were mostly in dialect—I realized at least four of my new neighbors were also named Angela. Growing up, I was the only Angela for miles. No one in school shared my name, nor anyone in our tree-lined neighborhood. It was lonely back then. But it made me unique. Here, I soon learned there were six Angela's on this small stretch of via Fontana alone. I guess you could say I was drawn here. For someone who grew up entirely without reference for her own name, save the one never mentioned, it was transcendent.

꧁꧂

Zia Maria then invited me to my first Sunday lunch. It was quite a long walk from the old village to her apartment house on the other side of town, so zio Vincenzo was dispatched to pick me up at the top of via Fontana where it met via Concezione. Somebody said something about a "chix cross." I just filed that away to call up later. Vincenzo was waiting faithfully in front of the old dry goods store in his vintage *cinquecento* station wagon when I walked up. I loved vintage cars and had driven them in Los Angeles, but of course to him it wasn't vintage. It was just his car; his diminutive country workhorse of a car. I'd often seen him and zia Maria zipping around town and country in it like two high school sweethearts getting their daily chores done.

He leaned his heavy frame over to open the tinny, hollow door from the inside. I climbed in and immediately gushed about how I loved the car—sunken bucket seats, floorboards nearly non-existent, and all.

"It's nearly as old as I am!"

He reacted as always with a hunch of his shoulders and his throaty laugh.

"Who knows? It's a long time ago now. Could be 1960 or '61."

Zio Vincenzo was definitely one of my favorite uncles here in Calitri. He was a big guy with an easy sense of humor and made a really good red wine. He was a good ten years older than zia Maria. The median age in this town between husband and wife. When he was not out with the guys in front of the post office, he would be holding court in the kitchen while Maria prepared their meal, never getting in her way or challenging her on anything.

It being a Sunday, I knew we were in for a big meal. I had dined at their table full of family a number of times since my first visit to Calitri. Each time, of course, with zia Concetta in attendance. This would be the first Sunday pranzo for me that Maria's mother wouldn't be there. So I wondered how it would feel.

We drove across town along the main Corso as I had seen Maria and Vincenzo do so many times. It was the first time I was in the passenger seat instead of Maria, or for that matter zia Concetta.

Still the ingénue in these small town Southern Italian

circumstances, I glanced over to Vincenzo but his eyes were locked on the road. At this hour on any given Sunday, the main Corso was alive with *i passeggiatori*; mostly suited men walking and waiting for their wives and children to be released from the church. Zio Vincenzo was no doubt aware of the implications our drive might have on the discussions in the piazza. He kept his head straight. Later, once my goods arrived in the port and were driven down from Livorno, he came by to haul away zia Concetta's old things. He simply tied the kitchen table, the 1970s cristalliere, the old and incredibly comfortable sheep's wool-stuffed mattress, including headboard, to the top of the tiny Fiat or folded them inside and then drove them down via Fontana—the entire piazzetta looking on. Yet he never registered it.

I modulated my ebullience as I entered their house. Zia Maria was a bit more serious than zio Vincenzo. And suddenly I was a little nervous about the transaction of buying via Fontana. We did the double kiss with a hug as she asked me how it was going.

"*Come va le cose?* Do you need anything? Has anyone said hello from the neighborhood?" It would be a while before I located the two *forni* and the small grocery store in my new neighborhood of la Cascina.

I immediately recounted the morning of the procession.

"*Ma certo!*" she said in acknowledgment. "It was the *Ascensione di Signore*." Then looked at me as if to say, But where have you been? I went on to say that I first heard the women singing from the balcony and how, when I realized they would walk by my door, I made it in time to get plenty of great photos, which was met with a sort of soft grunt of half disapproval.

"One was of zio Angelo, zia Giuseppina's cousin," I said. "He walked right by the door in his blue cape!"

"*Beh, sì.*"

But then I didn't want to push it. I had probably already gone too far. It hadn't been that long since her mother was gone. And here I was describing a photo-op from her house like some tourist in Rome.

She turned back to the stove. The kitchen table was set for three. I guess we were few for lunch today.

Vincenzo took his place at the table, setting down a large bottle of chilled white wine. I sat down too. Waited a moment, then said, "I'm really happy to be in the house.

You have been very kind to let me stay this first time. The sun comes in bright and strong every morning. Roosters call to each other from the fields below the balcony, like husband and wife." I beamed at them. "I love the house, I do. It's compact and cozy and perfect for one, for me."

Vincenzo listened attentively then repeated, *"Come marito e moglie."*

He glanced at Maria with an easy laugh. But Maria remained quiet. Her back was to us as she stirred the sauce. Twenty-one via Fontana was the house that she grew up in with her brothers; one who was buried four years ago, the other several years ago now. Zia Concetta was buried just last year. Her father Pasquale was long gone. I was here.

I looked down.

Vincenzo then deadpanned, "If the house was ours, we wouldn't have sold it."

I turned to look at him, wondering what he meant.

A few days later, we sat in their kitchen again to discuss the first terms of my down payment with their tall and somewhat serious son, Franco Vincenzo the bank manager. They informed me then that the house was the property of a sister-in-law of zia Maria's who lived in South America, and that I was actually buying the house from her.

Rina and her children had been bequeathed Concetta's house upon her death. So all paperwork would pass from Italy to Venezuela and back again with zia Maria and Franco Vincenzo serving as proxies.

I recalled that Rina and I had met last September in this same kitchen just days before Concetta died. She was visiting from Venezuela and was particularly taken with me, and with my love affair with the Handsome Man from Macchiursi. She was very kind and humble and seemed to have been a classic beauty at one time. She gently encouraged me, even counseled me about my relationship with Giuseppe. I had confessed that I—we—may be out of our league. She assured me then that our age difference should not matter. What mattered was how we felt about one another and not what others felt about our union.

"And his mother?" I asked.

Well, Rina had her own experience to recount. How when she was engaged, zia Concetta, her mother-in-law to be, was not all too keen on her son marrying a forestiera. That is, a girl not from Calitri.

The day after discovering who really owned the house, I initiated the bank transfer of ten thousand dollars as the first half payment and we agreed I would pay the balance once a few major repairs were done to the outside wall of the house. Franco Vincenzo issued me a bank promissory note. And just like that, owning a house in Italy was no longer a dream. True, 21 via Fontana wasn't entirely mine yet. But it was in spirit. And that was enough for everyone for now.

❧

The Tredicina di Sant'Antonio took me quite by surprise one afternoon in early June. The otherwise calm and long-light-filled afternoons seemed to pass without notice in the Centro Storico as I thought nothing much happened in la Cascina other than Mass on Sunday at the Immacolata when the little ladies in black passed by and then returned, in twos and threes in front of my door.

Turned out not to be true. When the solemn and steady clanging began it filled the lower valley with a somber yet hopeful sound, something you might hear in a 1940s movie about orphan boys in winter.

One afternoon, I decided I had better walk down the hill to the little yellow church I had never been to and put a photographic prayer in for myself to Sant'Antonio. It was well past the pranzo riposo. The aestival light was turning down behind the hill. I picked up my camera, walked out my door and down the lane to the right, taking the route that Thursday's procession had come up from. By the time I was on via Faenzari, Saint Antonio's bells had begun.

The bell rope was pulled steadily in five-minute intervals for at least forty minutes. It was the call to vespers for Sant'Antonio and the elderly women of la Cascina filed into the small yellow church for the evening's devotional prayer. Saint Anthony is one of the most revered and powerful saints in all Catholicism. His saint day falls on June 13th. The tredicina then means the thirteen days from the first of June up to and including the saint's day. His prayers and novenas, at least the popular versions, often go something like this:

> *Saint Anthony come around*
> *Something's lost that must be found*
> *Please help us bring it round.*

The *tredicina* is an extended novena in the number thirteen. Thirteen days to appeal to Saint Anthony, the patron saint of lost things. And a remarkable way to begin living in this little paese on the hill, I thought. Thirteen is a lucky number in Italy.

At the church, I found old Peppino, simple and devout, anchored between the double green doors with rope in hand, pausing to wipe his brow. Devotional prayer cards to Saint Anthony were on a narrow wood table to his right. A small rush basket held a few coins. He was dressed in an unlikely dark wool suit and cap, with a white cotton handkerchief tied round his neck.

It was a warm afternoon, yet the chapel was cool and dark. I walked around inside as invisibly as possible, trying not to call attention to myself. I was still a novice. L'Americana alone in a remote hill town in Italy. With a camera no less. Some people knew me well. But many still did not, and this was not my neighborhood. All those other visits I was sheltered within the confines of relatives in modern apartments or escorted with younger cousins dutifully in tow. Now I was on my own, at least for now, in the Centro Storico.

The rhythmic tolling began again deeply echoing inside the church, reaching down through my bones. Peppino's even strokes drew the double-knotted rope down, then it seemed to spring up all on its own. His work reverberated around the stone walls of the wide street arch as tall as the church, just to its right. The arch of Sant'Antonio supported the curving road above, one of the earliest and main entrances to the old village. Old women and men a few at a time began to appear from the road. They gathered in twos and threes at the threshold before walking inside to take their seats on simple wood benches. Votive candles were burning. Flowers, lilies in vases, and several small pots of young sprouting grasses—wheat grasses—as offerings, all on the floor in front of the makeshift altar. Saint Anthony himself was in his brown robe holding a baby lamb in one arm and a fresh white lily in the other.

Things quickly settled down to business as the women took to prayer. There was a call and response to the novena in a cadence that was at once primitive and expected. I stayed for a few minutes longer sitting on a bench, absorbing their sound, and then, before it got too crowded, quietly backed out the door into the light. The following days were the same. The tolling of the bell in early evening for vespers, then a Mass where the women prayed the novena at 6 p.m.

Then it was Tuesday, June 13, and Sant'Antonio was upon us. It was fairly early. I was still in bed in a kind of half sleep, listening to the town's ethereal summer silence, realizing today was the day when—*BOOOM, rattle, BOOOOMM, rattle, BOOOOOMMM.*

The thin glass panes of my balcony doors clattered as if there were a regiment of Roman soldiers, three thousand strong, marching through the streets of the Centro. Or were they out on my balcony?

BOOOOOOMMMM.

Stunned, I looked at the clock. Seven a.m. I flashed back to my first Festa season for the Madonna in Calitri, three years ago. I was startled in bed just like that morning as I lay sleeping in nonna Migliorina's bedroom.

It was festival cannon fire. But it felt like the heavens imploding. *Il fuochista* must be near the Immacolata just down my street. Then three rounds again. Louder than before.

BOOOM, rattle, BOOOOMM rattle, BOOOOOMMM.

Again the panes slowly clattered to a stop.

BOOOOOOMMMM.

Then finally a round or three of rapid gunfire and smaller popping cherry bombs scattered over the terracotta rooftops. I waited for a moment, anticipating. But it was over. I got out of bed, swung open my balcony doors as birds were taking frantic flight. And the bells of Saint Anthony began.

I was told there would be three masses said today in the little yellow chapel at the base of the hill, and then a procession with the saint and his followers through the Centro Storico in the afternoon. Again, they would proceed right by my door.

So, on my first afternoons living in 21 via Fontana, Sant'Antonio's tredicina spread through the valley, echoing across stone houses and filling the new rooms of my soul. It was a modern mantra in a lonely bell that seemed to be calling me home.

I am here, I said to myself. Not knowing yet what that would really mean. Yet something in my life that seemed lost was now found.

Fatta Bene (Well Done)

Sex, Food, Laundry

And the corredo.

I ran into Giuseppe's parents up at the one-hundred-year old dry goods store at the top of the street just a few steps up from my new house. They knew full well where I lived, and why, and yet I worried.

Did they approve or not?

Of course they didn't. I was an older woman and L'Americana who could easily lure their beloved eldest son away from the nest, the farm, the work, the loyalty that most Italian families demand. It took an especially strong person to break this bond, and Giuseppe had been straddling the fence for quite some time.

Was I giving him too much rope?

Clearly he wanted me and his Irpinian life too. Giuseppe, with his deep-country, wildwood ways, in his fealty, I knew now, would not ever think of leaving his town. Walking a hundred or so sheep since a grade-school boy on land so far out, so breathtakingly remote, he and his brother, teen shepherds, were raised just as all their grandparents before them, with wood fires in fields or to cook and heat the house, even today. What was I to do, though, to satisfy his old-world family?

Giuseppe's parents were farmers from long-standing Irpinia stock—at least two centuries on this land. I wasn't interested in pulling him from his roots. I want to live a quieter life. A slow country life with my man, waking up to views of the ancient dormant volcano its looming dense black presence on the horizon, with gold or shamrock green or rich black earth contrasting beneath and a pale whispering summer sky above.

"*E' meglio così, per te,*" Giuseppe liked to say. He meant to protect me from the future.

The future that was slow to dawn on me. The life as the wife of the eldest son to a family entrenched in centuries of traditional Italian farm life.

"Fresh honey!"

He shook his head. The dilettante emerged every so often.

"Baby lambs!"

The life of a daughter-in-law of an eldest son in Southern Italy was no walk in the park.

First there was the language barrier. Not just Italian, but a guttural ancient language, more than a dialect. I supposed I could learn more. Then there was the work expected, the devotion expected on the farm and in the farmhouse of the family. Then there was his mother. My American friends often joked about having an Italian boyfriend and they didn't even have experience with the native sons and what they thought it really meant dealing with the overbearing, overprotective, overlord mothers.

Bah, folklore, I thought. Not only that, I grew up with an Italian mother.

Giuseppe shook his head. His ranch hands to my city figure. We joked. His friends joked. Everyone else was scrutinizing our affair.

"*Se ti capita una figlia femmina, o maritale o scannala.*"

This I learned was a particularly specific old proverb from Irpinia, Southern Italy. A cruel blameful shaming that clearly defined daughters through family folklore and their world view. The rules and lack of rights or care of young women coming of age are defined for her when she is born: "If you have a daughter, let her marry or cut her throat." Simply, either she marries or she shames the family and the village by inference of scandal; by taking a lover or by leaving town for a brighter life. She can no longer be controlled. That is, no independence.

Scannale!

You cut her throat!

Nothing in between.

La Donnaccia. The bad woman, a danger to herself and her small-town women peers. The name came from the 1965 film directed by Silvio Siano, set in the neighboring town of Cairano.

Giuseppe, bless his alpha-male, old-world, deep Country Joe's heart, was either truly protecting me while bedding me—or just stalling for time. His parents had, I reminded everyone, accepted me not once but three times at their farmhouse before and after we started our love affair.

"*Come cambiare?*" zia Angelina demanded to know. She knew our history well. She was there that first day.

Franco later simply stated the obvious, "The life of a woman here is very hard. They are not a family for you."

And Giuseppe's father, Michele, bless his sly yet still very handsome heart—the man who started all this with the suggestion that I meet his son on my very first chance visit to his farm, staring down from his huge tractor—*furbo!*—did not even greet me cordially outside the dry goods store that summer day.

Giuseppe's uncle stood there too. I had greeted him on the street in the Centro for the last few days, not knowing his connection to Giuseppe's family. He smiled and nodded in complete acknowledgment of our friendly neighborliness. Giuseppe's mother, Rosa, was inside at the marble counter buying her goods, her back to the street. I had no choice but to enter. My hand was on the door. Though frozen at the sight of her matronly figure leaning heavily against her bags. A cold greeting from his father's sparkling blue eyes may have been the protocol, what with his wife right inside.

I pushed the door open, entered slowly. Rosa feigned cordiality in front of the shop owner with whom I was also neighborly acquainted. I reached out my hand to greet her as she double kissed my cheeks. I stiffened inside from wild, young-girl insecurity. I had been asking Giuseppe to take me to their homestead again for some days now, and he had gently refused. I didn't realize it was his mother's refusal.

I offered to carry her numerous and heavy purchases the few steps to the door. She was nearly lame in one leg from an ill-treated injury many years before. With the men still waiting on the other side of the wood and glass, she turned my offer down.

Girl indeed, I was a woman! An American woman! I didn't need to remind myself who and what I was to all of them, nor to Giuseppe. After the episode was over and his parents had left, I nearly buckled in front of the shop owner, Tomaso.

"How did I do?" I asked him.

"Why?"

"That was Giuseppe's parents." I confessed immediately.

"Yes, so? You were fine. What's the problem?"

So kind he was to see my distress at wanting to be liked or at least accepted by these hard-country people, who were probably quite lovely. I knew they could be lovely, if they would just give it up and let Giuseppe and me be.

That afternoon, warm and sunny, Giuseppe picked me up at that very spot in front of the dry goods store. I asked him if he had any news from his parents that they ran into me that day.

"No," he said, and looked away.

Clearly this was of concern to him yet he did not back me up. Did he think I was pressuring him to live with me? Marry? I had mentioned neither. Or was it that I was buying the house on my own. I knew it was no urban legend that young adults here lived with their parents until successfully matched. That no woman or man lived alone on their own, young adult, middle-aged or otherwise.

They never emerged as fledglings, as young adults do, to fly on their own. They were all *mammoni*. They all cultivated, needed, a sustained connection to la casa; parents, elders, and friends. They slept in single beds tucked in corners. I vowed to myself then, that I would not ask Giuseppe again for any inclusion to his home life. If they wanted me they would have to invite me.

Giuseppe drove me out to the north side, out to the hill fields that surrounded Macchiursi covered with grano, sparsely populated by fruit trees and olive forests. I loved our drives, loved being his passenger with the Irpinian countryside rolling by. In Los Angeles I was always behind the wheel of my car, albeit a roaring sexy Audi A6. I loved to drive too, but much better than that, I loved to be driven by this *cavaliere*.

Cavaliere. My grandfather Nicola, handsome sergeant in the king's cavalry in the early 1900s, or a plumed knight on a horse as in fairy tales, or the Paolantonio coat of arms from Gubbio on the wall in the loft apartment—women here use the term for their everyday men. Someone to carry in wood and then light your fire, take you out, take you dancing; to protect you and to serve. And as good Italian women, they in turn serve their men. Here a man needs a maid, a maiden. And I was told years earlier, a woman in Italy needs a man.

He turned off the unpaved country road between two fields low with early summer hay and young grasses. A lone tree beckoned in the middle distance. He swung the car onto a tractor path, rambling and wobbling along the uneven dirt tracks until he pulled right onto a breaking field and up to a cherry tree, gorgeous in its green leaf, a few bright orbs of fruit reddening in the sun. We alighted.

Like a sunflower reaching for the sun, I turned slowly, taking in the full view of undulating fields alternating green-golden and burnt umber. The hilltop of Calitri rose in the near distance in front of us. The seven peaks of Mount Vulture looming in its own deep blue haze behind.

Sensually warmed by the heat of the earth, out here I felt grounded and free. I leaned forward to rest against the car, gazing toward the eastern hillside of Calitri as he pointed to my balcony in the distance from over my shoulder. Then he held his hand over his heart. It was a gesture of fidelity.

Io ti aspetterò sempre. I will always wait for you.

A Stone, a Leaf, a Door

～

Here I was, first daughter of two Brooklyn kids with a lot of spunk and some good fortune, born to Italian immigrants in New York City in the early 1930s. Their adult lives seemed an American breeze comparative to their parents' hardscrabble youth here in Italy, and after they married in the mid-1950s, they settled into a comfortable duplex in a tony suburb of Long Island. Sadly, however, both their young childhoods were marred by the early deaths or abandonment of one parent each, leaving some fairly recognizable holes in their psyche.

It had become a soulful endeavor for me to unearth the buried family history that kept me traveling back to the hometown of my grandparents, born over one hundred years ago. After all these seasons, I had returned now as zia Concetta's protégé and my grandmother's rearguard to witness life and love as a new resident in the old village of Calitri.

Now the question beckoned, "Can I do this?" Live hilltop village life in remote Alta Irpinia, where historic religious processions and an old man pulling a pack donkey went right by my door? Could I let go of Los Angeles? Let go of a career, a comfortable home in the Hollywood Hills, to live the Roseto Mystery? A simpler, unharried life surrounded by the land and beauty that my grandparents once gave up for the heart loss and opportunities that came with emigrating to America?

The dream-vision of the woman in black, who I believe was Concetta thanking me, showering me with her unconditional love from above for securing the house, came as soon as I returned again to Los Angeles.

One night a woman in black appeared at the window at the foot of my bed. Overwhelmed by a powerful force, I felt a sustained wave of benevolence envelop me, pulling me beyond the borders of my consciousness and the room. She filled me with a kind of universal love. The unconditional love for a child from a godlike grandparent. I rose up to get a better look. Voiceless, my heart expanding, this compassionate love holding me fast, filling the room. It felt an eternity within a few moments. Then she was gone.

I dreamt of my grandfather Nicola too, on All Souls Day, back in November 2003—again in Los Angeles—after two thrilling months in the town as the new American girlfriend of the Handsome Man from Macchiursi, Giuseppe Zarrilli.

Clearly my grandfather saw that we had fallen in love, were completely thunderstruck with one another. Maybe in that dream he was acknowledging me, what I was doing, and why. While in the town that fall I had certainly felt that he was guiding me; finding his portrait tucked in a credenza drawer in nonna Migliorina's loft apartment, then unwittingly consummating my love affair with Giuseppe on his name day of San Nicola.

Living in the Paolantonio family's apartment, I had a beautiful view of the graceful arch of the old town. Those first mornings were memorable, bright and clear. Evenings, the glimmering lights played like stars on black velvet, deepening my romantic appreciation for the place. All pointing to this thin space opening between me and the town and the ghostly world of my ancestors, and whoever else was up there guiding me.

Now with this vision of the woman in black, it slowly dawned on me that I seemed to have a direct line to these ghosts of Italy. Nicola and little Mussolini, now Concetta. The princess? Whoever, and whatever was really going on I did not know, but I knew I loved the journey. Each time I traveled to the town I would just let go, let myself go, with whatever came down the road.

As I approached the town that very first day—seated alone, halfway back of a regional bus—I felt a pang deep in my chest, an alarm of the kind that alerted my brain that I was about to burst over the edge of some long-held loss. Loss slowly ascended on the switchback road with me, twisting and rising deeper into the town, carrying me through a sort of portal, once guarded, now wide open.

At forty-something I was still my father's daughter. I had always felt deep within me the Italian code of reverence and devotion to all things male in the Italian family nucleus. Whereas my mother was most times downright unruly to me, my father fueled my impressionable youth with a not unsubstantiated mantra—"Don't turn out like your mother." This ruthless denial of the importance of the women in his life propelled me away from the domesticated hearth. And set me wandering for years without maternal anchor.

Now I live in his mother's two-room stone house. Yet to me it was still and truly Concetta's house, since I never knew my grandmother, nor heard any warm personal tales of her; never possessed a single object to fawn over or create a childhood fantasy with. No hand-embroidered linens. No teacups or tea service. No wedding earrings or jewelry or any other collected ephemera from her humble boudoir. No favorite pottery or kitchenware. No painting of Jesus or rosary that may have hung over her ancient nuptial bed. "Nothing, and so be it," as Oriana Fallaci, the Italian journalist, said.

Where was the spirit of my grandmother?

Clearly someone possessed her things. But where they were squirreled away was not known to me, though I must have at some point inquired. I had only experienced one elder in the house on via Fontana, and that was Concetta. Warm spare kitchen with wood stove blazing in winter, some pot of ragu simmering up top, crowded balconied bedroom with an oversized Italian *comò* next to her matrimonial bed, archaic wedding photos and single portraits on the wall. Her husband Pasquale's framed portrait when younger, then when much older, perhaps the year or thereabouts of his death.

We would often sit on her bed sifting through the photos of her emigrated son's family, long since gone and rarely returned. Or on the balcony in warmer sunnier weather—calmly gazing over the rooftops and expansive view of the Ofanto Valley, and nearer, to a small circular parcel of land sketched out on a hillside of olive trees and flowering yellow broom.

She gestured once in that general direction and I took that to mean it was land her daughter Maria tended with her retired husband Vincenzo. But I came to know much later that it may indeed be the resting place of my grandmother's ashes.

The story was finally revealed to me when I called my father one day to ask him about the whereabouts of his mother. He said that he remembered his father's return to the town some short time after her death, yet when pressed, he "didn't recall an urn of ashes in the apartment in Brooklyn" where he continued to live, the youngest and as yet unmarried son, with his widowed father. So he guessed, that maybe on this return, his father brought her back to the village and scattered her someplace there.

"Scattered? What about the cemetery? Maybe she is buried in there?"

"Gee, honey, I don't know," my father said.

Non lo so!

The peasant's refusal to know the whereabouts of things, that I heard in so many of my relatives here, had been absorbed by my father. Had always been used by him, albeit in English. I had always hoped for something more. Though even Franco waved away my inquiries with the knowing pain of so much loss.

As a child, I could barely cajole more than a sentence from my father about his Italian-born mother. She remained locked inside his heart. And for years I could not find my way to forgive him for raising me with such a longing unanswered, until I adopted Calitri. Joseph Campbell writes of myth and mythologies: If one does not speak of a thing, it dies; that storytelling is paramount to the survival or the finding of one's soul.

On the other end of the phone, I felt my father's hesitation in all its arrested longing; his feelings resurfacing after all those years of forced internment by my quiet insistence that I learn something, bring something from him with me to the interview. I slowly realized what he was saying by not saying anything; never sharing anything of his mother all these years; that this once, and again now dearly devoted man, my father, lost his mother, not once, but three times—in body, soul, and spirit. She was lost to him early, in her illness, her manic depression. Then lost later, when he was in his late teens, when she was ritually hospitalized, and finally died there. The last was when his father returned her to Calitri.

Indigenous and old-world cultures of the Etruscans and the Romans believe in the seven generations principle. That as you pay reverence to your ancestors' spirit, their souls are healed seven generations back and seven generations forward, creating what they call fields of grace, through all time and space.

I said to my father gently, "Well, I suppose someone would have told me or showed me by now if she was buried there in the town?"

And then it hit me. Zia Concetta gesturing toward the circle of land that spring day on the balcony. I thought she was talking of her husband Pasquale and the land he worked back in years past. My grandmother was buried there.

Oh God, why didn't I understand this so much earlier?

Sometime ago, maybe while not understanding her dialect, she must have already told me and thought I had understood. She was surprised, I suppose, that I had not gleaned this fact by sheer association or subsequent deduction as the last remaining matriarch of our line of Cicoira's, albeit through marriage, and therefore the custodian of the family heritage and their original Centro Storico property.

Then I realized what her gesturing off the balcony, her quiet murmuring meant. But before even this, all their acceptance and tolerance of me—my returning again and again, taking photos yet never really questioning, just wandering, not even knowing I was looking for clues. Because they knew all along that my grandmother was here and that my grandfather had brought her back all those years ago. His incredible loyalty and love for both her and the town. And that the way you come into the world, is the way you go out. Concetta was trying to tell me. And it took me until after her death to understand.

The Chock Full O'Nuts can that held my grandfather's ashes was stored on a shelf in his son Tony's California garage for nearly thirty years, then tucked away forever into Tony's casket when he died, and was interred in godforsaken Simi Valley. Tony died in 1988. I had just arrived to live in Los Angeles and had attended his funeral with my parents. I had later gleaned from Tony's son that he and his younger brother had carried out their father's wish. But it was the first I had heard of a coffee can holding my grandfather's ashes. At the time I had no idea what it meant. My father never said a word. But I was sure now that it was a place my grandfather never meant to rest.

He meant to rest near my grandmother Angela Maria.

I think it prophetic that my grandfather died just weeks before I was born, just a few months after he returned from his last ocean voyage from New York to Calitri. He may or may not have had his entire life passing before him those moments before giving up the ghost: his New World accomplishments; the sacrifices he made to realize a better life; the emigration voyages from his hometown as a young man; his first voyage so young, alone, yet well protected by his personal patron saint of sailors and the sea, on the German schooner, the Prinzess Irene.

Arriving in New York harbor on the Fourth of July no less. A decidedly very intrepid and perhaps prescient young man. Perhaps these were some of his last thoughts with my father and pregnant mother, with me in the womb, at his bedside in the Brooklyn hospital. Releasing this passing film of his life to his impressionable, seemingly imperishable, youngest son with his new and growing family. How he left the village behind.

Little would he know, would anyone know how hard I would fall in love.

I fell for the thunder of fireworks at *mezzanotte*, the lucciole in the countryside, and for the handsome son of a local rancher. I'd like to believe our transoceanic courtship was encouraged with compliments from above, uniting the lost generations.

I fell for zia Concetta. For among all my parenti, it was she who came across town to find me that first November day only a few hours after my arrival, projecting strong allegiance to the memory of my grandmother. And now, after all these seasons I returned as Concetta's rear-guard, and my grandmother's protégé, as I begin to live and witness life and love in the town.

I always felt deep down that someday I would find the spirit of my grandmother. Between my first journey and today there have been several years of discovery in this small mountain village that I now call home. After buying her house on via Fontana, I had finally found her. My grandmother's spirit and my own were always with me, guiding me through life and love in the town. And now when I walk home from a day in the village, she will be right there with me, on the hillside, just beyond my balcony.

A Stone, a Leaf, a Door

Four Seasonal Alta Irpinia Recipies from Calitri

☙

In Los Angeles in winter, I'm a kind of forager: wildflowers from a field, persimmons or lemons from a community tree. Around the ranch on Mulholland Drive there are always desert flowers and winter greens and fruits to pick. And like the women in the old village of Calitri in Alta Irpinia, I conjure meals from my late garden with the staples in my kitchen. There's a pleasure in this that is satisfying and humble and real. But for them, it's a certain seasonal survival.

Winter bounty is bleak in Calitri with very little life in her streets. Men huddle in black wool caps and capes—*i coppoloni*—against the damp, bitter cold. Widow's live alone in deep grottos warmed by the meager fires from their fornacella stoves. They forage for bitter greens in spent gardens and live on acquasale, improvisational food. It's straight out of *Honey from a Weed*, Patience Gray's fasting and feasting travel book, which was an inspiration for me during my early visits to Calitri.

Now that I live on via Fontana, I am in the middle of all the artisanal traditions that are still kept up season after season. From the distant, steady clinking of a hand-pulled wine press deep in some tufa grotto, to the golden elixir that is a deliriously fruity grappa or fresh-pressed olive oil, to the aroma of woodsmoke from a fornacella at the height and heat of an August afternoon—for this reason, but not only, I love living around the older women of la Cascina.

Many of them still tend their own land out in fields far out from the town. They work hard all year round to produce the season's bounty that they still proudly put on their family's table year after year. Some of the older women of the village were born out there, raised out there. A few of their old rambling but simple homesteads have become successful *agriturismi* or vineyards. Whether it be how they put up their tomatoes for their sauce—*fac' buccac'*—or skin a rabbit for the Sunday meal, I am curious about their livelihoods, like an artist.

Here is a collection of seasonal recipes culled from what I have learned from the women of Calitri.

NOCINO *(Walnut Wine)*

"On June 24th you pick the walnuts," zia Giuseppina told me one day in November as I sat around her table with her family and a journalist from New York. June 24th is the feast of San Giovanni and the only day you begin the recipe for *nocino*, the dark, sweetly complex liqueur that is enjoyed here in winter.

> 16 large green walnuts
> 1 liter of 100 proof clear alcohol
> 1 stick cinnamon
> 2 whole cloves
> 1 teaspoon of fresh ground nutmeg
> 1 liter of bottled mineral water, *liscio* (or without gas)
> 750 grams Caster Sugar
> 6 "*tazze*" (small espresso cups) of fresh brewed espresso

Materials:
> 2-liter glass jar with cover
> 3-4 decorative glass bottles with cork or screw tops for the finished liqueur

Makes 2 liters.

Clean and prepare the glass storing bottles by boiling or washing well with plenty of hot water and a teaspoon of bicarbonate of soda. Let air dry and cover with a clean kitchen towel.

    Collect sixteen large green walnuts from a healthy walnut tree. The nuts should be harvested while a pin can still be pushed through them and the green stems snap softly yet easily to yield the fruit to your hand. If you have a fresh water well nearby, rinse and remove any small twigs or leaves, leaving the green husks on the fruit. Place the walnuts in a glass jar, which should be large enough to hold the walnuts covered in the alcohol. Add the spices. Pour the liter of alcohol over all, give it a couple of turns and cover tight. The alcohol mixture will turn a dark chocolate brown overnight. Put the jar in a cool dry place and soak the mixture for forty days.

After the forty days, strain the darkened alcohol mixture of walnuts and spices through a fine cheesecloth into a ceramic bowl. Discard fruit and spices. Set alcohol aside. Bring the liter of mineral water to a boil in a large saucepan. Combine the sugar with the boiled water, stirring with a wooden spoon to melt the sugar, then lower the heat.

When all the sugar has melted, turn off heat. Combine the walnut alcohol and the six espresso cups of coffee with the sugar water mixture. Mix gently with a wooden spoon. Let cool.

Decant the walnut liqueur—nocino—into the decorative bottles and *tappo* (close tightly with corks or tops). Let rest ten days.

Enjoy around a blazing fire in winter, or as an after-dinner digestivo for yourself and guests.

This keeps for a long time.

༄

PASTA CON PISELLI *(Pasta with Fresh Spring Peas)*

My neighbor Michelina called me over to her door one morning an hour before lunch.

"*Hai già preparato qualcosa?*" she asked.

She likes to thank me every now and then for running errands for her up in the town with a plate of prepared pasta for lunch. Usually something simple and in season. Today she had fresh local peas.

Peas are best harvested in late April or early May in Irpinia, but as always, it depends on the position of your garden on the hill and when you planted the seedlings. They are often garnished with fresh mint, the herb that is in season with the peas. It's nice to shell a basket of fresh young peas, on your lap outside in the sun on a cool stone bench.

"*Sono magnifici!*" Michelina said of her peas. "*E tanto saporiti! Li vuoi?*"

She and her husband had a large orto at the very bottom of Calitri's hill in the lower valley that runs along the Ofanto River. They sold their fruits and vegetables, displayed in her husband's handmade baskets, in spring and summer on a small rise on the street just outside their front door. These peas were gifted to her from a long-time friend who still tended her rows, and she wanted me to try them.

Michelina transferred the petite, brilliant green peas to a small bowl, then asked me if I knew how I would cook them. Before I could tell her, she said, "*Si fanno cosi.*"

She then measured out about 100 grams of small *lumache*, or little snail-shaped pasta, in a large aluminum kitchen ladle. I have this kind of ladle myself. I inherited it from zia Concetta. It was left in her kitchen along with a few other useful cooking utensils when I bought her house. I had no idea it measured 100 grams of pasta. Italians measure their pasta precisely at 100 grams per person for lunch every day. She then poured the dry pasta into a small rush basket that hung in her kitchen for me to carry across to my house. The basket was made by her husband; he was at one time *un cestaio*. Since I moved in, she has so far gifted me a few of his baskets of various sizes and ages.

"*I piselli con questa pasta sono davvero buoni. Provali,*" Michelina said. And she sent me on my way. She was completely sure that these small lumache-shaped pasta would be the best for the dish.

80 -100 grams fresh young peas, shelled
200 grams dry pasta lumache
Extra virgin Italian olive oil

2 small top sprigs of fresh mint, coarsely chopped
Salt
Cracked pepper
Fresh grated pecorino or parmesan cheese
Coarsely cut flat leaf Italian parsley to garnish

Serves 2.

Rinse the peas briefly in cold water, drain, and set aside.

Measure 80-100 grams of small lumache pasta for each person. Salt the water for the pasta and bring it to a boil. Cook the pasta in boiling water for a minute or two, then add the fresh peas. Boil together until the peas have changed color to a lighter green and the pasta is slightly *al dente*. Take down the pasta and peas together in a colander to drain. Return the pasta and peas to the pot or a wide serving bowl. Drizzle in olive oil, fold in a small handful of grated cheese, the chopped mint, and toss gently. Garnish with cut parsley, a bit more grated cheese, and pepper to taste.

Serve immediately.

FAC'BUCCAC *(Tomato Puree)*

One summer I tried my hand, ever so cavalierly, at putting up a few jars of fresh tomato puree. The inspiration came from a gifted bucket of passed-over San Marzano tomatoes, just picked, perfectly aromatic and ripe-red, with just a few blemishes that needed to be trimmed and they would be as good as new.

I remember my mother using tomato puree on Sundays while I was growing up on Long Island. That of course, came out of a large can: Nina, Tuttorosso, or Contadini. Here in Southern Italy, only a very few households use tomatoes from a can. Everyone else makes their own. Those who don't have time are usually gifted a crate of bottles of homemade puree from their mother or grandmother or aunt, including, occasionally, lucky me. And here, they are not making only a few jars from castoff fruit. They put up several quintali of tomatoes at a time at peak harvest season. That is, hundreds and hundreds of pounds of tomatoes, and who knows how many bottles yielded for the year—cooked over a wood fire, on a cantina stove, in the heat of an August afternoon.

This preserved tomato puree can be used in any dish that calls for tomato sauce, or prepared for pasta simply with olive oil or cooked with meat: beef braciole, pork, or *coniglio* (rabbit).

2-3 kilos of ripe red San Marzano tomatoes, whole
Bunch or two of fresh basil with large, healthy leaves
Sea salt

Materials:
A *passatutto*, (food mill)
Large, deep pot with lid
A half a dozen medium-size jars with lids cleaned and dried
Makes about a half dozen medium-size jars.

Clean and prepare the glass jars by boiling or washing well with plenty of hot water and teaspoon of bicarbonate of soda. Let air dry and cover with a clean kitchen towel.

Put all the fruit in the pot and toss in a handful of salt. On low gas heat, slowly bring the tomatoes to a boil. Boil lightly covered for twenty to thirty minutes, turning occasionally, being careful not to scorch.

After cooking down the fruit, pass the tomato pulp and liquid a ladle or two at a time through a hand-turned passatutto, to get a lovely, dense consistency of tomato puree.

Once all the tomatoes are passed through the passatutto,

assemble the clean, opened jars on a table and separate the basil leaves from their stems, leaving them whole.

Ladle the puree into the jars. Place one basil leaf on top of each jar and lightly cover with the lid. Let cool a few hours. After they are cooled, close the lids tight and set the jars a few at a time, lid side down, into a tall pot and cover completely with cool water. Bring to a boil. Boil rapidly for at least 20 minutes. This is the sealing process. Once the jars are boiled to a seal, they can be stored for up to one year.

Qua non si paga.

∞

PASTA ASCIUTTA *(Pasta in Tomato Sauce)*

Pasta asciutta is the local way to say "pasta with tomato sauce." If you asked someone here what they had for lunch that day, they would more than likely respond, "pasta asciutta," meaning a steaming plate of spaghetti with homemade tomato sauce, and that's it. And the only thing that arrives on an Italian's table hot is the plate of pasta. All other *secondi* are served room temperature.

>200 grams of dry pasta
>Spaghetti #8 or #16
>Your own freshly preserved tomato sauce, see recipe for fac'buccac
>Italian extra virgin olive oil
>Fresh basil
>Sea salt
>Freshly grated pecorino or parmesan cheese
>Coarsely cut parsley for garnish

Serves 2.

Bring a large pot of salted water to a boil, then toss in the pasta. Cook the pasta according to the instructions on the box.

As the pasta is boiling, heat a jar of your freshly preserved tomato sauce in a small sauce-pan, drizzle in some extra virgin olive oil, and a fresh leaf of basil.

Once cooked, drain pasta into a colander, then return to the pot with a ladle of sauce and a small handful of grated cheese.

Transfer the dressed pasta immediately to individual bowls, add another half ladle of sauce and grated cheese to taste, and some freshly cut parsley.

Serve immediately.

Qua si mangia bene.

VINEYARD PEACH JAM

The French call them *pêche de vigne*—vineyard peaches. The name derives from the late season variety, an heirloom peach that ripens in late fall at the same time of the grape harvest. And also, I suspect, for the deep sultry crimson color, almost that of red wine, to the skin and flesh of the peach.

Zia Concetta planted her peach tree in a small enclosed garden just below her balcony. The garden once belonged to the Cicoira family but was sold along with the tufa cantina below the house some thirty-five years ago. The family who bought the cantina and garden emigrated to France returning only in summers, perhaps the origin of Concetta's vineyard peach. Concetta's peach tree flowers glorious deep pink in early summer, and is the lone tree in la Cascina.

Simple fruit jams and tarts can be made with vineyard peaches fresh or preserved in this simple way.

2 kilos of vineyard peaches
400 grams caster sugar
Star anise, whole dried
Italian grappa

Materials:
Large, deep pot with lid
A half a dozen small jars with lids cleaned and dried
Makes about a half dozen small jars.

Clean and prepare the glass jars by boiling or washing well with plenty of hot water and a teaspoon of bicarbonate of soda. Let air dry and cover with a clean kitchen towel.

Bring a large pot of fresh cold water to a rolling boil. Put the fruit in the pot a few at a time for a minute or two to loosen skins. Pull them out with a slotted spoon and immerse immediately in cold water. As they cool, slowly peel the skins from the fruit. Cut in halves and remove stones.

Place the peeled, halved fruit into a large empty pot with a quarter cup of water. Bring to a slow, melting simmer over medium high heat. Add the sugar and two whole dried star anise and lower the heat. Stir the peaches continuously over the lowered heat, being careful not to scorch, until they are fully softened and the sugar has melted. A tablespoon of water at a time may be added if needed to keep from burning.

Ladle the fruit into the jars. Pour a tablespoon of grappa over the top of each open jar and cover tightly with the lid. Let cool. The grappa preserves the fruit without having to seal the jars by the boiling method. They will keep up to one year.

Leftover fruit can be used in tart recipes or spooned over gelato.

Four Seasonal Alta Irpinia Recipes from Calitri

Author's Note

~~~

Love, passion, and a quest for the triumphs of life were expressed and felt through Franco, zio Franco, the day I blew into town to prepare for the interview with the *New York Times*.

'Ah, but you come only for carnal passion,' he mocked. As I unlocked us from my hearts winning embrace.

He knew my gleeful ardor lay not only with wrapping my arms around him, as much as he loved my attention, but also for his family, Giuseppe and the entire town. Still, I laughed girlishly denying I understood what he meant.

I had been looking for him for a day and night. Just missing him in his home, his office and here near his club on via Francesco de Sanctis—finally spotting him alone on the street smoking a cigarette in the dark. News always spread like wildfire. He was standing there I knew, to make himself available, to be found.

" 'This is life,' he said. 'Is it not?' " And I had to acquiesce.

Tall, refined, handsome. The honored father and grandfather of a tightly corralled family, Franco Paolantonio had been with me from my very first journey to his village. It was clear to most we shared a bond, kindred spirits of mutual reverence and a playful lust for life. And he always allowed ample irony for and benevolent approval of my love affair with the handsome and younger rancher—concerned as he was since my first arrival to town alone, of not being settled. It was a source of gentle sparring between us each season, of who might be the new or real prince in my life.

But there never was another prince.

Questo è la vita was the working title of my stories of the town for all this time. A time honored Southern Italian idiom expressing acceptance, often veiled, of the triumphs and crushing defeats of life. Irony always at work in Franco's, he revealed to me then that he knew all, would always know all, before I knew that he knew, so bestowed his approval again.

This is my story of finding love and embracing it, and life, in the Italian mountain village of my spiritual roots, my emotional history and my beloved grandparents.

Franco Paolantonio perished in a fatal car accident and was buried one month to the day of our shared triumph—the *New York Times* Thanksgiving Day article about my journey home. And as anyone in the town might offer a questo è la vita as a balm to me for such a heart breaking tragedy it would be my turn to respond, *infame*.

Acknowledgements

Grateful acknowledgment to my *parenti lontani,* family and friends on both sides of the pond—this book is proof of my affection for you all. Special thanks to my editor Wendy Lee without whom I would not have believed; Doug daSilva whose design helped bring these pages to life; and to Angela G. Di Maio of Calitri for her perseverance with the Italian translation. Many early thanks go to Anna Haro, Enza Cubelli, Mariangela Tateo, Marlene Dunham and Susan Vastano who kept the vestal fires burning, and the many other dear friends near and far who believed in *Ghosts* from the beginning. A steaming plate of Filomena's ravioli awaits you. Come. Visit. *Vi aspettiamo.*

About the Author

Angela Paolantonio, whose grandparents landed at Ellis Island, was born in Brooklyn and raised on Long Island. Her love of photography began as she watched her father expose and develop contact sheets on the family kitchen table.

She holds a Bachelor of Fine Arts and Art History degree from Long Island University, Southampton, New York. She is a writer and photographer, curator, and consultant for art and photography exhibits, books, and events, both in Italy and the U.S.

Angela lives in Calitri, Italy, on via Fontana, in the house where her grandmother was born.

MARIANO DI CECILIA

Made in the USA
Middletown, DE
12 September 2016